ADVANCE PRAISE FOR *THE BIG*

"If Hunter S. Thompson had been a b ... is the book he would have written. But don't let the fear and loathing fool you: this book is a love letter to the American West—that is, what's left of the West in the wake of fracking, toxic waste, the gunning down of grizzlies and wolves, the hypocrisy of Democrats, and the venality of Republicans. There are passages here that will break your heart."

— Ted Nace, author of *Climate Hope: On the Frontlines of the Fight Against Coal*

"Here's the real story of our privatization of free-living animals. Of the federal malpractice of forestry. Of every bit of pious and charitable pandering that got us the weird EPA leadership and toxic militarism controlling our lives today. Jeffrey St. Clair and Joshua Frank tell all that unfolds when political parties share "the same lethal ideology" of infinite consumption. In this important folio of essays, these two legendary investigative writers tell the urgent story of vast open lands, of mighty waters yearning to flow free again, of elk and grizzlies.

Their perspective is informed here by Foucault, and thereby the down and out in Las Vegas and the lonely worker who retrieves their bodies from the Colorado River. This hardworking book is the antidote to today's obsequious political journalism. Buy extras. Put copies in the hands of those ready to shake off complacency, to struggle for human decency, to champion the Earth's atmosphere and the great, global biological community within it, from the glaciers to the plains to the cities."

— Lee Hall, environmental attorney and author of *On Their Own Terms: Animal Liberation for the 21st Century*

"Many thanks to Jeffrey St. Clair and Joshua Frank, who have elegantly highlighted the lives and actions that matter most in the

21st-Century struggle to keep it real. In a culture of artifice and "unreality" where everything's for sale, stories like these exemplify how persistence and focused resistance inspire a new generation of radical dissent. Ask any oligarch, CEO, opposing bureaucrat, or government attorney what "melts their glacier," and they will all tell you about that unique artist, poet or grassroots activist that can't be bought, won't cave in and never gives up."

— Steve Kelly, co-founder Alliance for the Wild Rockies

"Jeffrey St. Clair and Joshua Frank connect the dots between environmental destruction and Big Oil, Big Timber, Big Meat, "Hydro-Imperialists" and other greedy expropriators of our land and water. *The Big Heat: Earth of the Brink* names names, names policies and give readers an essential overview of the culprits in our environmental crisis and what can be done about it."

— Martha Rosenberg, author of *Born With a Junk Food Deficiency: How Flaks, Quacks, and Hacks Pimp the Public Health*

"While the reigning media-politics culture blares on about the latest bizarre White House drama, the ecological commons is being sacrificed on the bipartisan altar of a deranged state capitalism. Jeffrey St. Clair and Joshua Frank have been brilliantly ad righteously depicting, explaining, and denouncing this deeply political, man-made calamity from the environmental front lines for many years. The names and party configurations in nominal power change, but the eco-exterminist beat marches on at an ever-escalating pace, bringing us to the cusp of extinction. A collection of the authors' finest individual environmental essays over the last decade plus, *The Big Heat: Earth on the Brink* is left environmental writing at its eloquent, state-of-the-art best. It is also a stirring call to meaningfully militant action."

— Paul Street, author of *They Rule: The 1% v. Democracy*

ALSO BY JEFFREY ST. CLAIR AND JOSHUA FRANK

Hopeless: Barack Obama and the Politics of Illusion

Red State Rebels: Tales of Grassroots Resistance in the Heartland

THE BIG HEAT

Earth on the Brink

COUNTER PUNCH

CounterPunch
PO Box 228
Petrolia, CA 95558
www.counterpunch.org

First published by *CounterPunch* 2018.

AK Press
370 Ryan Avenue #100
Chico, CA 95973
www.akpress.org

ISBN: 9781849353366
E-ISBN: 9781849353373
Library of Congress Control Number: 2018932447

Typography and design by Tiffany Wardle.

Typeset in Minion Pro, designed by
Robert Slimbach for Adobe Systems Inc.
and Founders Grotesk, designed by Kris
Sowersby for Klim Type Foundry.

THE BIG HEAT

Earth on the Brink

JEFFREY ST. CLAIR & JOSHUA FRANK

COUNTERPUNCH

SITTING SUN

The cover image on this edition is a rendition of the Sitting Sun pictograph on the basalt cliffs of the Columbia River Gorge near Maryhill in what is now Washington state. The image was painted by a shaman of the river tribes more than 300 years ago, when the first European plagues began to sweep across the Pacific Northwest, killing upwards of 80 percent of the tribal people. The sun was a holy image found across the region, often depicted as a rayed arc by the Northwest tribes. But the Sitting Sun is distinct. Each of sun's rays is barbed with a smaller sun and those smaller suns are painted not with red ochre, the color of life, but in white clay, the shade of death. The Sitting Sun burns with the heat of 20 suns, forever rising over Miller Island, an ossuary of the river tribes, the isle for a new kind of dead.

PHOTO BY SCOTT DIETZ

ACKNOWLEDGMENTS

This book, which spent many years in the germination stage, started out as one thing and morphed into something quite different. As a consequence, *The Big Heat* had many midwives, but none more vital to its existence than Becky Grant, whose head for figures and eye for aesthetics keeps CounterPunch fresh, feisty and solvent. Sitting beside Becky in Petrolia are Deva Wheeler and Nichole Stephens, both of whom can be counted on to do the impossible on little notice. As usual, Tiffany Wardle's crisp and fluid design makes our prose look better than it probably reads. Up in Stumptown, Nathaniel St. Clair zealously promotes our heresies whether he agrees with them or not. We are deeply indebted to Zach, Lorna, Bill, and rest of the gang at AK Press, for working with us over the last dozen years and for running one of the most vibrant and fearless publishing companies on this (or any other) continent. We are indebted to Scott Dietz for the use of his photograph of the Sitting Sun rock painting. For more of Scott's work check out his website The Narrative Image (https://thenarrativeimage.blogspot.com). Our book tries to give voice to the thousands of activists and organizers who are putting their hearts, minds and bodies on the line in what may prove to be the ultimate battle for the fate of the planet as we know it. Among those who have educated and inspired us, we'd like to extend a special note of gratitude to: Clarke Abbey, Mike Bader, Martin Billheimer, Denise Boggs, Barbara Brower, Patricia Clary, Ted Nace, Tom Carpenter, Michael Colby, Karen Coulter, Stan Cox, John Davis, Susan Davis, Michael Donnelly, Mike Garrity, Marnie Gaede, Keith Hammer, Tim Hermach, Robert Hunziker, Steve Kelly, Owen Lammers, David Mattson, Arlene Montgomery, David Orr, Scott Parkin, Doug and Andrea Peacock, Lauren Regan, Mike Roselle, Dr. Robin Silver, Chris

Simon, John Weisheit, Louisa Willcox, and George Wuerthner. On the homefront, Chelsea Mosher and Kimberly Willson-St. Clair kept the creative fires stoked, the egos grounded and the honey dripping. We've lost some companions in the last few years whose friendship shaped our thinking on nature, political struggle and about how to live: David Brower, Tom Cannon, Alexander Cockburn, Dean Frank, Margot Kidder, Franklin Lamb, Saul Landau, Norman Pollack, TH St. Clair, John Trudell, and Larry Tuttle. We dedicate this book to them. *The Big Heat* was written under the influence of Peter Tosh, Blue Mitchell, Townes Van Zandt, David Vest, Joe Strummer and ¡Moxie Tung!

TABLE OF CONTENTS

FORWARD

SECTION 1 LANDSCAPES

SECTION 2 WATERSCAPES

SECTION 3 POLITISCAPES

FORWARD: IT'S GETTING HOT UP IN HERE

By Jeffrey St. Clair and Joshua Frank

> "The world is turning, I hope it don't turn away."
> — Neil Young

When the overnight low (109F in Oman) would be a record high in most places on Earth, you know your planet is in trouble. The evidence of our warming climate is all around us. At times it feels as if our world is unraveling. Ice shelfs melting. Seas rising. Rivers flooding. Wildfires broiling. Hurricanes destroying. Droughts devastating. It's not as if these events haven't been around since the dawn of time, but man-made global warming is undoubtedly making matters much, much worse. There's little hope that we can stem the rising tides and turn back the damage carbon has wrecked on our little blue planet. But there is plenty to keep fighting for.

It doesn't matter that the odds aren't in our favor. We've all seen the numbers. 2016 was the warmest year on record. 2017 the third warmest. In fact, seventeen of the 18 warmest years on record, *ever*, have occurred since 2001. NASA predicts that by 2020 global temperatures will have risen more than 1 degree celsius over the past 140 years. Of course, this is directly correlated to CO_2 concentrations in our atmosphere. Carbon dioxide levels are higher today than at any point in the past 800,000 years, and the rate is going up.

Many climate scientists, including James Hansen, believe the CO_2 tipping point is 350ppm. As of April, 2018, NASA measured a ratio of 407ppm. Methane isn't helping matters either. Levels of atmospheric methane have also been rising exponentially. While methane doesn't stick around as long as carbon dioxide, it's far better at absorbing heat and is considered 84 times more potent than its carbon brother.

The Earth as we know it, is changing forever. And it's not just polar bears that are suffering. Coral worldwide is disappearing. Grizzlies are scarce. Salmon aren't returning to spawn. Antarctic penguins are dying. North Atlantic cod, which have survived decades of over-fishing, are now failing to adapt to their changing ecosystem. Snow leopards, tigers, Green Sea turtles, African elephants and many more are facing extinction as they struggle to survive in their altered environments.

It can feel dire. But the anger and fear climate change evokes must be cultivated into action to fight for what's remaining. Standing Rock, by all accounts the greatest uprising against the American fossil fuel industry in decades, ought to be a rallying cry for us all. It doesn't matter if Big Oil sends its goons to crack our skulls, or the Feds put us behind bars. The precedent has been set, and despite setbacks, the fight for Standing Rock, and all that it symbolizes, will continue.

There are still trees to save, oceans to protect, dams to break, bears to defend and the same greedy bastards to defy. Yet, there are plenty of reasons to remain a "half-hearted fanatic" as Edward Abbey once warned, let us not be consumed by it all. While the glaciers may be melting, there are still mountains to climb, rivers to float, beaches to roam and community gardens to tend.

What we've attempted to cultivate in this volume of reports, essays, profiles and investigations, is fodder for the soul and cautionary tales of what it means to be an environmentalist in the late stages of capitalism. The point is not to feel overwhelmed by [redacted] all the shit, but to be invigorated by it to fight back—to take a stand like our brothers and sisters at Standing Rock.

The world may be changing faster than humans can properly grasp, which only means we must alter our perspective and change our tactics to defend it. In short, it's time to get radical.

– June 25, 2018

SECTION 1
LANDSCAPES

THE WOLF AT TROUT CREEK

By Jeffrey St. Clair

The bison are in rut at Alum Creek.

Two or three hundred of the shaggy beasts are crowded in the little valley. The bulls have left their normal bachelor groups and joined the big herds of cows and calves to parry each other for preferred mates. They are antsy, kicking up dust devils that swirl around them like brown mist.

I walk slowly up the creek to a group of five dark bison, three females and two males. One of the bulls looks ancient. His eyes are crusty, one of his black horns broken. He is large, but unsteady on his legs, which look too thin to support his bulk. He sucks breaths deeply and raggedly. His lower lip is extended and quivering as he approaches one of the young cows. He shakes his head, his tongue flicks repeatedly at the air, as if tasting the estrus.

As the old patriarch struggles to mount the cinnamon-colored female, a young bull rushes over, butts him in the side, nearly knocking him down. The young bull kicks at the ground, snorts aggressively. The old bull stands his ground for a moment, drool stringing from his mouth. Then finally he turns away from what will almost certainly be his last summer. He staggers downstream towards me, his head hung low, flies gathering at his eyes.

I am less than a mile from Yellowstone's main road through the Hayden Valley, an artery thickly clogged with vans, mobile homes and the leather-and-chrome swarms of weekend motorcycle ganglets. There is no one else here in the pathway of the great herds. Even the metallic drone of the machines has faded so that I can hear the heavy breath of the bison in their annual ceremony of sexual potency.

Even bison, the very icon of the park, aren't safe here in their last sanctuary. The shaggy bovines are victims of rancher panic and a gutless government. Like cattle and elk, bison can carry an infectious bacterium that leads to a disease called brucellosis which can, rarely, cause cows to abort fetuses.

There's no evidence that Yellowstone bison have transmitted the disease to Montana cattle, grazing cheaply on public lands near the park. But as a preventive strike, all bison that wander outside the boundaries of the park in search of forage during the deep snows of winter are confined in bison concentration camps, tested and either killed on site or shipped to slaughter-houses.

Not to worry. Ted Turner is coming to the rescue. I read in the morning paper that Turner is offering to liberate the bison quarantined at Corwin Springs, ship them to his 113,000 acre Flying D Ranch south of Bozeman, fatten them on his vast rangeland grasses and serve them up for $18 a plate at his restaurants.

Suddenly, the old bull turns my direction, angry and frustrated. He snorts, paws at hard dirt and feigns a charge.

I retreat and stumble south across the slope of stubborn sagebrush, over a rounded ridge and down into the Trout Creek valley, leaving the bison to settle their mating preferences in peace.

I'm leaking a little blood. The day before I took a nasty plunge down the mossy face of an andesite cliff at a beautiful waterfall in the Absaroka Mountains, ripping the nail off my big toe.

Each time my foot snags a rock an electric jolt stabs up my left leg. I stop at a at the crest of the ridge, find a spot clear of bison pies, and sit down. I ease off my boot and bloody sock, untwist the cap from a metal flask of icy water and pour it over my swollen toe, already turning an ugly black.

Even in late summer, the valley of Trout Creek is lush and green with tall grasses in striking contrast to the sere landscape of the ridges and the broad plain of the Hayden Valley. The creek itself is an object lesson in meander, circling itself like a loosely coiled rope on its reluctant path to the Yellowstone River. Once acclaimed for its cutthroat trout, the creek has been invaded by brookies, rainbows and brown trout—though these genetic intrusions are viewed with indifference by the great blue heron that is posing statuesquely in the reeds, waiting to strike.

Fifty years ago, Trout Creek was an entirely different kind of place. This valley was a dump, literally, and as such it was then thick with grizzly bears. The bears would assemble in the early evening, after the dump trucks had unloaded the day's refuse from the migration of tourists to Fishing Bridge and Canyon and Tower Junction. Dozens of grizzlies would paw through the mounds of debris, becoming conditioned to the accidental kindness of an untrustworthy species.

The bears became concentrated at the dump sites and dependent on the food. This all came to a tragic end in 1968 when the Park Service decided to abruptly close the Trout Creek dump, despite warnings from bear biologists, Frank and John Craighead. Denied the easy pickings at the trash head that generations of bears had become habituated to, the Craigheads predicted that the grizzlies would begin wandering into campgrounds and developed sites in search of food. Such entanglements, the Craigheads warned, would prove fatal, mostly to the bears.

And so it came to pass. The dump-closure policy inaugurated a heinous decade of bear slaughter by the very agency charged with protecting the bruins. From 1968 to 1973, 190 grizzly bears in Yellowstone were killed by the Park Service, roughly a third of the known population. That's the official tally. The real number may have been twice that amount, since the Park Service destroyed most of the bear incident reports from that era. Many bears died from tranquilizer overdoses and dozens of others were air-dropped outside the park boundaries only to be killed by state game officials.

The situation for the great bear has scarcely improved over the last forty years. There are more insidious ways to kill, mostly driven by the government's continued lack of tolerance for the bear's expansive nature. New park developments have fragmented its range, while cars, trashy campers, gun-toting tourists and back-country poachers rack up a grim toll. And now the climate itself is conspiring against the grizzly by inexorably burning out one of the bear's main sources of seasonal protein, the whitebark pine.

Yellowstone is a closed system, a giant island. Genetic diversity is a real concern for Yellowstone's isolated population of bears. So is the possibility of new diseases in a changing climate. The death rate of Yellowstone grizzlies has been climbing the last two years. The future is bleak. So, naturally, as one of its parting shots, the Bush administration delisted the Yellowstone population from the Endangered Species Act, stripping the bear of its last legal leverage against the forces of extinction. The Obama administration showed not the slightest inclination to reverse this travesty.

During the very week I was hobbling around Yellowstone one of Montana's most famous grizzlies was found by a rancher, shot and killed on the Rocky Mountain Front near the small town of Augusta. He was a giant, non-confrontational bear who weighed more than 800 pounds and stood more than seven-and-a-half feet tall. He was beloved by grizzly watchers, who called him Maximus. His anonymous killer left his corpse to rot in a field of alfalfa in the August sun. The government exhibited only its routine apathy at this illegal and senseless slaying. Let us pray that the great bear's DNA is widely disseminated across the Northern Rockies and that his killer meets with an even more painful and pitiless end.

I catch a flash of white circling above me. Osprey? Swainson's hawk? I dig into my pack and extract my binoculars and am quickly distracted by a weird motion on the ridgeline across the valley. I glass the slope. Four legs are pawing frantically at the sky. It is a wolf, rolling vigorously on its back, coating its pelt in dirt, urine or shit. Something foul to us and irresistible to wild canids.

The wolf rolls over and shakes. Dust flies from his fur. He tilts his head, then rubs his neck and shoulders onto the ground. He shakes again, sits and scans the valley.

His coat is largely gray, but his chest is black streaked by a thin necklace of white fur. He presents the classic lean profile of the timber wolf. Perhaps he is a Yellowstone native. He was certainly born in the park. His neck is shackled by the tell-tale telemetry collar, a reminder that the wolves of Yellowstone are under constant surveillance by the federal wolf cops. He is a kind of cyber-wolf, on permanent parole, deprived of an essential element of wildness. The feds are charting nearly every step he takes. One false move, and he could, in the antiseptic language of the bureaucracy, be "removed," as in erased, as in terminated.

This wolf is two, maybe three years old. His coat is thick, dark and shiny. There is no sign of the corrosive mange that is ravaging many of the Yellowstone packs, a disease, like distemper and the lethal parvo virus, vectoring into the park from domestic dogs.

It has been nearly fifteen years since thirty-one gray wolves were reintroduced into the park, under the Clinton administration's camera-ready program. With great fanfare, Bruce Babbitt hand-delivered the Canadian timber wolves to their holding pens inside the high caldera. Of course, it was an open secret—vigorously denied by the Interior Department—that wolves had already returned to Yellowstone on their own—if, that is, they'd ever really vanished from the park despite the government's ruthless eradication campaign that persisted for nearly a century.

These new wolves came with a fatal bureaucratic catch. Under Babbitt's elastic interpretation of the Endangered Species Act, the wolves of Yellowstone were magically decreed to be a "non-essential, experimental population." This sinister phrase means that the Yellowstone wolves were not to enjoy the full protections afforded to endangered species and could be harassed, drugged, transported or killed at the whim of federal wildlife bureaucrats. Deviously, this sanguinary rule was applied to all wolves in Yellowstone, even the natives.

The Yellowstone packs, both reintroduced and native, are doing well, but not well enough considering the lethal threats arrayed against them, even inside the supposedly sacrosanct perimeter of the park.

This young wolf might well be a member of the Canyon pack, a gregarious gang of four wolves frequently sighted at Mammoth Hot Springs on Yellowstone's northern fringe, where they dine liberally on the elk that hang around the Inn, cabins and Park Headquarters. This close-up view of predation-in-action agitated the tourists and when the tourists are upset, the Park Service responds with a vengeance. The federal wolf cops were dispatched to deal with the happy marauders. When the wolves began stalking the elk, Park Service biologists lobbed cracker grenade shells at them and shot at the wolves with rubber bullets. Finally, the small pack left Mammoth for less hostile terrain, showing up this summer in the Hayden Valley, throbbing with elk and bison.

But the non-lethal warfare waged on the Canyon pack wolves came with a bloody price. The wolves lost their litter of pups, a troubling trend in Yellowstone these days. Pup mortality in Yellowstone is on the rise. In 2008, on the northern range of the Park only eight pups survived. Several packs, including the Canyon and Leopold packs, produced no pups. Over the last two years, the wolf population inside the Park has dropped by 30 per cent. Even so, the Bush administration decided to strip the wolf of its meager protections under the Endangered Species Act in Montana and Idaho, opening the door for wolf hunting seasons in both states. Then Judge Donald Molloy, a no-nonsense Vietnam Vet, placed an injunction on the hunts and overturned the Bush administration delisting order.

Revoltingly, the Obama administration redrafted the Bush wolf-killing plan and again stripped the wolf of its protections under the Endangered Species Act. So now both Montana and Idaho are set to killing hundreds of wolves in state authorized hunts—unless Judge Molloy once again intervenes to halt the killing. Both states have brazenly threatened to defy the court if Judge Molloy rules in favor of the wolf. The putatively progressive governor of Montana, Brian Schweitzer, has been especially bellicose on the matter, vowing: "If some old judge says we can't hunt wolves, we'll take it back to another judge."

In Idaho, the state plans to allow 220 wolves to be killed in its annual hunt and more than 6,000 wolf gunners have bought tags for the opportunity to participate in the slaughter. Up near Fairflied, Idaho rancher vigilantes are taking matters into their own hands. In August of 2009, six wolves from the Solider Mountain pack in the wilds of central Idaho were killed, probably from eating a carcass laced with poison. Don't expect justice for these wolves. Rex Rammell, a Republican candidate for governor of Idaho, has placed wolf eradication at the top of his agenda. He has also made repeated quips about getting a hunting tag for Obama. After catching some heat for this boast, Rammell sent out a clarifying Tweet: "Anyone who understands the law, knows I was just joking, because Idaho has no jurisdiction to issue hunting tags in Washington, D.C." Welcome to Idaho, where Sarah Palin got educated.

Across the valley, the wolf is standing rigid, his ears pricked by the bickering of a group of ravens below him on the far bank of Trout Creek. He moves slowly down the slope, stepping gingerly through the sagebrush. He stops at one of the looping meanders, wades into the water and swims downstream.

He slides into the tall grass and then playfully leaps out, startling the ravens, who have been busy gleaning a bison carcass. Earlier in the morning a mother grizzly and two cubs had feasted here, I later learned from a Park biologist. Perhaps the Canyon wolves had made the kill, only to be driven away by a persuasive bear. Perhaps it was an old bull, killed during the rut.

The wolf raises his leg and pisses on the grass near the kill site. He sniffs the ground and paces around the remains. Then he rolls again, twisting his body violently in mud near the bison hide and bones. The ravens return, pestering and chiding the wolf. He dismisses their antics and grabs a bone in his mouth.

I lurch down the hillside for a better view, bang my aching foot on a shard of basalt and squeal, "Fuck!"

The wolf's ears stiffen again. He stares at me, bares his teeth, growls and sprints up and over the ridge, his mouth still clamped tightly on the prized bone, and down into the Alum valley, where he disappears into the dancing dust of mating bison.

– September 1, 2009

BURN A TREE TO SAVE THE PLANET? THE CRAZY LOGIC BEHIND BIOMASS

By Joshua Frank

Fire up your chainsaw and cut down a tree. Not so you can decorate it for the Christmas holiday; so you can set it on fire to help combat global warming. That's right, burn a tree to save the planet. That's the notion behind biomass, the new (yet ancient) technology of burning wood to produce energy.

It might seem crazy that anyone would even consider the incineration of wood and its byproducts to be a green substitute for toxic fuels such as coal. Yet that's exactly what is happening all over the country, and it has many environmentalists scratching their heads in disbelief.

Wood waste, such as forest trimmings and other agricultural debris, is being used in numerous power plants across the country with the impression that it is a renewable, green resource.

"People get easily confused by biomass because it is always lumped in with other green technologies," said environmental activist and filmmaker Jeff Gibbs, who co-produced Michael Moore's "Fahrenheit 9/11." "Burning our trees in the name of renewable energy to produce power is about as Machiavellian as it gets."

NASA's James Hansen says that the burning of coal is the single largest contributor to anthropogenic global warming, so any alternative fuel source must decrease the amount of carbon dioxide (CO_2) released into the atmosphere if we are to put the breaks on climate change. Biomass, despite its label as a renewable energy source, does not solve the problem because burning trees actually emits a large amount of CO_2.

Proponents counter that biomass only releases as much CO_2 as the trees absorb while growing in nature. So as long as replacement trees are grown at the same rate they are burned in incinerators, biomass will always be carbon neutral.

"Emissions from a biomass facility are substantially lower than those from fossil fuel-based energy sources," Matt Wolfe of Madera Energy, developer of the Pioneer Renewable Energy project, said in a public hearing in Massachusetts earlier this year. "Is biomass perfect? No, of course not," Wolfe added.

"But you have to consider what the alternatives are. Low-emission, advanced biomass technology is a much cleaner source of power than coal or oil. We should not let the perfect be the enemy of the good."

An article in *Science* released October 2009 attempted to debunk the myth that biomass is a good alternative to traditional coal and oil burning. The study, authored by climate scientists, claimed that when an existing forest is chopped and cleared to produce fuel, the ability of those harvested trees to absorb CO_2 is eliminated entirely while the amount of greenhouse gases in the atmosphere actually increases.

"The game is up," stated biomass skeptic Ellen Moyer, a principal of green engineering firm Greenvironment, after the release of the report. "The problem has been identified, and the clarion call for course correction has rung out around the world. The days of biomass burning ... are numbered and pending legislation needs to be corrected before perverse incentives to burn our forests are enshrined in law."

Moyer's proclamation that the jig is up may be a bit premature. Biomass is largely subsidized by state and federal governments, and with the help of the Obama administration seems to have a bright future as a significant source of energy in the United States. In fact, a recent federal report says that approximately 368 million tons of wood could be removed from our national forests every year. The current climate legislation hung up in Congress also includes biomass alongside wind and solar power as a source of renewable energy.

In the summer of 2007, Agriculture Secretary Tom Vilsack confirmed that the government would invest $57 million on 30 different projects that support the development of biomass from trees.

"Emerging markets for carbon and sustainable bioenergy will provide landowners with expanded economic incentives to maintain and restore forests," Vilsack said.

This new government initiative was likely marshaled by Forest Service veteran Tom Tidwell, who was Vilsack's pick for the powerful slot of Undersecretary of Agriculture for Natural Resources and the Environment, a position that, among its other responsibilities, places Tidwell in control of the U.S. Forest Service.

"We know [Tidwell] well and we look forward to working with him," Montana Wood Products Association President, Chuck Roady, told *Evergreen* magazine after Tidwell's confirmation.

"He certainly understands the plight of western Montana's sawmills and he understands our forests and their biomass potential," added Roady, who is also the general manager of Montana's oldest lumber company, Stoltze Lumber, which hopes to construct a biomass power plant at its milling site in the Big Sky state.

Another problem with biomass is that it is typically mixed with substances like coal to produce energy. In Nevada, for example, NV Energy is set to use a mix of coal and wood at its Reid Gardner coal-fired power plant. As a result, the company hopes to qualify for the state's renewable energy credits. The 750 tons of wood chips that will be used in the initial test project at the coal plant will be harvested from a section of Arizona's Kaibab National Forest in an area that was hit by a wildfire three years ago.

If a coal-fired power plant receiving energy credits isn't mind boggling enough, take what is happening at biomass facilities in Michigan that are burning not only old homes and construction debris, but also tires. The Lincoln and the McBain power stations in Michigan both burn tires as a secondary fuel source in their green biomass plants.

That's not all. The Greater Detroit Resource Recovery Biomass Facility, located in the heart of Motor City, doesn't only use wood and tire fragments, it also burns trash, and lots of it; over 6 million pounds every single day. That's right: "renewable" garbage: soiled diapers, old cereal boxes, filthy mattresses and even motor oil go up in flames in order to provide electricity to Detroit residents.

"Most of the trash is not Detroit's trash," lamented City Councilwoman Joann Watson, who is joining environmentalists to fight the plant, noting huge increases in asthma rates around the facility. "Why should our children, our elderly, our people have to breathe it? What level of toxicity is acceptable?"

Down in North Carolina the situation does not seem much better. A biomass plant there even plans on firing up chicken shit along with wood to produce power.

"They are burning more than trees because wood is simply not a good energy source," said Jeff Gibbs, who resides in Michigan and is fighting the state's six operating biomass plants. "Look, wood produces 50 percent more CO_2 than coal, for the same amount of energy output. We have to stop this before more plants begin to pop up."

Not only is biomass not a good source of power, claims a 2007 paper presented at the European Aerosol Conference, it's also not a healthy alternative to coal. The paper claimed that particulate matter (particles, such as dust, dirt, soot or smoke) was actually higher for a 7 megawatt wood gasification plant than it was for a large coal-fired power station.

And particulate matter (PM) is very dangerous. The EPA asserts that it can cause asthma, chronic bronchitis and even premature death in people with heart or lung disease. On the environmental side, PM can change the nutrient values in water bodies, turning streams and lakes acidic.

"At every turn biomass is a complete and utter train wreck," added Gibbs. "Chopping up and burning whole trees will not conquer global warming, it will only exacerbate the problem beyond the point of no return."

– December 8, 2009

GLACIER NATIONAL PARK MAY NEED A NAME CHANGE SOON

By Joshua Frank

Glacier National Park may soon need a name change. One of Montana's most majestic places is fast disappearing; at least its glaciers are—at a clip of 90 feet every year. The park's remaining glaciers will be gone in a little over two short decades.

Perhaps there is no better confirmation that the earth is heating up than the glacial retreat taking place in this northwestern corner of Big Sky country. As a teenager I used to venture through the park in search of wilderness and solitude. A chance to catch a glimpse of a Canada lynx, my favorite bobtailed wildcat, was worth the risky journey through these treacherous Rocky Mountain ranges.

Montana was home and snow-capped Glacier Park my refuge.

Times have surely changed. Those glaciers I took for granted 15 years ago have now mostly vanished, leaving barren rock behind as their earthly tombstones. In the late 19th century, when conservationist George Grinnell dubbed this place the "Crown of the Continent," there were approximately 150 glaciers. Today, less than 30 remain. And sadly their deaths are imminent.

Glaciers in the park have been slowly melting since the 1850s, with a cooling period during the 1940s–1970s, but since then the pace has been a rapid, perpetual decline. It's a tale Westerners are becoming accustomed to these days. Our wilderness is dying and the species it cradles are evacuating, or going extinct as a result.

In 2006 a dozen environmental organizations petitioned to designate Glacier National Park and the adjacent Waterton National Park in Canada endangered. Together both parks are known as the Waterton-Glacier International Peace Park, which was deemed a World Heritage Site in 1995 by the United Nations.

"The effects of climate change are well documented and clearly visible in Glacier National Park, and yet the United States refuses to fulfill its obligations under the World Heritage Convention to reduce greenhouse gas emissions," said Erica Thorson, an Oregon law professor who authored the petition submitted to the UN's World Heritage Committee.

The park was never designated endangered, and the glaciers keep melting.

The glacial disappearance in the park follows a pattern that has accelerated around the world since the early 1980s. Mt. Hood, a Cascade statovolcano that can be seen from nearby Portland, Oregon on a clear day, has also fallen victim to our warming climate—all 11 of Mt. Hood's glaciers are vanishing.

In 2006 a team of researchers at Portland State University reported that the mountain's glaciers lost approximately 34 percent of their volume since 1982. When glaciers disappear rivers begin to dry up; any increase in melting can have extreme impacts on local water supplies.

Glaciers in the Pacific Northwest reside in lower elevations and in different climates than those situated in the high-altitude Montana Rockies. Heavy snowfall keeps these glaciers thriving, but when snow turns to rain and temperatures increase so does the melting of glacial ice. "Everything is now retreating, and the smaller glaciers are disappearing," said Philip Mote, a research scientist at Oregon State University. "The decline in snowfall in the Northwest has been the largest in the West, and it is clearly related to temperature."

In the western continental United States there are slightly over 1,700 glaciers, 1,225 of which are located in the state of Washington. Glaciers in the Evergreen State provide over 470 billion gallons of water in runoff each summer.

"In some watersheds, melt water from glaciers makes a large contribution to stream flow," said Christina Hulbe, a professor of geology at Portland State University. "As we lose glacier ice we lose that water supply, or at least its seasonal distribution. You can think of a glacier as a reservoir for water. Snow falls on the top and if it is not melted the next summer, will over time densify to become glacier ice."

Yet snowfall in the Pacific Northwest is declining while temperatures in the region are rising, and this has many scientists concerned.

Interestingly enough, the seven glaciers that sleeve up the slopes of Mt. Shasta are actually growing. While climate change is increasing the drying up of glaciers all over the world, this solitary, dormant volcano in California is benefiting from consistent temperature changes off the Pacific coast. Shasta's are the only glaciers in the Lower 48 that are not in retreat. It's a different story in Alaska, however, where almost 99 percent of all glaciers are shrinking.

"When people look at glaciers around the world, the majority of them are shrinking," said Slawek Tulaczyk, an earth science professor at UC Santa Cruz. "[Mt. Shasta's] glaciers seem to be benefiting from the warming ocean."

Professor Tulaczyk, whose research team has been studying glacial activity on Mt. Shasta, believes that increased precipitation on the mountain is resulting from the Pacific Ocean heating up. This is causing spring snow accumulation to be heavier in Mt. Shasta's higher elevations. In turn, this snow increase helps Shasta's glaciers grow instead of shrink.

Back in the Northwest, not only is habitat at risk because of global warming, but so are human water supplies. Stream flows are shrinking as a result of glacial melt and in places like Washington it is beginning to affect summer drainage into man-made reservoirs.

"Some reservoirs [in Washington] get 20, 30 and even 40 percent of their water during the summer from glaciers," said Joe Reidel, a 15-year veteran as a park geologist for the North

Cascades National Park. "Without a doubt, global warming is real. We need to get past that debate."

Unfortunately, as demonstrated in Copenhagen last month, even those who believe man is contributing to climate change still cannot agree on which method will best reduce greenhouse gas emissions. Cutting carbon dioxide output remains the best approach to minimizing the impact of global warming.

But even if we do so, as the renowned climate scientist James Hansen and others have argued, many of these glaciers, like the ones I traversed not long ago in Montana, will still be gone by the time I turn 50.

The next generation of nature lovers may wonder why the 16,000-square-mile Glacier National Park does not have any glaciers left. They may also ponder why we didn't do more to save them when we had the chance. As debate rages on about how to handle climate change, precious time is being wasted. Even so, we all know who the real villains are.

"I reserve my true hatred for the PR thugs and scientific guns-for-hire (going rate: $2,500 a day) at Big Coal, the rapers of West Virginia and Black Mesa, and Shell Oil, the killers of Ken Saro-Wiwa," writes Jeffrey St. Clair. "They can all roast perpetually in Hell's Cul-de-Sac, otherwise known as Phoenix, Arizona, circa 2050."

– January 20, 2010

THE PRIVATIZATION OF WILDLIFE: HOW TED TURNER SCORED YELLOWSTONE'S BISON HERD

By Joshua Frank

It is just one more battle in the century-and-a-half-old range wars, where land and wildlife have come into direct conflict with selfish, private interests. It's also a story of privileged ethnocentrism, where a once proud indigenous culture and the wild species it depended on have been all but eviscerated.

Welcome to the Interior West, the land of selective freedom and prosperity.

"I love this land and the buffalo and will not part with it," wrote the great Kiowa Chief Santana, who later killed himself while imprisoned in Texas after being tricked by General William Sherman into believing a peaceful council meeting was in his tribe's future. "...A long time ago this land belonged to our fathers, but when I go up to the river I see camps of soldiers on its banks. These soldiers cut down my timber, they kill my buffalo and when I see that, my heart feels like bursting."

The betrayal continues. American bison once roamed these Great Plains in such large numbers that Lewis and Clark noted seeing 10,000 head in a single glance. Their observation no doubt sealed the species' fate. As anyone who has driven down Interstate 90 through Wyoming from Montana today can surely attest, these awe-inspiring creatures no longer dominate the Plains.

Instead hormone-infested cattle and genetically engineered crops occupy this lonely, dry landscape. Water has been stolen for profit. Impoverished Native Americans have been quarantined while oilmen keep drilling for more cash. The only remaining wild buffalo inhabiting these parts roam in places like Yellowstone National Park. But it is certainly no safe haven. When the buffalo migrate past the park's invisible boundaries (perhaps in an attempt to escape fanatical summer tourists sporting binoculars and high-powered cameras), they are killed under the pretext of "disease control." More than 3,000 have been killed since the 1980s by state agents and hunters who have purchased buffalo tags.

The illness that has prompted the State of Montana and Yellowstone Park to embrace such a vicious policy is called brucellosis. Management officials declare that most of Yellowstone's buffalo test positive for brucellosis, a disease where intracellular parasites cause chronic ailments. What these wildlife professionals won't tell you, however, is their field-testing only demonstrates that the buffalo possess antibodies to the disease, and not full-blown brucellosis. This means they've been exposed (like humans who were exposed to polio as kids) but are not necessarily able to transmit the disease.

Even more alarming is the fact that spreading of the brucellosis rarely occurs among free roaming herds. Transmission only happens in very specific, unusual cases, where a domesticated animal like a cow comes into contact with living brucellosis bacteria. One such instance where this might happen is when an infected fetus is miscarried (or aborted, as scientists term it) in the open range by a buffalo and then licked clean by a cow shortly thereafter. The likelihood of such an encounter is minimal at best, as a cow would have to discover the fetus well before scavengers consumed it. The solution is simple: Keep cattle and buffalo separate.

"[N]early all bison abortions—and abortion in wild bison is an extremely rare event—occurs in the late winter. In most of the habitat used by bison at this time of year, cattle are not present. They are back at the home ranch being fed hay," says Montana-based ecologist and author George Wuerthner. "That is why simply keeping cattle and bison separated is a fairly easy solution to conflicts—if a solution were something that the ag boys were interested in creating."

Yellowstone buffalo, despite being on the verge of extinction, have virtually no protections in the West. It's rather telling then, that the current Yellowstone Buffalo Management Plan is carried out by the Montana Department of Livestock (MDOL) and the U.S. Department of Agriculture (USDA) and not the U.S. Fish and Wildlife Service, the federal agency that enforces the Endangered Species Act. Buffalo aren't seen as a threatened species by our government, despite alarmingly low numbers when compared to the historical records. They are viewed as expendable property.

"These are native wild animals but they are treated as livestock," Stephany Seay of the Buffalo Field Campaign, an advocacy group based in West Yellowstone, recently told me. "Brucellosis is a livestock disease, plain and simple. The ranching community doesn't want buffalo on public lands, so they are willing to spread the lie that brucellosis is a killer."

The Buffalo Field Campaign and others believe this is what's at the core of the State's buffalo management policy; the battle over which type of animals have the right to roam free and eat the grasses that sprout up on our public lands. For example, if buffalo are reintroduced into areas that have typically been dominated by cattle, then the grazing rights of ranchers on these public lands is threatened.

What's driving the buffalo killings outside Yellowstone is the fact that a handful of ranchers graze cattle on the public lands adjacent to the park. The USDA and MDOL claim these livestock are at risk of contracting brucellosis, even though there has never been a single documented case of a wild buffalo transmitting the disease to cattle. Down in Wyoming's Grand Teton Park buffalo that carry brucellosis antibodies commingle with cattle on a daily basis, yet there has not been a single contamination instance ever recorded.

"The so-called random shooting at the Montana borders is actually eliminating or depleting entire maternal lineages, therefore this action will cause an irreversible crippling of the gene pool," warned Dr. Joe Templeton of Texas A&M University's Dept. of Veterinary Pathobiology back in 1998. "Continued removal of genetic lineages will change the genetic makeup of the herd, thus it will not represent the animal of 1910 or earlier. It would be a travesty to have people look back and say we were 'idiots' for not understanding the gene pool."

In what the government livestock managers claim to be a study to help save the last remaining wild buffalo in the region, they developed a Quarantine Feasibility Study, where buffalo from Yellowstone are captured, probed, tested and killed in an attempt to study brucellosis as well as to create a so-called disease-free herd. The ultimate goal, as stated in the study guidelines, is to release brucellosis-free bison onto public lands.

The study, now into its sixth year, has turned out to be a utter failure. To date, none of the buffalo studied have been released back into the wild. At the study's onset officials promised that the herd would be placed on public or tribal lands and that none would be used for commercial profit. But when the study was coming to an end late last year, the ranching community flexed their lobbying muscle and put their cattle interests above the welfare of this biologically threatened species.

As the Montana Department of Fish, Wildlife & Parks (MFWP) asserted at the time, the buffalo from Yellowstone were captured to "determine if bison that have successfully completed quarantine are reliably negative for brucellosis and suitable for the establishment of new tribal and public herds." The Park's permit clearly states that buffalo collected "may be used for scientific or educational purposes only, and shall be dedicated to public benefit and be accessible to the public..."

Nonetheless, after the quarantine, the buffalo had to go somewhere, yet MFWP had no plans for what to do with the herd. The

Buffalo Field Campaign and others have opposed the Quarantine Feasibility Study from its inception. The groups argued that the experiment would "manipulate and sacrifice the wild integrity and unique behavior of America's last population of migrating buffalo."

But as the 11th hour of Feasibility Study struck, a backroom deal was hatched. The ranching community had been successful and forced the agency to backtrack on its original promises. Not once were there public discussions on whether or not to let the bison roam free on tribal lands, even though the Northern Arapahoe said they would allow their lands to be grazed. Millions of acres could have been considered for the buffalo's relocation in Montana and Wyoming alone.

Instead, Montana Governor Brian Schweitzer picked up the phone and called a uber-wealthy rancher to bail the agency out.

Ted Turner, the media mogul-turned-Montana buffalo rancher, answered the governor's call. In exchange for 75 percent of the herd's offspring, Turner would allow the buffalo to live on his Green River ranch for the next five years. In all, there could be upwards of 400 buffalo born into his possession. Turner certainly had to be excited about the opportunity to improve the genetics of his own domestic herds. In February 2010, 88 Yellowstone buffalo were transported, protected by Homeland Security, to Turner's property. One calf from the herd has already perished.

"MFWP and the media would have us all believe that the only options that these buffalo had were going to Turner or to slaughter, and if you are opposed to them going to Turner then you must be for slaughter," the Buffalo Field Campaign wrote shortly after the announcement. "Ironic, coming from one of the agencies that participate in the slaughter of wild Yellowstone buffalo."

There are many reasons, aside from Turner's own greed, to oppose the relocation of the quarantined herd to Green River. Just two years ago a major anthrax outbreak occurred at Turner's Flying D ranch, which is located just down the road from where the buffalo are today. Anthrax, a deadly bacteria, occurs in soil and remains dormant until it rains when the spores can become lethal. The anthrax on Turner's ranch in 2008 took the lives of 257 of his domestic buffalo. It was also reported that at least two deer and 14 elk fell victim to the outbreak. A state veterinarian even recommended that cattle ranchers in the area vaccinate their cattle against Turner's anthrax.

On March 23, opponents of the bison relocation to Turner put their complaints to the test and field a lawsuit against MFWP, asserting that the Turner agreement violated commitments made by the agency throughout the quarantine process. Western Watersheds Project, Buffalo Field Campaign, Gallatin Wildlife Association and the Yellowstone Buffalo Foundation filed the legal challenge.

"By removing these bison from Yellowstone, holding them on private lands where the public is not allowed to see them, and selling their offspring to a private corporation, the State of Montana is in clear violation of its public trust responsibilities," says Joe Gutkoski, a representative of the Yellowstone Buffalo Foundation, "How did the promise of wild buffalo in Yellowstone National Park for the enjoyment of future generations become ranched buffalo fenced behind PRIVATE, NO TRESPASSING signs?"

MFWP had no comment on the lawsuit or the feasibility study.

When it comes to buffalo, indigenous rights and the welfare of the land, special interests typically rule the day. Yet it is worthy fights like this that remain the wild buffalo's last chance at genetic survival.

"This is simply a clear violation of the public trust and the offspring of these wild buffalo do not belong to Ted Turner," Stephany Seay of the Buffalo Field Campaign told me. "Livestock don't own our land. We, the people and the bison do."

– April 5, 2010

THE NEW WESTERN TRAVESTY: CLIMATE CHANGE AND WILDFIRES

By Joshua Frank

As my wife Chelsea and I drove through Arizona on our annual pilgrimage from California to Montana, orange smoke billowed along the darkened horizon, signals of hearts shattered and landscapes scorched. Days earlier nineteen hot shot firefighters died together as they battled the intense blazes near the mountain town of Yarnell. It was the most lethal wildfire America had witnessed in 80 years.

The Yarnell flames were so erratic and intense the team became suddenly trapped, and despite each of the men deploying their individual fire shelters, all fighting the flames that day perished. The lone survivor was out fetching a truck for his crew, only to return to the gruesome scene. It was the single deadliest incident for firefighters since the 9/11 attacks on the World Trade Center.

Fires like the one that charred the small Yarnell community are only growing in size and ferocity in the West. According to the National Interagency Fire Center, the number of wildfires every year in the U.S. has remained relatively steady, but their size has increased dramatically. In 1987, a little over 2.4 million acres burned across the country whereas 2012 saw over 9.3 million acres go up in flames.

That's more than the size of Rhode Island and Maryland combined and it's a trend many see as only increasing as more droughts plague Western states and climate change continues to rear its ugly head.

"Today, western forests are experiencing longer wildfire seasons and more acres burned compared to several decades ago," says Todd Sanford, a climate scientist at the Union of Concerned Scientists (UCS). "The greatest increase has occurred in mid-elevation Northern Rockies forests, which are having higher spring and summer temperatures and earlier snowmelt. These conditions are linked to climate change."

Seven of the largest fires since 1960 have occurred over the last twelve years. As these fires get larger more homes, particularly those built in fire zones, are being lost. For example, this year's Black Forest Fire in Colorado consumed over 500 homes, while last year's Waldo Canyon Fire, only a few miles away, burned almost 350 houses. Even the U.S. Forest Service is beginning to hone in on the real culprit behind the intensified flames.

"We're seeing more acres burned and more burned in large fires," says Dave Cleaves, climate-change adviser for the U.S. Forest Service. "The changing climate is not only accelerating the intensity of these disturbances, but linking them more closely together."

Rising summer temperatures are exacerbating drought conditions and increasing pests like mountain pine beetles, which are ravaging Western forests and killing trees that in turn provide fuel for wildfires. Drought conditions in Arizona have been so bad over the past twenty years that trees like evergreens, manzanitas, oak and mahogany are drying up, becoming increasingly susceptible to fire.

"Even a degree or so warmer, day in day out, evaporates water faster and that desiccates the system more," says University of Montana fire ecologist Steve Running.

Professor Running knows his numbers. Over the past 10 years temperatures have risen 1.6 degrees Fahrenheit across the continental United States, with certain states out west seeing an even larger jump. Arizona's average annual temperature, for instance, has risen 2.3 degrees. Yet, even as it gets warmer and fires burn hotter, people are continuing to build homes in fire-prone areas. And no real entity is putting a stop to it. Banks are not evaluating loans based on the potential for wildfire and homeowners are having little trouble insuring their properties despite being built in the path of potential flames.

Arizona is no doubt partially to blame for its own warming climate. The Navajo Generating Station, near Page, pumps out 2250 megawatt coal-fired power every year and all the carbon that goes with that amount of dirty energy production. Arizona also imports coal from New Mexico, Colorado and Utah, producing nearly 90 million metric tons of carbon dioxide annually from its 16 operating coal-fired power units.

As climate change increases fire activity, it is also contributing to the Forest Service's efforts to battle fires. In the last ten years fire fighting staff at the agency doubled. Currently 40% of the Forest Service's annual budget is allocated toward battling wildfires at over $2 billion a year. The agency's staff has a lot of ground to cover, about 231 million acres of public forest land alone has a moderate to high fire risk. Of course, most of the focus is on protecting areas where homes are vulnerable.

Forest Service Chief Thomas Tidwell reports that the number of houses built within half a mile of national forests exploded from 484,000 in 1940 to 1.8 million in 2000. That's a lot of property to protect at taxpayer's expense.

According to the Fannie Mae Foundation, which is not exactly a foe to development, Denver ranked forth in the country for urban sprawl in 2000, trailing only Atlanta, Miami and Detroit. Fannie Mae cited these cities as spreading outside their urban centers at a dangerous rate. Strip malls line the Denver suburbs, where the housing developments are reminiscent of the endless tract homes of Orange County, California. Much of this vast expansion has pushed communities into fire prone habitat that is affected by pine beetle infestations.

Winter temperatures aren't as cold as they used to be in the Rocky Mountains, glaciers are melting and snow packs are decreasing faster than normal. As such, insects like the native pine beetle are surviving the winter months and thriving once spring rolls around, which is becoming earlier every season. The Forest Service estimates that areas in Colorado affected by pine beetles is around 3.4 million acres, which almost matches the combined 3.7 million that presently impact Wyoming and South Dakota. The Forest Service notes that the pace has slowed somewhat, but that's only because mature trees in the outbreak hotspots have already been killed off.

Having grown up in and around Western forests, the epidemic is apparent at first glance. Discolored trees pepper forest landscapes with brown and orange hues. It's as if these coniferous pines have somehow turned deciduous. It's certainly a spooky climate change omen.

Colorado's ritzy Beaver Creek Resort, 100 miles west of Denver, is one of the many places where the pine beetle has left its deadly mark. "We can't stem the tide," Tony O'Rourke, executive director of Beaver Creek's Home Owners Association told Newsweek in 2008. The solution to protect Beaver Creek's multi-million dollar homes O'Rourke represents? Clear-cutting. No trees means no fires. Of course, allowing fires to burn would be a healthier way to manage the problem, but O'Rourke and others aren't about to risk losing their mountain mansions.

According to a study by CoreLogic, Colorado is number three of 13 Western states for the most high-risk homes insured, trailing only California and Texas. The study indicated there are over 121,000 homes in Colorado that were built in or near forest land. A whopping 2,000 structures have been burned in these so-called "red zones" since 2002. However, this hasn't staunched development. From 2000 to 2010 almost 100,000 new homes were built in wildfire prone areas of Colorado, bringing the total number to 556,000.

Colorado, aside from refusing to put the brakes on home development in red zones, is also not doing much to combat the very problem that is making their fire seasons longer and more intense. In 2006, Colorado ranked seventh in the nation in coal production, with over 36 million short tons of coal produced. Burning of coal in Colorado produces around 90 million metric tons of carbon dioxide emissions every single year. Like Arizona, you could call Colorado its own worst enemy.

***

After traversing state highways out of Colorado and north through Wyoming's coal-country, stopping off in South Dakota's Custer State Park, Chelsea and I head on up to my hometown of Billings, Montana. A dozen hours on these lonely highways and it is easy to see that the coal barons, developers and their allies are the West's biggest menace. No longer is the air fresh, Wyoming's unfettered gas drilling has made parts of the state's air quality worse than Los Angeles' on its worst days. Endless streams of coal trains roll past, piled to the brim with black rock bound for incinerators here and abroad. Wyoming's Black Thunder mining pit, operated by Arch Coal, is the first mine to ship out 1 billion tons of coal. It's a disgusting sight to see.

Author William Kittredge calls Montana the "Last Best Place," but I often wonder how long his phrase will remain apt. The majestic ice formations of Glacier National Park have been in retreat for years, victims of a warming climate. Some of the very glaciers I enjoyed in my youth, less than twenty years ago, are no longer around. Fish too may soon be casualties of a climate in peril.

On the Madison River, where I cast my first fly, the number of days where the water temperature is dangerous for trout species (around 70 degrees) increased from six days a year in the 1980s to 15 per year over the past decade. It's a sad reality for those that make their living entertaining wealthy Hollywood producers and Wall Street brokers on weeklong fishing expeditions along Montana's mighty rivers: if trout numbers decline so will tourist dollars.

Pine beetles, as in most other Western states, are also destroying trees in Montana along with a staple food source for threatened grizzly bears. As author Doug Peacock has written, "During 2008, the bears suffered a double disaster: grizzlies died in record numbers and global warming dealt what could be a death blow to the bear's most important food source. Some 54 grizzly bears were known to have died in 2008, the highest mortality ever recorded ... Related to the high mortality of 2008 was the massive die off of whitebark pine trees, whose nuts are the bear's principal fall food. Mountain pine beetles killed the trees; the warm winters of the past decade allowed the insects to move up the mountains into the higher whitebark pine forests."

Wildfires in Montana have also increased over the past several decades. Over 2 million acres of forest land burned in 2007 and nearly 2 million more in 2012, a significant increase from the worst years of the 1980s and 1990s.

As humans continue to spew more carbon dioxide into the atmosphere, the world's climate will continue to be altered. In fact, as many scientists believe, there may already be no turning back. Warmer winters, hotter summers, drought and burning forests (and the homes built in them) may soon be the new norm for the Western United States. The signs are already all around us. If you don't believe me just take a little road trip through the Rocky Mountains to see the travesty first hand. Just remember to take your camera, it's all going fast.

– September 23, 2013

ILLEGAL MARIJUANA OPERATIONS ARE DESTROYING PUBLIC LANDS: COULD LEGALIZATION HELP?

By Joshua Frank

It was the largest pot bust in one of the most weed-friendly states in the country. Last spring a SWAT team, with National Guard choppers hovering overhead, broke up a mammoth grow operation and confiscated 91,000 marijuana plants in Eastern Oregon. In total, the weed had a street value of over a quarter of a billion dollars.

Dozens of weapons were found and six individuals were arrested. However, no doors had be to kicked in and no grow lights were hauled off during the raid. In fact, the grow operation, like an increasing number in the United States, wasn't set up in an urban building or across the border in Mexico. It was taking place outdoors on our public lands.

The scene law enforcement uncovered that day in Oregon was one of ecological devastation. Several miles of plastic drip lines, piles of trash and hundreds of pounds of chemicals and herbicides were discovered in a remote part of the state's scenic Wallowa County. Dozens of trees were cut along the valley floor to bring in sunlight for the plants. The growers, who happened to be spotted by bear hunters a few months prior, had also formed well-worn pathways that meandered along a riverbed through thousands of their water-sucking plants.

"Many people would be outraged at the damage to our public lands caused by illegal marijuana growers," said Sgt. John Shaul of the La Grande Police Dept. shortly after the raid.

The illegal farm crew will face charges for growing pot as well as for environmental damages. Their case, maintains U.S. Drug

Enforcement Administration, illustrates a trend that is spreading across the country.

According to the Office of National Drug Control Policy, for every acre of land where marijuana is grown, approximately 10 more acres are polluted with toxic chemical fertilizers and herbicides. Water diversion from streams is also intense, with an estimated hundreds of thousands of gallons of water being illegally drained from streams that may contain endangered species like salmon and trout. However, the long-term toll these farms inflict on the environment is hard to gauge.

Government officials contest the pot-growing outbreak is being orchestrated largely by so-called "drug trafficking organizations" from our neighbors in Mexico. The DEA says these drug cartels' business model is to maximize profit by reducing delivery expenses. Pot smokers can then buy cheaper weed because the growers are able to avoid the costs associated with smuggling hundreds of pounds of product across the border. Fortunately for these producers, the cannabis plant can flourish in many types of conditions. All they need is some remote land with access to water and they are up and running in no time.

Most of federal eradication efforts have thus far been focused on seven states: Hawaii, Washington, Oregon, California, West Virginia, Kentucky and Tennessee, with almost 60 to 65 percent of these outdoor crops being planted on public lands. In the last two years alone, law enforcement agencies across the country seized over 20 million pot plants, an annual increase of 5 million compared to 2005. Growers have expanded their growing business into other states as well, including Michigan, Wisconsin, Alabama, Colorado and Virginia.

It's not just public lands that are being used for clandestine pot farms. Last summer, owners of the Korbel Winery in Sonoma County, California were startled to find that 15 of their protected redwood trees had been chopped to the ground by trespassers who were growing over 100 pot plants on their land. To top it off, bags of fertilizer were dumped along a nearby creek.

"It was sad to see those nice redwood trees down," said Sonoma County Sheriff's Sgt. Mike Raasch after looking over the wreckage.

A large number of the marijuana gardens are located up and down the West Coast, with a majority sprouting up in California. The High Intensity Drug Trafficking Area (HIDTA), a federal program that oversees drug enforcement across that country, reported in June 2010 that "California produces more marijuana than Mexico." Officials estimate that in 2009, California's seized plants would have had a retail value of $17.8 billion. The cost to taxpayers to clean up the razed lands where the weed was grown reached as much as $1 million per farm.

The crops that provide these considerable profits are often protected by heavily armed guards. On August 28, 2011, former Northern California city councilman Jere Melo was shot and killed while investigating an outdoor marijuana-growing operation in Mendocino County. Melo was hired by a timber company to investigate reports of a pot farm being constructed on their land. When Melo and his friend got close to the farm, a man protecting the plants popped up and opened fire. While his partner was able to escape, Melo was not so lucky.

In 2010 HIDTA estimated that almost 121 square miles of land was being used throughout California to grow illegal pot. As the report noted, "For every acre that is 'Impacted' (the actual growing area) there are another two to 10 aces that are considered 'Constrained.' The Constrained area is that which is marked by trails, waterlines, campsites and other areas trampled by growers ... The City of Sacramento is 97 square miles in size and the amount of area used for growing marijuana exceeds the size of the state's Capital city ... Why do the drug trafficking organizations grow so much marijuana in California? The answer is simply the demand by users and unrestrained profits."

Sequoia National Park, well known for being home to some of the world's most gigantic trees, is also residence to hundreds of pot growers during the prime harvesting months of April to October. Several parts of the park are closed to visitors during this time, including the pristine Kaweah River drainage, where drug cartels are cultivating massive amounts of pot. These operations, which would place the industry high on NASDAQ if it were a single legal company, are by no means environmentally benign.

"It's so big that we have to focus our resources on one or two areas at a time, because otherwise it's beyond our scope," Sequoia's special agent assigned to the ordeal, told the *Los Angeles Times*. It is estimated that California's marijuana trade accounts for $14 billion in annual sales.

Such environmental devastation has placed many marijuana advocates into one of two camps: Those who want to keep pot illegal so they can continue to profit without taxation and regulation, and those who want to legalize the plant in order to reduce these sorts of environmental impacts—not to mention incarceration associated with non-violent drug crimes.

"This kind of destruction, lack of respect for nature and the area, and elaborate scheming to hide their efforts is only possible because marijuana remains a profitable, underground drug rather than being a profitable, legal one," wrote Aaron Turpen for *CannaCentral* following the incident at Korbel Winery. "Legalize marijuana and then the need to hide it—destroying old growth trees and a natural setting in the process—goes away."

Not all agree with Turpen's assessment. When Californians voted on Prop 19, the initiative to legalize marijuana in November 2010, the state's main pot-growing region actually voted against the measure. The weed-rich "Emerald Triangle" counties of Humboldt, Mendocino and Trinity all said no to legal pot.

There is good reason why these illegal growers (not to be confused with legal, medicinal producers) embrace libertarian ideals when it comes to their bustling industry: without government involvement they can rake in millions in profit. No environmental studies have to be done and no taxes will ever be paid. The only thing these growers have to worry about is being raided by drug enforcement cops.

President Obama, while admitting to have toked a little ganja years ago, has taken up Bush's hard-line stance against legalization of the herb. Recently the president dismissed any medical value of the substance, and in a 2010 Drug Control Strategy report, the White House explained why marijuana ought to remain classified as a dangerous, illegal drug:

> We have many proven methods for reducing the demand for drugs. Keeping drugs illegal reduces their availability and lessens willingness to use them. That is why this Administration firmly opposes the legalization of marijuana or any other illicit drug. Legalizing drugs would increase accessibility and encourage promotion and acceptance of use. Diagnostic, laboratory, clinical, and epidemiological studies clearly indicate that marijuana use is associated with dependence, respiratory and mental illness, poor motor performance, and cognitive impairment, among other negative effects, and legalization would only exacerbate these problems.

Many of those who want to see pot legalized envision a future where their drug of choice is viewed more like wine than heroin. They want to know where their marijuana is coming from and how it was grown. Many want it to be organic and eco-friendly. They may even want to visit farmers and take a tour of the crops. However, as long as weed remains illegal, they claim, ecologically damaging operations on public and private lands will only become more prevalent. Violence over market share will ensue and more taxpayer dollars will be wasted.

Longtime legalization advocate, Orange County Superior Court Judge James Gray, estimates that legalizing pot could save California at least $1 billion a year by reducing arrests and prosecution, with that number only increasing if other states are taken into consideration.

"We couldn't make this drug any more available if we tried," Judge Gray said during the battle over California's Proposition 19. "Not only do we have those problems, along with glamorizing it by making it illegal, but we also have the crime and corruption that go along with it … Unfortunately, every society in the history of mankind has had some form of mind-altering, sometimes addictive substances to use, to misuse, abuse or get addicted to. Get used to it. They're here to stay. So let's try to reduce those harms, and right now we couldn't do it worse if we tried."

– December 11, 2011

SACRIFICIAL WOLVES

By Jeffrey St. Clair

I was prone on my stomach on a small knoll above the Lamar River, peering through my field glasses toward a stand of tall cottonwoods, their leaves a shimmering bronze in the autumn light. The morning air was crisp, hinting at an early snow in the dark, distant peaks of the Absaroka Range. The summer tourists had evaporated; I felt alone in the Big Empty.

I had ventured to this remote Northeast quadrant of Yellowstone National Park looking for wolves.

One particular wolf, in fact, a female called 832F, the grand-daughter of one of the original pairs of wolves reintroduced into the park in 1996. She was the unrivaled leader of her pack, a gregarious and inquisitive creature, graceful and athletic, capable of taking down a mature elk by herself. She was also, by all accounts, a dutiful mother, caring, doting, fiercely protective.

I had seen her once before, a fleeting glimpse, two years earlier, a few miles from the Lamar Valley in the green meanders of Slough Creek, with two pups, a few months old, nipping playfully at her heels. Instead of merely watching them, I stumbled clumsily for my camera. Her ears pricked, she turned to me, gave a stern growl, as if to say "you blew it, buddy," and vanished with her brood into a thicket of willows.

This was to be my shot at redemption and I left my Canon, with its intrusive lens, locked in the car. I had chosen a spot about 200 yards downwind from the fresh corpse of a bison, which was being picked at by a grouchy group of ravens. I had been settled in for two hours or so, crouched low in the tall grasses, when they came, silent as shadows, down through the cottonwoods, to the decaying body by the river. Even the ravens, those caustic critics of authority, quelled in the presence of the pack.

The two pups had grown. They raced each other to gnaw at the flank of the bison. Six other wolves, followed casually, waded into the river, lapped water and then began to feed on the carcass. After twenty minutes or so, the satiated wolves curled up near each other and napped in the sunshine. But Wolf 832F didn't join the feast. She sat on a ledge above the river, her head held high, surveying the valley as the fall winds bristled across her shining coat.

Two months later, two of these wolves would be killed, shot by hunters in Wyoming, who were gunning for "radio-collared wolves," which identified them as originating in Yellowstone. One of the wolves was 832F, the other was her mate.

Arguably the most famous wolf in the world, 832F had the misfortune of slipping across the invisible boundary of Yellowstone Park into the state of Wyoming, a free-fire zone. There she encountered an anonymous hunter, who had been camped out in the forest for 20 consecutive days, just waiting for one of the Yellowstone wolves to cross the sights of his rifle. There is compelling evidence that anti-wolf hunters in Wyoming had been honing in on the telemetry frequencies from the radio collars to track and kill the wolves as they crossed the boundary of the park.

In May of this year on the northern border of Yellowstone, a wolf-hating rancher lured another pack of Yellowstone wolves out of the park to his ranch. He baited the wolves by setting out sheep carcasses on his property. The rancher waited until park wolves showed up and opened fire, killing a black two-year old female, who had been born and reared in Yellowstone's Hayden Valley.

In the past two years, since the Obama administration shamefully gave the green light to legal wolf hunting in the Yellowstone region, fourteen of the Park's wolves (about 12 percent of the total population) have been shot or trapped outside the park's boundaries.

The decision was shameful because we now know the decision to delist the wolf was motivated solely by politics not science. The review panel met in secret with Democrats from the state of Montana who vigorously pushed for the delisting, which they argued would be a crucial factor in tight senate and gubernatorial races. Meanwhile, ecologists who objected to the plan were ignored and three scientists on the review panel who were viewed as "pro wolf" were summarily removed.

The consequences for wolves and the integrity of the Endangered Species Act itself have been grim. In Yellowstone itself, the wolf population is in free-fall. Ironically, wolf populations in the park hit their high point during the Bush administration, with a count of 174 wolves in 2003. When Obama took office in the winter of 2009, there were an estimated 146 wolves in Yellowstone. That number has declined sharply each year. This year the park's population has fallen to 70 wolves, marking a more than 50 percent reduction in Obama's four years in office.

Even wolves in Oregon, where wolf hunting is outlawed, are not safe. OR-16 was a young black male, a little over a year old, born along the upper Walla Walla River. He had been radio-collared and photographed to great fanfare by Oregon wolf biologists in November 2012. Three months later, a wolf hunter shot the black pup near Lowman, Idaho. There is speculation that Oregon ranchers may have deliberately chased the wolf across the Snake River into Idaho during the height of the state's wolf hunt. A posting by a Bill K. on an anti-wolf email group bragged: "If us pushing that wolf back over to be shot in Idaho works. We will continue to push many more back for the shooters. Hell we will even pay for the ammo. Ha ha ha ha."

OR-16 was just one of more than 500 wolves legally killed in Idaho in the last two years. And the slaughter is just getting started.

All this blood sacrificed for what?

– October 25, 2013

GET YOUR WINGS

By Jeffrey St. Clair

Against the slate-colored Oregon sky, the bird's white-and-black markings almost shimmer. Its long, sharply pointed wings are cocked in a dihedral as it hovers over the choppy waters of Young's Bay. It hangs nearly motionless for a moment before plunging into a steep descent. The bird strikes the water, shudders and emerges with a small cutthroat trout in its talons. It wheels skyward and lands on the branch of a dead Sitka spruce and begins to consume its prey.

I don't need to consult my Sibley guide. There's no doubt about the species: it's that masterful fishing raptor, an osprey. But wait a minute. An element of doubt creeps in. Osprey's aren't supposed to be here, near the mouth of the Columbia River, up here on Parallel 46, in far northwestern Oregon. Not this time of year. Not during the third week of February. Yet there she is, casually flaying a trout, less than 100 yards away from me.

Osprey are neotropical migrants. Like many Californians, they summer in the Northwest and head south for sunnier terrain in the early fall. On the west coast, Osprey tend to winter in Honduras, Guatemala, Panama, Colombia and return north in the spring. Birders, an obsessive tribe of which I've long been a member, keep close watch on the first arrival dates for migratory birds like osprey. There's a fancy word for the science of monitoring these migratory timetables called "phenology."

In Oregon ornithologists have been assiduously recording the first arrival dates of osprey for at least the past 80 years. Up here in Astoria, the oldest American settlement west of the Rockies, those records, though spotty, go back even farther—to the Scottish botanist David Douglas, up and down the Columbia region from 1824 to 27, to the men of John Jacob Astor's American

Fur Company, founded in 1812, and the Corps of Discovery, also known as the Lewis and Clark Expedition, of 1805/6.

Lewis and Clark were meticulous note-keepers and relatively gifted naturalists, especially the moody Meriwether Lewis. It's worth noting that neither Lewis or Clark, nor the expedition's other diarist Patrick Gass, recorded seeing an osprey during their stay at Fort Clatsop, the remains of which are just a quarter of a mile from where I spotted my winter Osprey. They left the soggy outpost for their return to St. Louis on March 23, 1806.

And it makes sense that they didn't see an osprey that cruel winter of unrelenting rain, because over the course of the last 80 years the average first arrival date of Osprey at Young's Bay is around the first day of April. So this bird was at least 55 days premature. Turns out, she wasn't alone. Fifty miles south, at Tillamook Bay, an Osprey has been sighted all year long for the past three years. Similar year-round sightings have been made across Oregon: on the Columbia River near Bonneville Dam, at Detroit Lake in the Cascade Range and along the Illinois River in the Siskiyou Mountains. Over the past decade, across the Pacific Northwest, osprey have been arriving on average a couple of days early each year.

And the osprey aren't alone. Turkey vultures, swallows, warblers and all sorts of wading birds are also showing up, across the northern hemisphere, days, even weeks, ahead of schedule. For example, a recent long-term study by the Royal Society of London revealed that Black-Tailed Godwits are arriving to their nesting grounds in south Iceland more than 22 days earlier than they did in 1988. In all these cases, climate seems to be the driving force behind the early migrations northward.

Of course, it's been a peculiar winter here in Oregon. On that same week of February came news that Santiam Pass in the central Cascade Range was bare of snow. Santiam Pass sits at 3750 feet and since record-keeping began has averaged about 40 inches of snow on the ground in February and often much more.

A hundred and fifty miles to the south, Crater Lake National Park saw its thinnest snow pack in more than a century. Even more disturbing, the snow pack at Crater Lake is 50 percent lower than the lowest ever recorded. It's going to be a dry and crispy summer here in the Pacific Northwest.

Ecological bills are coming home to roost, though few seem to take notice. Down in Florida, a state in eminent peril from rising sea levels, the state's billionaire governor Rick Scott issued an executive diktat gagging state employees from mentioning the word's climate change or global warming. The man who blew the whistle on Scott's gag order was a long-time ecologist at the state's Department of Environmental Protection named Bart Bibler. After Bibler breached Scott's ludicrous injunction at a public meeting on coastal management issues, he was slapped with reprimand, suspended from his job and ordered to submit to a mental health evaluation. Apparently, Rick Scott has read his Stalin. But even Comrade Joe couldn't stop the seas from rising.

When we returned home to Oregon City from the coast a few days after sighting the Osprey, the forsythias were in bloom, daffodils were poking up and a Rufous Hummingbird was flitting around the backyard, already up from the Yucatan, two months ahead of schedule, in search of a nectar fix. The climate is changing in strange and inscrutable ways and the birds, at least, are racing to keep up.

– May 1, 2015

LONG TIME COMING, LONG TIME GONE

By Jeffrey St. Clair

On the day Pope Francis released his encyclical on the fate of the Earth, I was struggling to climb a near vertical cliff on the Parajito Plateau of northern New Mexico. My fingers gripped tightly to handholds notched into the rocks hundreds of years ago by Ancestral Puebloans, the anodyne phrase now used by modern anthropologists to describe the people once known as the Anasazi. The day was a scorcher and the volcanic rocks were so hot they blistered my hands and knees. Even my guide, Elijah, a young member of the Santa Clara Pueblo, confessed that the heat radiating off the basalt had made him feel faint, although perhaps he was simply trying to make me feel less like a weather wimp.

When we finally hurled ourselves over the rimrock to the top of the little mesa, the ruins of the old city of Puyé spread before us. Amid purple blooms of cholla cactus, piñon pines and sagebrush, two watchtowers rose above the narrow spine of the mesa top, guarding the crumbling walls of houses that once sheltered more than 1,500 people. I was immediately struck by the defensive nature of the site: an acropolis set high above the corn, squash and bean fields in the valley below; a city fortified against the inevitable outbreaks turbulence and violence unleashed by periods of prolonged scarcity.

The ground sparkled with potsherds, the shattered remnants of exquisitely crafted bowls and jars, all featuring dazzling polychromatic glazes. Some had been used to haul water up the cliffs of the mesa, an arduous and risky daily ordeal that surely would only have been undertaken during a time of extreme environmental and cultural stress. How did the people end up here? Where did they come from? What were they fleeing?

"They came here after the lights went out at Chaco," Elijah tells me. He's referring to the great houses of Chaco Canyon, now besieged by big oil. Chaco, the imperial city of the Anasazi, was ruled for four hundred years by a stern hierarchy of astronomer-priests until it was swiftly abandoned around 1250 AD.

"Why did they leave?" I asked.

"Something bad happened, after the waters ran out." He won't go any further and I don't press him.

The ruins of Puyé, now part of the Santa Clara Pueblo, sit in the blue shadow of the Jemez Mountains. A few miles to the north, in the stark labs of Los Alamos, scientists are still at work calculating the dark equations of global destruction down to the last decimal point.

This magnificent complex of towers, multi-story dwellings, plazas, granaries, kivas and cave dwellings was itself abandoned suddenly around 1500. Its Tewa-speaking residents moved off the cliffs and mesas to the flatlands along the Rio Grande ten miles to the east, near the site of the current Santa Clara (St. Clair) Pueblo. A few decades later they would encounter an invading force beyond their worst nightmare: Coronado and his metal-plated conquistadors.

Again, it was a prolonged drought that forced the deeply egalitarian people of Puyé—the place where the rabbits gather—from their mesa-top fortress. "The elders say that the people knew it was time to move when they saw the black bears leaving the canyon," Elijah told me.

Elijah is a descendent of one of the great heroes of Santa Clara Pueblo: Domingo Naranjo, a leader of the one true American Revolution, the Pueblo Revolt of 1680, which drove the Spanish out of New Mexico. Naranjo was half-Tewa and half-black, the son of an escaped slave of the Spanish. That glorious rebellion largely targeted the brutal policies of the Franciscan missionaries, who had tortured, enslaved and butchered the native people of the Rio Grande Valley for nearly 100 years. As the Spanish friars fled, Naranjo supervised the razing of the Church the Franciscans had erected—using slave labor—in the plaza of Santa Clara Pueblo.

Now the hope of the world may reside in the persuasive powers of a Franciscan, the Hippie Pope, whose Druidic encyclical, *Laudato Si'*, reads like a tract from the Deep Ecology movement of the 1980s, only more lucidly and urgently written. Pope Francis depicts the ecological commons of the planet being sacrificed for a "throwaway culture" that is driven by a deranged economic system whose only goal is "quick and easy profit." As the supreme baptizer, Francis places a special emphasis on the planet's imperiled waters, both the dwindling reserves of freshwater and the inexorable rise of acidic oceans, heading like a slow-motion tsunami toward a coast near you.

Climate change has gone metastatic and we are all weather wimps under the new dispensation. Consider that Hell on Earth: Phoenix, Arizona, a city whose water greed has breached any rational limit. Its 1.5 million residents, neatly arranged in spiraling cul-de-sacs, meekly await a reckoning with the Great Thirst, as if Dante himself had supervised the zoning plans. The Phoenix of the future seems destined to resemble the ruins of Chaco, with crappier architecture.

I am writing this column in the basement of our house in Oregon City, which offers only slight relief from the oppressive heat outside. The temperature has topped 100 degrees again. It hasn't rained in 40 days and 40 nights. We are reaching the end of something. Perhaps it has already occurred. Even non-believers are left to heed the warnings of the Pope and follow the example of the bears of the Jemez.

Yet now there is no hidden refuge to move toward. There is only a final movement left to build, a global rebellion against the forces of greed and extinction. One way or another, it will either be a long time coming or a long time gone.

– August 2015

MOUNTAIN OF TEARS: OREGON'S VANISHING GLACIERS

By Jeffrey St. Clair

> Slow-burning, life dies like a flame,
> Never resting, passes like a river.
> Today I face my lone shadow.
> Suddenly, the tears flow down.
> — From "Cold Mountain," by Han-Shan (Trans. A. Kline)

I've made this same climb up the rugged northeastern slope of Mt. Hood every year since we moved to Oregon. This is expedition 26. The route is challenging to the point of being cruel. It's even more demanding on an aging body that has spent far too many years bent over a Macintosh.

The trail up Cooper's Spur, a sharp ridge plunging off the volcano's pyramidal peak, is steep and treacherous. The slope is coated in fine steel-gray volcanic ash, ground down over the centuries by snow and ice. You take two steps up and slide one step back. The trail zigzags its way ever-upwards, gaining more than 3,000 feet, in dozens of switchbacks through ash and scree to a place called Hieroglyph Point, where the path finally peters out. According to mountain lore, Hieroglyph Point was named after a boulder featuring "mysterious markings." In fact, the markings aren't mysterious and they aren't hieroglyphics. They are beautiful kanji characters carved into the rock by Japanese climbers who summited Hood via this precarious route in 1908. This is the highest spot on the mountain that you can reach by trail. But having reached 9,000 feet, I usually scramble even further up the 45-degree slope to the Chimney, a near vertical passage through dark basalt to the summit.

At several vantages, the exposure along the deeply incised canyons that flank both sides of the Spur is extreme, dizzying.

The sense of vertigo is enhanced when the winds pick up, as they tend to do in the afternoon, whipping around the summit at speeds of forty to sixty miles an hour. Two years ago, I watched as group of four climbers a few hundred feet above me where blown off the Spur and into a boulder field, escaping largely unscathed. Others haven't been so lucky. This is the most lethal quadrant of a deadly mountain. Since 1980, at least 28 people have perished on and around Cooper Spur, many of them plunging headlong onto the Eliot Glacier 2,500 feet below, their corpses emerging months, sometimes years, later in the milky waters of glacial melt. Tears of the mountain, climbers call it.

The Spur itself is a massive moraine, formed by the advance and retreat of an ancient glacier. This is a testament to the power of ice and water to sculpt and shape landscapes on a vast scale. That transformative force is diminishing, year-by-year, as a warming planet works inexorably to eradicate mountain glaciers.

When I first climbed Cooper's Spur in the early 1990s, much of the ridge was still under snow well into August, the route visible only by following stone cairns and wooden posts. By 2005, these high slopes on Mt. Hood were clear of snow by mid-July, if not earlier. This spring, after a blistering run of days in April, the snowpack on Cooper's Spur had melted off by early May, exposing the mountains largest and most vulnerable glaciers to at least six months of unrelenting sun.

Even following a stormy winter of heavy rains and mountain snow, Oregon's snowpack was reduced to 56 percent of normal, a trend that has been getting worse for the past twenty years. The story is the same up and down the Cascade Range, from North Cascades National Park on the Canadian border to Mt. Shasta in northern California. One consequence of the dwindling snowpack is the fact that the soggiest part of the country is now facing the prospect of water shortages. The prospect of diminished snowpacks and early melt-offs is even more dire for the salmon and trout that spawn in the mountains small rivers and streams.

On my descent, I stopped at the elegant stone climber's shelter built seventy years ago, which has somehow survived rockfalls and avalanches, to get a little relief from the blistering sun and near 100-degree temperatures. Inside I met a Swedish glaciologist named Arne Sjöström, who has been studying Cascade glaciers for the past decade. He invited me to walk with him down into Eliot Canyon for a close up look at Oregon's largest glacier. On the floor of the canyon we crossed numerous small terminal moraines, the traces of the glacier's accelerated retreat. Eliot Creek was gushing, a white roar from the late afternoon melt.

Svensson told me that the Eliot Glacier has lost more than 140 feet in thickness over the last century and has retreated more than 1,000 feet from the first photos of the glacier taken in 1901. Across the Northwest, Svensson said, glaciers have retreated by more than 50 percent and the pace of retreat is quickening. Dozens of northwest glaciers have disappeared entirely, including ten named glaciers in Oregon, along with hundreds of other smaller perennial ice and snow patches.

The headwall of the Eliot Glacier is iridescent blue, a blue that casts an eerie glow in the summer moonlight. As we approached the wall of ice, we were struck by waves coolness emanating from glacier. The face of the glacier was deeply fissured and we could hear it rumble and crack, as if the mountain itself was moaning at the loss of ice that had coated its flanks for the last 20,000 years.

We live in a time when essential elements that have shaped life on our planet are vanishing before our eyes.

– September 8, 2016

OF GRIZZLY BEARS AND BUREAUCRATS: THE QUEST FOR SURVIVAL

By Joshua Frank

I've always been attracted to grizzly country, or in other words, I've always been drawn to wilderness. Perhaps there's no way around it, having grown up in Montana it's likely a key strain of my DNA. We don't call it real wilderness in Big Sky Country unless the place is inhabited by grizzlies, or at least what few still remain.

Arguably America's greatest apex predator, no animal symbolizes the "wild" more than the grizzly bear, which thrives if given a roaming range of 70–300 square miles for females and up to 500 for males. Of course, humans (read colonial settlers) being attracted to the land of the grizzly is exactly what's put this majestic wandering creature on the verge of extinction today.

Take the case of the Southern California grizzly (Ursus horribilis), which up until the late 1800s dominated the state's southern coastline, where for centuries the great bears scavenged along the region's rivers and wetlands hoping to snag the once abundant salmon and trout. As Mike Davis writes in *Ecology of Fear*, during a "national orgy" of killing between 1865–1890, upwards of 95% of California's "wild game" was slaughtered. California grizzlies all but vanished during this short span of 25 years, likely the largest wildlife kill-off in history. That's right, before orange groves and fruit orchards began to dominate the dry California landscape, there were grizzlies. Tens of thousands since the Pleistocene age, supported by an abundant, healthy ecosystem.

"In this canyon were seen whole troops of bears; they have the ground all plowed up from digging it to find their sustenance in the roots, which the land produces," Pedro Fages, a Spanish soldier and explorer wrote in his diary in 1769. "They are ferocious brutes, hard to hunt ... They do not give up."

The last known grizzly in So Cal was shot in 1916 by Cornelius Birket Johnson, an industrious farmer living at the foothills of the San Gabriel Mountains in north Los Angeles. The hungry bear trampled the man's newly planted vineyard, chomping on his young grapes for three straight nights. Ol' Johnson wasn't about to let the pesky bear get away with such thievery and destruction, so one night he lured the grizzly with a slab of beef and snagged him in a trap, but like all feisty grizzlies, this young guy wouldn't go down easy. Johnson later shot the bear dead after finding it gravely injured, exhausted, bloodied and suffering, having dragged the metal trap far from where it was originally set. Thus, at the hands of Johnson, the extinction of the So Cal grizzly was complete.

It's the same sad story virtually everywhere one looks across the West. Between the mid-1800s up until the 1920s, grizzlies were killed off in 95% of their native habitat by European settlers in the Lower-48. The only bears that survived this period lived in remote, mountainous regions like the Montana wilderness. As David J. Mattson and colleagues write for the National Biological Service, "Unregulated killing of bears continued through the 1950s and resulted in a further 52% decline in their range between 1920 and 1970. Altogether, grizzly bears were eliminated from 98% of their original range in the contiguous United States during a 100-year period."

The numbers are startling. Scientists estimate there were at least 50,000 grizzlies living in the contiguous United States in the mid-1800s. Today that number has dropped to a measly 1,100. Certainly, it's a miracle any grizzlies are alive today at all, and the ones that are continue to live under constant assault. While over-hunting and obscene Western expansionism has worked in tandem to annihilate the grizzly, which was listed as threatened in 1975 by the federal government—climate change is just one of the latest obstacles the bear faces in its quest for survival, despite the fact that the U.S. Fish and Wildlife Service (FWS) doesn't believe so.

"[We] conclude that the effects of climate change do not constitute a threat to the [Yellowstone grizzly bear population] now, nor are they anticipated to in the future," the FWS declared in the Federal Register in March, after concluding another "study" on the health of the grizzly in Yellowstone.

Leave it to the paper-pushers at FWS to deny the fact that grizzlies are impacted by our warming climate. Indeed that's exactly what they are doing when it comes to Yellowstone's grizzly bear population. Over 10 years ago the grizzly's most important high-energy food source in Yellowstone, the whitebark pine nut (*Pinus albicaulis*), ceased to exist as winter temperatures rose. Warmer winters, a solid 2 degree rise since the 1970s, allowed pine beetle larva to survive the winter months and mature as summer approached. And we all know the devastation the pine beetle has wrought on Western forests—now these important high-altitude trees are essentially non-functioning and no longer a food source for hungry grizzlies that dig up and munch on these pine cones prior to hibernation. In total, more than 60 million acres of forest from Northern Mexico through British Columbia have been killed by the pine beetle. Indeed, the death of the whitebark pine is just one indicator that climate change is forever altering the fragile Yellowstone ecosystem and the species that depend on it.

Today greater Yellowstone, which comprises of 31,000 square miles, sustains an estimated 600 grizzly bears. That's 1 bear per 52 square miles. FWS actually believes this is a healthy number and is working hard to delist the bear, which they've attempted to do for the past two decades. FWS's own staff initially believed only 16 percent of Yellowstone's whitebark pines were infected by the pine beetle.

Therefore, the FWS claimed, the little beetle served no real impediment to the survival of the grizzly. This estimate was later shattered by Dr. Jesse Logan, a decorated entomologist who is the former head of the FWS's bark beetle research team. Logan's own independent study suggested that nearly 95 percent of Yellowstone's whitebark pine tree population was impacted. Following Logan's analysis, FWS subsequently altered their estimate to 74 percent.

"The whitebark pine is both a foundation and a keystone species," Jesse Logan tells *Scientific American*. "The health of the whitebark pine is very closely related to the health of the entire ecosystem."

When the whitebark pines die off, so does a vital food source for bears. And when grizzlies go for good, there is no returning. Perhaps that's FWS's intention, despite their claims to have the best interest of the grizzly at heart. If they did actually give a shit, they'd learn from their own past mistakes. In 2007 FWS delisted the Yellowstone grizzly and the move had devastating impacts. In 2008, 54 Yellowstone grizzlies died—37 of which were killed by hunters. It was likely the highest mortality rate of the Yellowstone grizzly in over 40 years.

"'Known' mortality is, as a rule of thumb, generally about half of actual grizzly bears dead. A hundred dead bears per year, no matter if the total number in the ecosystem is 200 or 600, means the [Yellowstone grizzly] population is crashing downhill," writes author and bear advocate Doug Peacock. "This is especially true for the grizzly, one of the world's slowest-reproducing mammals."

Fortunately, in 2009 U.S. District Judge Donald Molloy ruled that Yellowstone's grizzlies were not fully recovered, and cited the whitebark pine die-off as the reason the bears deserved to be protected by the Endangered Species Act once again. One major problem, noted Molloy, was there were no regulatory protections in place if the population began to decline, which clearly was happening.

"Even if the monitoring were enforceable, the monitoring itself does nothing to protect the grizzly bear population," Molloy wrote. "Instead, there is only a promise of future, unenforceable actions. Promises of future, speculative action are not existing regulatory mechanisms."

Now, FWS argues that it's again time to strip these bears of their frail legal protection. No matter that the whitebark pine epidemic is far worse than it was ten years ago. No matter that the bear population is essentially the same size as it was in 2007. The delisting a decade ago shows us that the government does not have the capability to manage the delicate balance of grizzlies and their diminishing habitat. In fact, as climate change continues to kill off one of these bear's main food sources, grizzlies will need more land to survive, not less.

Of course bears have no idea humans have drawn arbitrary lines around their habitat, dictating where they are allowed to roam and live. Whitebark pine trees are nearly gone in Yellowstone National Park and won't be returning in our lifetimes. Sure grizzlies are highly intelligent, and will work hard to survive under adverse conditions. But if delisted, FWS will be setting up a major impediment that will forever devastate the grizzly as they face the bloodlust of trophy hunters near the park's boundaries when they leave Yellowstone in search of food and new mates.

By denying that Yellowstone grizzlies are threatened by climate change (or greedy sport hunters for that matter), FWS is turning its back on science. It's also turning its back on common sense. Delisting the grizzly serves no decent purpose whatsoever. There is no question that history will repeat itself if these short-sighted bureaucrats can pull it off—in this case a history of avoidable extinction.

When we lose grizzlies, we lose wilderness, and when we lose wilderness we lose a piece of ourselves that can't ever be replaced.

– January 14, 2017

THE FIRES THIS TIME

By Jeffrey St. Clair

As Hurricane Irma was charging across the Caribbean, 3,500 miles to the Northwest the Columbia River Gorge, one of the continent's natural marvels, had exploded into flames. The Gorge, a National Scenic Area largely under the management of the U.S. Forest Service, is a 4,000-foot deep chasm in the Cascade Mountains through which the Columbia River forges toward the Pacific. The western half of the Gorge is temperate rainforest, dominated by 300-year-old Douglas-fir and western hemlock trees.

The fire had started on September 2. It was a suffocatingly hot day in a record run of hot, dry days. Northwest Oregon hadn't seen measurable rain since the first of June. The forest floor was crisp, arid and flammable. A group of teens had ventured into Eagle Creek Canyon seeking refuge under its tall trees, emerald pools and waterfalls. Goofing around, one of them shouted, "Hey, watch this." Then he lit a pack of fire-crackers and tossed it down to the canyon floor, where it detonated like a bomblet. Within hours, the Eagle Creek Fire had raced across 3,000 acres of old-growth forest, stranding more than 100 terrified hikers on the Pacific Crest and Eagle Creek Trails. By the next day, the river town of Cascade Locks was under evacuation orders.

Three days later, I awoke to a sickly-sweet smell in Oregon City, 70 miles west of the Gorge fires. Outside, a gray scrim of ash coated the porch and my ancient Subaru. Our house was enshrouded in a pall of smoke so thick I could barely detect the vague outlines of the house across the street. The night before the winds had shifted and the fire had surged 14-miles to the West in a few hours. I-84, the main east-west Interstate in Oregon, was closed and would remain so for three weeks. The ash and debris, still warm to the touch, continued to fall for the next five days, until the winds shifted and the fires raged to the east menacing the town of Hood River. In three weeks, the Gorge fires had burned nearly 50,000 acres. And, after nearly 30 years spent scrambling up and down each trail, I had come to know nearly each acre intimately.

As Multnomah Falls, Oneonta Gorge, Angel's Rest and dozens of other natural jewels went up in flames, popular rage against the fire-starter intensified. There were vengeful calls for the kid to be arrested, tried as an adult, fined millions of dollars and hauled off to prison for decades. The anger toward the tyro pyro is understandable, but misplaced. The Gorge was primed to burn. If it hadn't been firecrackers, it would have been a cigarette butt, a campfire, a spark from a truck engine, a lightning strike.Forests, even rainforests, are born in fire. Ecologically, fire is a regenerative force.

Mature Douglas-fir trees have thick, furrowed bark that makes them resistant to most fires, which historically have tended to burn in a patchwork, mosaic-like pattern, that tends to clear out the understory and reduce the fuel load but leave the big trees unscathed. The Gorge had burned before, but never like this. These fires are different. They consume whole stands of trees. They burn hotter, longer and spread faster.The wildfire season in Oregon has expanded by 75 days since 1980. In the 1970s, the average Oregon wildfire burned for about a week before petering out.

Now, forest fires here in the Northwest rage for an average of 56 days, until they are extinguished by the fall rains and snows, which come later and later each year. The number of acres burned in Oregon each year has more than doubled since 1980. What has changed in those 37 years? The climate.

If you're looking for a culprit to blame, blame the Blob, the vast patch of warm surface water in the Pacific Ocean that has been expanding off the Northwest Coast for the past six years. The warm air currents percolating up from the Blob, which now seems less like a freakish phenomenon and more like a twisted new reality, has derailed the jet-stream. The low-pressure systems that have brought rain, fog and cool temperatures to the region for millennia have been diverted, replaced by a stubborn high pressure system that tends to stick over the Northwest from June through October. This was Oregon's hottest and driest summer in history. The fifth such record in the last seven years. You get the picture.

But the politicians don't. They see fire as an opportunity for plunder. Sonny Perdue and his wrecking crew at the Agriculture Department, which through a bureaucratic quirk controls the Forest Service, are portraying old-growth trees as standing weapons of mass destruction. Taking the Vietnam approach to the National Forests, which Perdue calls the "woodbasket of the world," Perdue intends to save the forest by clearcutting it, without any restraint from troubling environmental laws. "We're not going to roll over at every 'boo' from the environmentalists," he vowed in Montana in July. How convenient for the timber industry.

Denial prevails, coast-to-coast. In Houston, the Feds are aerial spraying the wreckage of Harvey with pesticides, preparing for reconstructing in the floodplains and marshes. In Oregon, the plans are already being scripted to log the scorched forests for their own good, which is the ecological equivalent of pouring acid on a burn patient. If they succeed, the Columbia Gorge will become a sylvan necropolis to greed and climate change.

– November 24, 2017

SECTION 2
WATERSCAPES

DAMBUSTERS: RESISTING THE HYDRO-IMPERIALISTS

By Jeffrey St. Clair

More than 700 feet below the surreal steel span of Glen Canyon Bridge, the Colorado River bursts loose from the spillways of Glen Canyon Dam. The current of this once mud-red river is now a strange cartoon-blue, deathly cold, as it courses through the last 17 miles of Glen Canyon. Now, it is a river in name only, its every minute fluctuation controlled by hydro-engineers and water bureaucrats. The Colorado is finally loose, but it is not free.

To the north stands the implacable concrete plug of Glen Canyon Dam: smooth, white, indifferent. Behind the blond wall stretches a dead lagoon of stagnant water 200 miles long, burying one of the most glorious canyons on Earth. Knowing that the one-armed explorer John Wesley Powell was something of a heroic figure to the conservation movement aligned against the Colorado dams, Floyd Dominy, chief hydro-imperialist and then-head of the Bureau of Reclamation, impishly decided to name Glen Canyon's watery grave Lake Powell, Jewel of the Colorado.

Radical environmentalists, such Edward Abbey and David Brower, viewed the naming as kind of final sacrilege. But sticking Powell's name on the reservoir is probably apt. The big hydro dams clotting the rivers of the world have always been pushed by progressives under the false promise of tamed rivers, cheap water for irrigation, and cheap power. Native ecosystems and native peoples be damned. Even Powell, a humane man by most accounts, thought this way. He would have dammed every river in the American West. Does it matter that he would have done so in the name of democracy?

In 1869 John Wesley Powell began his first venture down the Green and Colorado Rivers. This wasn't an Army expedition. It didn't enjoy the backing of the federal government. Powell wasn't the hired errand boy of an eastern-industrialist-turned-philanthropist. He wasn't searching for gold or oil. He was merely a largely self-educated teacher at a small college in rural Illinois with a consuming interest in geology. His expedition to the Colorado Plateau consisted of four small boats and a crew of nine other men: hunters, drifters, friends, and shell-shocked Civil War vets. It was financed by the Illinois Natural History Society he headed. Powell had neither the educational pedigree of Clarence Dutton nor the imperial ambitions of John Fremont.

Powell was the oddball on the roster of explorers of the American outback. His trip was as close to pure science as the West had yet seen. His conclusions from that trip, and his subsequent career, highlight the dangerous impurities bundled into that science, and the blind spots Powell shared with his cohorts. He presents us with a parable of intrusiveness, heedlessness, and self-aggrandizement that often escapes the notice of an environmental movement more willing to iconize him for relative virtue than analyze his ultimately disastrous failures.

The trip took Powell and company through some of the world's deepest and most beautiful canyons-including Lodore, Desolation, Labyrinth, Cataract, and the Grand-and over vicious rapids and through sizzling uncharted deserts and Indian country to the Colorado's confluence with the Virgin River, at Grand Wash in southeastern Utah, 1,000 miles downstream. In 1875 after a second, federally-funded expedition crewed by geologists, photographers, and painters—and rooted on by the booster press and Congress—Powell produced his self-glorifying bestseller *Exploration of the Colorado River*. Three years later his *Report on the Lands of the Arid Region of the United States* called for a reorganization of the development of the West under the auspices of a new government agency—which he, of course, would lead. Powell got to head the US Geological Survey; but the West's fate ended up in the hands of the Bureaus of Reclamation and Land Management.

However awed he might have been by the landscapes he traversed, Powell never shared Thoreau's belief in the redemptive power of wilderness and of wild, untamed rivers. Rather, he knew that the arid wasteland itself must be "redeemed": by the judicious application of irrigation principles. Mid-life, the amateur geologist who collected seashells on the banks of the Mississippi became a technocrat fascinated with harnessing the water of the West. Like Jefferson, Powell held that democratic values flourished from small farms and ranches. An appropriately irrigated West, Powell believed, would keep the interior reaches of the country from falling into the hands of monopolists and robber barons.

Powell dreamed of capturing the river's power for utilitarian service. At various turns he could be called a progressive, a realist, a technocrat; under any label he was consistently ready to re-engineer nature and western society, an advocate of centralized planning on a vast scale. Powell was one of the first apostles of scarcity. Laudably, he would reject Jefferson's gridded township system for political boundaries contoured to hydrographic basins. Still he was willing to impound nearly every drop of the Colorado River's water behind dams—built high in the mountains in order to minimize evaporation. "All the waters of all the arid lands will eventually be taken from their natural channels," he wrote. Note the double "all."

Powell advocated this gargantuan water-impoundment even though he estimated that all of that water would yield viable crops or pasture on less than 3 percent of the arid Western lands. He sought to rationalize and control the development of these irrigation lands by reserving them in the public estate, making most of the West a kind of federal commons interspersed with homesteads and small communities.

"I early recognized that ultimately these natural features would present conditions which would control the institutional or legal problems," Powell wrote in his *Report on the Arid Lands*. That is, the harsh terrain would form a natural safeguard against over-population and economic exploitation. He was wrong, of course. Soon he saw the power elite capture the government and use it to redesign the plumbing of the West—training the spigots to their own enterprises, irrigating the vast plantations of the Imperial, San Joaquin, and Sacramento valleys, worked by the West's equivalent of slave labor. Irrigation led to servitude, not liberation; to cartels, not small-scale democracies; and the centralized water bureaucracy was a servant of the hydro-imperialists, not an honest broker of the public interest.

Powell began to see the shape of the future, and objected. He engaged in fierce congressional combat with Senator William Stewart of Nevada, the Ted Stevens of his time. Powell was one of the first whistleblowers and he met the fate assured most of his kind: he was chased out of office, running from trumped-up charges of corruption and financial malfeasance.

Was this disaster of water control the perversion of Powell's vision, as he thought? It was different from anything the maverick explorer and politician had wanted or worked for. But it was in another way the culmination of his vision-of his deeper vision, which differed not at all from that of those he fought. The vision characterized enterprises of the era, from rail-laying, to buffalo-killing, to dam-building, to homesteading promotion, to forced relocation and outright massacres of Native peoples. It Is the vision of Manifest Destiny.

When the Manifestly Destined looked out over the land, they saw deficiency: an incongruity between what was there and what was familiarly usable. The reflex thought after such vision is always, how to clear the slate and close that gap. Pre-existing human relationships to the land-honed over millennia of necessity, of error, of success-was invisible to the various explorers' eyes. The functioning commons, the dynamic equilibrium of fire-managed forests and prairies, the intricate stewardship and sharing of a river's salmon runs between dozens of autonomous peoples: rejected as impossible, these had to be denied and if necessary eradicated, with the plow, the canal, the cattle ranch, the grid of 160 acre wheat farms. As the US runs up against its borders, it begins to recognize the magnitude of loss incurred in its expansionist rampages.

The Colorado, the great river of the West, is now experiencing a perilous decline. The annual floods of the Green, Grand, and Colorado Rivers have been neutered, as upstream dams straight-jacket the flow of the rivers. The river channel is narrowing. The seasonal wetlands are vanishing. Springs and seeps are drying up. Beaches are disappearing. The water table is dropping. The cottonwood groves are dying off, and so are the sand and coyote willows, squeezed out by tamarisk. The river is losing its organic nutrients, as driftwood and other debris are entombed behind the dams. Endemic species of fish, like the humpback chub, which evolved only in the Colorado Basin, are sliding toward oblivion, replaced by catfish and carp. The water behind the dams is evaporating, turning saline, loading up with pesticides, petrochemicals, and fecal matter. The reservoirs are silting up, losing storage capacity and electrical generating capability.

On the Klamath River, the decline has reached bottom, giving us a glimpse of the Colorado's near-certain future. The salmon of the Klamath River, once one of the mightiest runs on earth, have been for decades in a slow, steady slide toward extinction. Then, in 2002, 30,000 salmon died as they ascended the broiling river, deprived of water by the political antics of farmers in the Upper Basin who demanded full deliveries in a drought year. The gory front-page photos of mass death suggested a sudden catastrophic event, a singular tragic mistake. In fact, the salmon of the Klamath, which flows some 200 miles from southern Oregon to the northern California coast, are the victims of a system that has conspired against them since the 1940s at least. Industrial agriculture, backed by the federal government, has free reign to de-water the Klamath River to irrigate alfalfa, potatoes, and onions.

That the Yurok, Hoopa, Karuk, and Klamath tribes enjoy treaty rights to the river's salmon and depend on those fish for food, income, and ceremonial rites has meant nothing to the irrigators' agribusiness backers. The salmon are a looming impediment to their increasingly frail economic hold. Once the fish provided leverage for legal threats—via tribal lawsuits and the Endangered Species Act—the masters of the river plotted their final doom. With the troublesome fish out of the way, they believed that their precious waterworks would be safe.

In the wake of the fish kill, the Klamath River tribes stepped up their campaign against PacifiCorp's relicensing of the four hydroelectric dams. The implausible latest addition to the alliance of tribes, environmentalists, fishermen, and Pacific Northwest ratepayers is the ultra-conservative Klamath Basin Water Users Association. The farmers, many of whom lost contracts after the 2001 water shutoffs, say that they have finally joined with the tribes because removing the dams would pull the basin back from the brink of crisis. (The alliance is praiseworthy, powerful, and barely precedented, but it must be noted: Farmers irrigating this dry cold land, trying to save their way of life, still ride in the same wooden boat going over the waterfall with John Wesley Powell.)

In the face of such united pressure, PacifiCorp has agreed to discuss dam removal. Those dams coming down would make the Klamath conflict—until now considered a hopeless battle—a turning point in the water wars. We already see farmers in the Deschutes River basin heeding the Klamath's terrible warning.

Deranged models of U.S. water control have been cloned across the developing world, always with the same bottom line: drowned riverine ecosystems, displaced communities, flooded sacred sites, extinctions, and resource privatization. Third World nations buying the hydro-power rap must hock their futures to the merciless cadre of global bankers, submitting to the neoliberal stricture of the IMF and World Bank. Water and power must be privatized, jacking up the price for basic necessities. The dams are vulnerable to catastrophic breaches and terrorist attacks-and I don't mean terminally ill river-rats with a houseboat and 17 beer coolers packed with C-4 explosives. Object to the dictates of your imperial overlords and your brand-new dam might well become an inviting target for cruise missiles.

Worldwide, threatened river systems are crying out for a new generation of whistleblowers, for government biologists, hydrologists, and geologists willing to risk their own careers to save river ecosystems on the brink of collapse. Like Dai Qing in China, they will, almost certainly, be vilified, ridiculed, investigated, and threatened by the international cliques profiteering on the waters' demise. In the U.S., the George W. Bush administration, in collusion with its stacked Supreme Court, axed the last frail protections federal whistleblowers enjoy. These scientists, should they ever step into the public spotlight, will need cover and protection. Can they look to Gang Green—the big DC enviro groups like the Sierra Club and the Wilderness Society—the ones that gave you Glen Canyon Dam (and so many more)? Fat chance.

But we must leave these brave whistleblowers to their fates for the moment. Their alarms alone will never be enough. We learn from the example of John Wesley Powell that science, vision, and conscience will not suffice against the Leviathan's momentum and might. Nor can any Bureau of Reclamation fish-saving compromise truly threaten the hegemony of the megadammers, wherein any water that makes it to the sea is water wasted, and no trickle goes unlevied. In just the same way, the hero model favored even by many eco-warriors actually perpetuates the mega-dam mindset. Those who would save the rivers must take the rivers for their heroes, and the salmon and chub, and look not to iconized individuals for leadership but to one another and to the earth itself for partnership. The Klamath River tribes, like the Mun River protesters and Cochabamba's "Defenders of Water and Life" win more lasting victories than Gang Green. It will take a network of river consensus and the forging of a new water culture to bust the dams and to scour away their poisoned silts.

So here is my clarion call for a new global movement of resistance against the hydro-imperialists: a movement to stop new dams, decommission existing ones and restore wild rivers. A real reclamation movement whose compelling mantra is: Let the rivers flow and the river peoples be.

– April 14, 2007

LET THEM EAT OIL: THE POLITICS OF DEEPWATER HORIZON

By Jeffrey St. Clair

The mood in the Alaska office of the Minerals Management Service (MMS) was festive. Word had just reached Anchorage that the president was preparing plans to expand offshore drilling in Alaska. John Goll, the service's regional director, summoned his top lieutenants to his office for a briefing of the joyous news. After confirming the rumors that had circulated all morning, Goll invited "all hands" in the office to join him for coffee and pastries. At the center of the table, the cheering staffers were greeted by a large cake, with "Drill Baby Drill" scrawled across it in chocolate icing.

The year was not 2004. The president was not George W. Bush. This scene took place in 2009, a few months into Barack Obama's first term as president.

As it turned out, Goll had several reasons to be upbeat. Not only had the new administration steamrolled its environmentalist allies and decided to move forward with new drilling operations along Alaska's fragile coastline, but Goll and his troubled agency had survived the presidential transition intact. Goll, who was appointed to the powerful post of Alaska regional director in 1997 during the Clinton administration's drive to escalate drilling on the North Slope, had come into his prime as a bureaucratic facilitator of big oil under George W. Bush.

As detailed in a Government Accountability Office investigation of the Alaska Office of the MMS under Goll's tenure, the relationship between the government regulators and the oil industry was incestuous. The report revealed an agency that approved nearly every drilling plan without restrictions, muzzled internal dissent and gagged agency scientists. Environmental reviews, when they were undertaken—which was rarely—were cursory and fast-tracked. The only obligation for the oil companies was: just drill. Drill where you want, how you want.

There's nothing to indicate that after Ken Salazar piously declared that he was going to weed out and reinvent the MMS as a fierce regulatory watchdog, Goll and his cronies did anything but chuckle.

Perhaps Goll knew more about the real Salazar than the mainstream environmental groups who had blindly lauded the man-in-the-hat's appointment as interior secretary. In the first year of the Obama administration, Salazar's Interior Department had put 53 million acres of offshore oil reserves up for lease, far eclipsing the records set by the Bush administration. This staggering achievement probably came as no surprise to Goll and his oil industry cronies. When Salazar served in the U.S. Senate, he publicly chided the Bush administration for the lethargic pace of its drilling operations in the Gulf of Mexico. Peeved, Salazar co-sponsored the Gulf of Mexico Energy Security Act, which opened an additional eight million acres of the Gulf to new drilling.

In this optimistic spirit, Goll's office proceeded to swiftly and blithely approve one of the most contentious oil drilling plans of the last decade—a scheme by Shell Oil to sink exploratory wells in Beaufort and Chukchi Seas, crucial habitat for the endangered bowhead whale.

The drilling plan was hastily consecrated on the basis of a boilerplate environmental review despite the fact that even minor oil spill in these remote Arctic seas would prove to be an uncontrollable ecological catastrophe. Indeed, under Goll's direction, the Alaska office of the MMS was so uninterested in environmental analysis that it had failed to even develop a handbook for writing environmental reviews as required by the Department of Interior. Why bother, when Shell Oil could be depended on to write its own environmental analysis? That's efficiency.

Goll wasn't the only Bush holdover at MMS to survive the Obama transition. There is the curious case of Chris C. Oynes. Oynes served for 12 years as the director of oil and gas leasing operations for the MMS in the Gulf of Mexico. Those were buxom years for the oil industry. During his tenure in the Louisiana regional office, Oynes approved nearly 1,000 new oil drilling permits, roughly a fifth of all the current drilling sites in the Gulf of Mexico. Few of these operations underwent even the most simplistic environmental reviews or on-site inspections. Instead, as detailed in a blistering report from the Interior Department's inspector general, under Oynes' watch the repeat offenders in the oil industry were allowed to police themselves, writing their own environmental analyses, safety inspections and compliance reports, often in pencil for MMS regulators to trace over in ink.

The inspector general concluded that the agency fostered a "culture of ethical failure." That may be putting it mildly. For Oynes and his colleagues, it wasn't about ethics but serving the interests of big oil. And he did that in a big way that meant billions for Gulf oil drillers.

Here's how it went down. In 1995, Congress, in collaboration with the Clinton administration, passed the Deep Water Royalty Relief Act, a bill meant to encourage oil companies like BP to begin the risky proposition of drilling for oil more than a mile beneath the surface of the Gulf. As an incentive to drill, the deepwater operators were exempted from paying royalties until the amount of oil produced hit certain price and production triggers. These triggers were supposed to be written into the lease contracts. For example, the price trigger was set at $28 per barrel. The companies were meant to pay royalties to MMS on all oil sold above this rate, which was substantially below the market price of crude in the late 1990s. But this language mysteriously disappeared from the contracts. One MMS staffer later told investigators with the inspector general's office that he had been instructed to remove the price trigger language from the leases.

The man who signed off on most of the 113 deepwater leases offered in 1998 and 1999 was the MMS's regional director at the time, Chris Oynes, who duly told investigators that he simply overlooked the missing language. But executives at Chevron, ever conscious of the bottom line, noticed the absence of price triggers and met with Oynes three times to discuss the matter. Apparently satisfied with the terms of the deal, Chevron plunged into the deepwater bonanza in the Gulf. For his part, Oynes said he had no recollection of these meetings.

A year later, officials at the Interior Department discovered the mistake. Panicky emails flew back and forth inside the agency. But instead of exposing the debacle and trying to rectify the problem, they covered it up for the next six years. The assistant director of MMS decided not to inform the head of the agency, and the sweetheart deal with deepwater drillers remained buried until 2006, when it was unearthed by Inspector General Earl Devaney, who called the affair "a jaw-dropping example of bureaucratic bungling."

Devaney put dozens of MMS officials under the microscope in an attempt to identify the official who ordered that the price triggers be removed from the deepwater leases. Oynes himself was made to take a polygraph test. But, in the end, Devaney found no smoking gun, largely because of the convenient death of one of the central players in the affair. Frustrated at every turn, the inspector general ended his investigation, appalled at the entire agency: "Simply stated, short of a crime, anything goes at the highest levels of the Department of Interior."

What Devaney termed a "blunder" ended up allowing the deepwater drillers to stiff the federal treasury out of an estimated $12 billion in royalty payments. Some might write this off as a monumental mistake. But at the MMS, these kinds of screwups always seem to end up bulging the pockets of the oil companies.

As for Oynes, he survived the royalty affair unscathed. He escaped indictment. He wasn't forced to resign. He wasn't even demoted. Instead, in 2007 Johnnie Burton, Bush's head of MMS, appointed Oynes assistant director of MMS in charge of offshore drilling. His charmed career continued a year later, when Ken Salazar, ignoring furious protests from environmentalists and former Interior Department staffers, decided to retain Oynes in that fatal post.

Oynes is the one constant figure in the Deepwater Horizon catastrophe. The project originated during his term in the Bush administration and was approved under his watch in the Obama administration. Despite the highly experimental nature of the drilling operation, the MMS's approval came without environmental review. It contained no special restrictions or impositions on BP's operating plan. Just like old times.

On May 16, however, after the explosion of the Deepwater Horizon rig and with a new damaging new IG report on criminally lax safety inspections by the MMS at Gulf drilling sites during Oynes years as head of the Louisiana regional office looming, he quietly resigned his post.

As Oynes skulked from his office, with oil tides coating the marshes of coastal Louisiana in an indelible brown crude, he must have looked back on his 30-year career with a sense of pride. Servicing big oil is precisely what MMS has always been about. The agency was created during the Reagan administration by James Watt as a bureaucratic handmaiden for the oil and gas industry. Oynes had done his job and done it well. As an MMS press release noted, "During his tenure in the Gulf of Mexico he conducted 30 lease sales and oversaw a 50 per cent rise in oil production."

And that, after all, is the name of the game.

– November 19, 2010

EMBRACING THE URBAN-NATURE ETHIC

By Joshua Frank

As I walk along the Los Angeles River on a cool fall afternoon, I gaze across a graffiti-ridden concrete embankment and imagine what this landscape must have looked like less than 100 years ago. The LA River today, which dumps the area's urban runoff directly in the Pacific Ocean, serves as a paved flood control channel for the city. It carries litter, bacteria and other nasty pollutants from the streets of LA straight into the nearby sea, without ever being treated.

This is certainly not the type of roaring river I grew up appreciating in the wilds of Montana, but it is rugged in its own right. The engineers that designed this industrial behemoth missed the ecological boat when they drew up plans to channelize this once expansive waterway. Intent on protecting property and allowing for development as close to the river as possible, the LA River—in its original state—was destroyed in the name of work relief and ambitious flood control. This is not to say the river, once the sole provider of fresh water for the city, was killed off entirely. But it will never again resemble the stream and wetlands the Gabrielino Native American tribes enjoyed for well over a thousand years.

The legendary Olmsted Brothers were two men who envisioned something starkly different for the LA River than what exists now. If you've ever traversed the vast parkway system in the Emerald City of Seattle, strolled along the Delaware River in Philadelphia's gorgeous Franklin Delano Roosevelt Park, or spent a quiet evening in New York City's Central Park, you've experienced the works of the Olmsteads up close. While their imaginations were progressive at the time, these two brothers were not radicals. The Olmsteds were advocates of open space and the preservation of natural aesthetics in urban areas, but they did not wish to halt western expansion.

Nonetheless what the Olmsteds and partner Harlan Bartholomew put forth in the 1930s would have made Los Angeles one of the most ecologically attractive cities in the United States, with the LA River as its crown jewel. Instead of trucking in concrete and tearing out the river bottom, they sought to keep the LA River as natural as possible. The brothers argued that greenbelts ought to surround the meandering streambed with a broad network of wetlands, some 440 miles worth, providing flood control and serving as recreational parks for working class families that lived in nearby neighborhoods. Central to their hope in keeping the LA River free, was to limit, if not entirely eliminate, private development in its 50-year floodplain. Natural channels would be protected and the river would flow unimpeded all the way to the Pacific.

Sadly, the Olmstead/Bartholomew plan had two substantial obstacles in its path: a dearth of local funds and morally bankrupt regional planners. Instead, the New Deal era federal government came to LA's fiscal rescue by employing massive public works projects to the determine of the environment—and LA wetlands in particular. No large parks-building program was ever employed, let alone given much consideration. On the contrary, New Deal funds were explicitly used to eliminate hundreds of square miles of wetlands and pave the majority of the LA River's vast alluvial plain.

One could blame manifest destiny on the developers' innate greed and government backing for what happened to the LA River. Certainly their desire to capitalize by building on virtually every square inch of land in the basin played a role. They sought to tame the river, which in the infamous flood of 1938 killed 87 people and swamped out 300,000 acres of land. Of course, it's far cheaper to avoid building in a flood zone than to build in it. Yet, as any land speculator will tell you, it's never quite as profitable to protect as it is to exploit. So building they did.

For half a century the LA River fell into utter disrepair. While it became the location for classic films like *Grease* and *Chinatown* (ironically centered around the corruption of the region's water wars), the river was a mere afterthought for many who called Los Angeles home. It wasn't until the mid-1980s that a movement to revitalize the waterway came to a head, recognizing, not only its historical significance for the region, but its ecological importance as well. The group leading the charge, Friends of the LA River (FoLAR), is still succeeding despite the perception that the LA River isn't an actual river.

"FoLAR's founder, Lewis MacAdams and two friends, Patt Patterson and Roger Wong, cut the chain-link fence in downtown Los Angeles near First Street and walked upstream to the Arroyo Seco / Los Angeles River Confluence—the birthplace of Los Angeles," explains FoLAR's executive director Shelly Backlar. "They decided that someone had to speak on behalf of the River and it would be them. Lewis envisioned the gospel tune, 'Let's All Gather at the River' as his inspiration for the organization. When he started he thought his job would be to convince people that the River had the potential to unite and inspire communities but he soon realized that he had to convince people that there is a river in Los Angeles."

The City of LA didn't catch on immediately. It took almost two full decades before the City officially adopted a comprehensive Los Angeles River Revitalization Master Plan, which occurred in May 2007. The process was arduous, but the result of the 18 month process was substantial. With the Master Plan, LA now has a vision for transforming the 32 mile stretch of the river within the City's jurisdiction into something a bit closer to what Olmstead and Bartholomew believed was possible.

As I stroll along a littered stretch of the LA River in the neighborhood of Echo Park I contemplate what could have been but also recognize what the river is today, and more importantly, what it means for the city tomorrow. Blue heron and mallards inhabit the river during winter months, along with hundreds of other species, many of them endangered. FoLar has also documented largemouth bass, Amazon sailfin catfish and more. In Ballona Creek, which at one point connected with the LA River, steelhead have been spotted, a sign that, in the most optimistic of scenarios, could perhaps return to the river one day in the distant future.

While the habitat the LA River provides for these animals is not optimal, it is still habitat, and an improving one at that.

***

Urban waterways, like wetlands, not only provide refuge for migratory birds, they also give people a sense of place—a small connection to the wild. Nature is not confined to the locations we designate as wilderness—more environmentalists need to expand their perceptions in order to recognize how important urban nature is for many species survival.

Along with protecting native ecosystems, we shouldn't turn our backs on the environments that have the potential to be revitalized in dense cities like Los Angeles. I am certain the animals that depend on these little slivers of nature, many of them struggling to survive, would echo similar sentiments.

It is this urban-nature ethic that thrust Joe Linton's kayak into the LA River four years ago to demonstrate that the waterway was indeed navigable, a requirement for all rivers that fall under the protection of the Clean Water Act. Linton, who writes for the popular LA Creek Freak blog, and others, paddled their way through concrete debris and sometimes dangerous passageways to make their case.

Their message did not fall on deaf ears. The EPA in July 2010 declared the LA River navigable, giving it the full protection of the Clean Water Act.

"This is a watershed as important as any other," said the EPA's Lisa Jackson, as she stood in front of Compton Creek, an almost destroyed tributary to the LA River. "So we are going to build a federal partnership to empower communities like yours ... We want the LA River to demonstrate how urban waterways across the country can serve as assets in building stronger neighborhoods, attracting new businesses and creating new jobs."

Now the entire 834-square-mile LA River watershed might be given the attention it deserves after nearly a century of neglect and abuse. While a place like Ballona Wetlands, which is one of the most intact wetlands in the area, has long been given the respect it rightly deserve—fending off development but not always coming out victorious—the LA River is primed for revival.

***

In 2004 voters in Los Angeles passed Proposition O, which authorized the City of LA to issue a series of general obligation bonds of up to $500 million for clean water projects in the city. The main goal of the measure was to help the City meet clean water requirements known as TMDLs (Trash Total Maximum Daily Load), which were set by originally passed by the Regional Water Quality Control Board. As a result, there have been many numerous public works projects funded and more to come.

"It showed that the people of Los Angeles really care about water quality," said David Nahai, former head of the Los Angeles Department of Water and Power. "Five hundred million dollars is not chump change." Early this year the City drained Echo Park Lake, which acts as a retention basin for local runoff. The lake, which is manmade, is being relined and improved, allowing the water collected in it to be less polluted. Likewise, Machado Lake in industrial Harbor City is slated to receive Proposition O funds to address water quality and pollution issues that plague the water body.

While the City doles out money for these projects, controversy occasionally follows. Speaking of one such project in the community of Wilmington that included the construction of an artificial-turf baseball field, Mark Gold, who served as President of the local conservation group Heal the Bay at the time, was quoted as saying, "It was politically popular, No one's going to say Los Angeles doesn't need more ball fields. But it's not a new ball field. It's not diverting water from anywhere. So is it appropriate that Prop. O funds pay for it?"

Keeping the City Council's use of Proposition O funds honest is what Mark Gold and other environmentalists are attempting to do. Nonetheless, even Gold admits Proposition O, which passed by an overwhelming 76% of the vote, was a step in the right direction for LA.

"Although the pace of the projects isn't as fast as I would have hoped, the vast majority of Proposition O projects are good projects that reduce runoff pollution and provide other benefits such as greening the City, reducing flood risk and augmenting local water supplies," writes Gold. "Unfortunately, Proposition O only pays for building the projects themselves. The funds can not be used for operations and maintenance so the new projects are actually adding to the watershed protection programs ongoing budget difficulties."

The other major issue when dealing with water quality, especially in a coastal city like Los Angeles, where runoff drains into the ocean, is minimizing litter, especially the big killer—plastics. Los Angeles County Board of Supervisors voted to ban plastic bags in November 2010. The ban will affect 1,000 stores in unincorporated areas. Long Beach also passed a plastic bag ban, which the city hopes will drastically decrease the amount of litter on its streets.

Will the LA River one day have a larger abundance of life? Will wetlands in the area be revitalized and protected as they should be? Not if people are complacent. One thing is for sure, allocating money for restoration work is a good thing, but ensuring that future development and redevelopment projects don't negatively impact what little wetlands and waterways remain, is imperative.

Nonetheless, as Heal the Bay notes, water quality in the area is slowly improving along many of our local urban beaches. With continued diligence and a growing awareness about the importance of clean water, perhaps these beaches, and the runoff that pollutes them, will only get better.

Whether they are year-round residents or just stopping over on their long flight from Canada to Mexico, many species rely on these littered waters for survival. That's enough for me. Let's tear out this concrete and bring the LA River back a little closer to the way nature intended.

– October 17, 2012

THE BLOOD-STAINED SHORES OF TAIJI

By Joshua Frank

The shores and ocean waters were stained a blood red as the annual dolphin slaughter in Taiji, Japan commenced. As of late-January, over 250 dolphins were netted this month, including a very rare albino calf. Another three dozen were killed for their meat, and the killing, despite media reports to the contrary, continues.

The Taiji dolphins suffer an unspeakably savage death. In shallow waters fishermen stab the dolphins with metal spikes through their blowholes. It usually takes several strikes to sever the dolphin's spine. It's a slow, painful and soul-wrenching death. It often takes as long as 30 minutes before the dying dolphin inhales its final breath.

The helpless animals are driven to the killing cove by boat, made infamous by the Academy Award-winning documentary *The Cove*, in a barbaric ritual that is void of even the slightest ounce of compassion. This year, after five horrific days in captivity, families of bottlenose dolphins were ripped apart, mothers screaming in agony as their babies were stolen away. Others fought to get free, only to be corralled back into the cove.

Currently the International Whaling Commission (IWC), the toothless non-governmental body that oversees whaling activities, does not protect dolphins and porpoises, which is why Japan can kill dolphins by the thousands with impunity. In fact, the IWC affords no protection for nearly 90% of all cetacean species. While Taiji may be the most notorious of the hunts that takes place in Japan, many other killing operations are equally cruel. These ruthless Japanese "drive hunts" murder nearly 20,000 dolphins, porpoises and small whales every year.

Activists noted that this winter's Taiji slaughter was one of the largest in years. In all they reported at least 50 "show-quality" specimens would be shipped off to aquariums around the world from China, the Middle East to inland Mexico and beyond. The animals fortunate enough to avoid being killed for their meat were released back to sea, where they will spend the rest of their emotionally traumatized lives.

The albino dolphin, named "Angel" by long-time activists Ric O'Barry and Karla Sanjur, was first spotted as she swam nervously alongside her mother into the cove. Soon after the first sightings of the pale white Angel, she was netted by Japanese fisherman, taken from her pod, and, as of this writing, remains locked inside the dreary Taiji Whale Museum, where she waits to be sold to an aquarium that will put her up on display, no doubt marketing her unique skin tone.

International pressure is mounting in hopes of putting a halt to the murders and kidnappings of Taiji. US Ambassador to Japan Caroline Kennedy, daughter of JFK, expressed her dismay on Twitter.

"Deeply concerned by inhumaneness of drive hunt dolphin killing. USG [US government] opposes drive hunt fisheries," tweeted Kennedy, who was nominated to her post last November. It was a first for a US government official to criticize the hunt.

Some have denounced Kennedy and others that oppose the mass killing as cultural imperialists, even though the practice has only been going on in Taiji since 1969. Why is that? It's true that marine parks in the US are guilty of exploiting marine life, as well documented in the 2013 film *Blackfish* (snubbed by the Academy), which exposes the dark reality of SeaWorld, where cruel entertainment is passed off as conservation. Even so, this reality doesn't diminish criticism of the dolphin killings in Taiji or the fact that the dolphins are fighting for their lives as they are chased to their deaths by eager fisherman.

We empathize with the dolphin's pain as biological similarities abound. Like humans, dolphins are social creatures. They give birth, they breathe air and warm blood flows through their veins. Someone more spiritual than myself may say there is a primal connection between dolphins and humans that evokes something sacred in us.

While I wish the heartless killings of dolphins would end, the cynic in me can't help but wonder how that will ever happen. One would think it is much easier to convince humans that killing other humans is unethical and morally bankrupt. But we live in a morally bankrupt, compassionless society, where our liberal president deploys drones, bombs weddings and kills scores of innocent children with scant public opposition. If we can't put an end to these killings, how will we ever save the dolphins from those damn lethal pikes of Taiji?

Nonetheless, perhaps dolphins can teach us more about humanity than we can teach ourselves. Perhaps dolphins can show us the true innocence of life and re-connect us to the natural world, in its wild state. Perhaps dolphins symbolize real freedom—freedom from our petty needs and material excesses.

Ordinary people everywhere, including many Japanese, have voiced their outrage over the slaughter in Taiji. The conservation group Sea Shepherd and others continue to protest the killings and vow to one-day end the hunt. Their success hinges on whether or not tough international pressure can be waged, which in the end funds programs to transition these Japanese fisherman into new lines of work. Let's join them.

Until this happens, the dark red blood of innocent dolphins will continue to stain our souls and the sands of Taiji.

– January 24, 2014

OCEANS WITHOUT FISH

By Jeffrey St. Clair

The SS *Gijon* cuts through the slate-colored swells, trailing a white V in the waters of the Bering Sea. The trawler lowers its giant pelagic net from the stern of the ship and it unfurls into the waters below. The vast net, thousands of yards of nylon mesh, sweeps in a lethal curtain across the depths.

Hours later, the nets are cranked up to the piercing whine of straining engines. Inside: more than 400 tons of fish, crabs and squid. A Stellar's sea lion and a few fur seals, indiscriminately snared while foraging for salmon, are also part of the haul.

The sea lion and seal are not spared. Indeed more than forty percent of the haul is considered worthless by-catch and will simply be ground up and spewed in bloody currents of saturated chum from the bilges of ship back out into the sea. Some 500 million pounds of marine life are wasted in this way in the North Pacific every year.

The Bering Sea is now the most productive fishery in North America. More than one-third of the United State's commercial catch come from these frigid waters near the top of the world. Among the species sought by the fishing fleets of the North Pacific are yellowfin, sole, herring, halibut and ocean perch. But the most cherished target is pollock, the tofu of fish. Pollock, craved by the Japanese for surimi, turns up in American markets as fish sandwiches at Burger King and McDonalds and as imitation crab in the fish freezers at Safeway.

The SS *Gijon* is registered to the Seattle-based American Seafoods Corporation, a subsidiary of Resource Group International, a Norwegian conglomerate. The ship is a floating factory, longer and wider than a football field. The $40 million trawler can process 80 tons of fish mass a day, turning sole into fish meal and pollock into surimi. The catch is stored in huge freezers, where it can linger for months.

Resource Group International's primary competitor in the lucrative pollock fishing grounds of the North Pacific is the Arctic-Alaska Fisheries Company, another Seattle-based outfit. Arctic Alaska was acquired in 1992 by Don Tyson, the chicken mogul and Clinton patron from Springdale, Arkansas. Since then Tyson's company has bought up three other Alaska seafood operations and, as a consequence, began fending off anti-trust investigations by the Federal Trade Commission.

The incursion of the big factory trawlers into the icy waters of the North Pacific began in the late 1970s and early 1980s. By 2000, there were 45 factory trawlers operating in the Bering Sea fishery. The big ships are powered by super-charged diesel engines fed by massive fuel tanks that permit the trawlers to remain at sea for months without returning to home ports to refuel or off-load their catch. Often the processed surimi is simply transferred at sea to smaller ships owned by Japanese fish merchants. The long range of the factory ships allows them to operate in several distance fisheries in a single season and evade the catch quotas that saddle smaller operations.

The arrival of the industrialized super-trawlers spelled an almost immediate cultural and economic disaster for the communities of coastal Alaska. For decades the flourishing Alaskan fishing industry had been characterized by independent ship owners and small processing plants, sprinkled down the coast in towns like Kodiak, Cordova and Ketchikan.

In the 1970s, nearly 80 percent of the Alaskan pollock catch was made by small operators. Now the situation is almost entirely reversed. More than 70 percent of the pollock in Alaskan waters is taken by factory trawlers and dozens of independent boat owners have gone bankrupt. But it's the shore-based factories, making value-added fish products, that have been hit the hardest by the new generation of trawlers. The canneries, surimi plants and frozen fish processing factories provided year-round high wage jobs, an important stabilizing force for rural Alaska's predominantly season economy. Today many of those plants and jobs are gone, replaced by the factory trawlers, which increasingly tend to employ Mexican and Vietnamese laborers at sweatshop pay rates.

Many of the Artic-Alaska Company's ships unload their catch not in Seattle, but in Shanghai, China, where Tyson purchased a fish factory in 1994 from the Chinese government. The deal was brokered with the help of Commerce Secretary Ron Brown and was back by federal government insurance and loan guarantees from the Overseas Private Investment Corporation (OPIC). In fact, the growth of the American factory trawler fleet was heavily underwritten by the US treasury, thanks to effective inside work by the congressional delegation from Washington state. Tyson's company alone swept up more than $65 million in low-interest loans to fun the construction of 10 factory trawlers. In total, the Seattle-based factory trawler fleet raked in more than $200 million in so-called Fisheries Obligation Guarantees and other federal subsidies.

The economic dislocation brought about by the invasion of the mega-trawlers into Southeast Alaska is grimly paralleled by an ecological catastrophe in the waters of the Bering Sea and North Pacific. Again most of the blame can be laid squarely on the industrial behemoths. Using sophisticated sonar and electronic tracking devices, factory trawlers like the *Gijon* can swiftly zero in on new spawning grounds and fish them to near extinction. This is called pulse trawling. A particularly outrageous example of this genocidal method occurred in the 1980s in the Shelikoff Strait off the Aleutian Islands, when a newly discovered pollock stock was relentlessly fished to the point of collapse. According to a report on factory trawlers by Greenpeace, in less than a decade the Shelikof pollock fishery had declined from an estimated biomass of 3 million tons in 1981 to less than 300 thousand tons in 1988.

Every since the factory trawlers began flocking to the Alaskan waters the pollock season has closed earlier than planned. In the late 1970s, the pollock fishing season regularly ran for 10 months. In 1994, it closed after 70 days. It's not surprising. The annual harvest capacity of the trawler fleet may well be greater than the entire pollock population of the Bering Sea. The ramifications of this dire situation were contemplated in an internal assessment by executives at the American Seafood Company: "the catching capacity of vessels operating in the Bering Sea fishery appears to be double or triple the annual quota." And these were quotas that most marine biologists considered to be dangerously inflated.

It's not just the species targeted by the trawlers, such as pollock and sole, which are depleted. Crab, halibut and arrowtooth flounder are also in trouble. The consequences extend even to fish-eating seabirds, such as puffins, thick-billed murres and black-legged kittiwakes, as well as marine mammal, such as Stellar's sea lions, fur seals, and sea otters. Pollock, for example, accounts for nearly 70 percent of the rare sea lion's diet. A report by the National Research Council warns: "It seems extremely unlikely that the productivity of the Bering Sea ecosystem can sustain current rates of human exploitation, as well as the large populations of all marine mammals and bird species that existed before human exploitation—especially modern exploitation—began."

The trend toward over-exploitation of the Alaskan fishery will be difficult, if not impossible, to reverse. For one thing, even the most stringent federal fishing laws have often served only to exacerbate the problem. Take the Magnuson Act, passed in 1976 as a way to protect American off-shore fishing grounds from growing incursions by foreign fishing fleets. The measure, rammed through Congress by the acerbic Senator Warren Magnuson, a Democrat from Washington, extended the federal government's jurisdiction over fish matters from 3 miles to 200 miles off the US coastline, a move that was bitterly denounced as an act of ecological imperialism by the Japanese and Norwegians. In reality, it was simple economic protectionism.

The Magnuson Act established regional fish management councils to determine fishing seasons and allocate catch quotas. These councils, which soon came to be dominated by fishing industry lobbyists, were expressly exempted from federal conflict-of-interest laws, allowing industry flacks to direct as much of the haul back to their own companies and clients as they could get away with. And they did just that.

Exacerbating this situation is the archaic management philosophy of the federal agency charged with maintaining the health of ocean fish stocks: the National Marine Fisheries Service, which, curiously enough, is under the purview of the Commerce Department. Instead of viewing marine ecosystems as vibrant, diverse and inter-connected environments, NMFS attempts to manage ocean fish stocks through a species-by-species approach. This benefits the bottom lines of the fishing fleets, but flies in the face of current ecological thinking. By focusing only on the commercial fish stocks, NMFS ignores the toll industrial fishing methods exact on non-target species and on the marine habitat itself.

Medical researchers, backed by hefty grants from companies like Arctic-Alaska, continue to churn out reports touting the health-enhancing benefits of diets laden with pollock, salmon and perch. Fish seems to lower bad cholesterol, reduce heart attack risks (especially for men) and suppresses the advance of free radicals, those frenzied compounds that stimulate cancer cell growth.

All this is undoubtedly true. Yet there are also health dangers associated with fish consumption. Fish can be contaminated with heavy metals, pesticides and other chemical toxins. One recent study estimated that consumption of PCB-laced fish from the Great Lakes may lead to 40,000 new cases of cancer over the next

25 years. Seafood products also carry a host of food-borne pathogens, including listeria, vibrio vulnifcus and, yes, salmonella. Testing for such dangers is even more lax and rudimentary than that in the beef industry. One local seafood merchant in Portland, Oregon told me: "What it comes down to is smell. When it starts to stink, we yank it off the shelf. What else can you do?"

But even the most accomplished sole sniffers would be unable to detect that there is something terribly wrong with many of the fish being hauled out of the Bering Sea. Thousands of tons of pollock, perch and black sole taken by ships like *Gijon* may—metaphorically, at least—glow; they may make Geiger counters erupt into a chilling stutter of clicks. In short, a considerable part of the haul from this last, great productive fishery may be radioactive.

What's going on here? The story dates back to 1971, during the glory days of the Nixon administration and the nuclear sabre-rattling leading up to Henry Kissinger's détente with the Soviets. In order to send a message of "American resolve," Nixon ordered the Atomic Energy Commission and the Department of Defense to detonate the largest underground nuclear explosion in US history on Amchitka Island, a volcanic extrusion in the Bering Sea, halfway down Alaska's Aleutian Islands.

The five-megaton hydrogen "device" detonated on November 6, 1971 exploded with such shattering force that the middle of Amchitka Island fractured and collapsed, forming what the mad scientist Edward Teller delicately termed a "nuclear-excavated lake." In the wake of the blast, hundreds of dead puffins were found with their legs driven through their chests, while sea lions, resting on sea rocks miles from the test site, were discovered with their eyes blown out of their sockets. Within months, there was ample of evidence that the test site, called Cannikan Lake, had begun to steadily leak radioactive waste, despite assurances from James Schlesinger, then head of the Atomic Energy Commission, that it would take "a thousand years or more" for transuranic uranium to dribble into the sea.

Thousands of pages of recently declassified documents released by the Department of Energy to the Alaska Department of Environmental Conservation reveal that Amchitka blast site began to leak Iodine 131 and Crypton 85 within two days of the nuclear explosion, draining into the groundwater and then to the sea through underground fissures in the island. Soon after the disclosure of these damaging documents, Alaska Senator Ted Stevens discreetly told Clinton's Energy Secretary, Hazel O'Leary: "Madame Secretary, we've got a real problem up here. There's leaking from the Amchitka test site and it might endanger our North Pacific fisheries."

Now disturbing levels of Americum, Plutonium and Tritium are showing up in plants samples on the island. "If we're finding these levels of radioactive waste, then the potential for severe harm is there," said Pam Miller, a Greenpeace scientist who wrote a detailed report on the radioactive leakage on Amchitka. "This stuff appears to be leaking into the most important commercial fishery in the world."

Even so executives at Arctic-Alaska Seafood remained tranquil. "We've never once found any radioactive fish," a company spokesman told me. Moments later, however, the PR man admitted that the company had never tested its fish for radioactive waste and had no plans to start.

No wonder the surrealists adopted the fish as a symbol of their movement.

– May 9, 2014

FIELD NOTES FROM A MIRAGE

By Jeffrey St. Clair

> The scientists say
> It will all wash away
> But we don't believe any more
> Cause we've got our recruits
> And our green mohair suits
> So please show your I.D. at the door
>
> —"Sin City," Gram Parsons and Chris Hillman

The sidewalk is so hot the soles of shoes are melting, leaving faint footprint traces on the concrete. On this late June afternoon, the air temperature is 112 degrees in Las Vegas and considerably hotter down in the mirrored chasm of the Strip.

The merciless heat works its spell, luring the hordes into the cool labyrinths of the casinos, where even Ariadne could get lost amid the flashing neon, the hypnotic swells of electronica, the eerie moans of the losers at the tables.

Inside is right where they want you. That's where your pockets get picked on high-tech slots (the funniest machine: KISS; the creepiest: the Joker, featuring video of Heath Ledger), Cirque du Soliel shows (at $155 a ticket) or extravagantly priced and barely digestible food prepared under the trademark of the omnipresent Mario Batali.

We came here for the American Library Association's annual conference, where my wife Kimberly and her colleagues at Portland State University's Millar Library are slated to receive a major award for innovation. After enduring the tedium of 1001 PowerPoint demonstrations on subjects like "Threshold Concepts" and the bibliographic perils of e-publishing, normally prim and sedate librarians are primed to cut loose for a week of licentious abandon in the desert. Las Vegas offers a celebration of the uniquely American version of the Id, a perpetually uncoiling knot of simulated desire with strobe lighting and a cheesy soundtrack.

What is a Threshold Concept, you inquire? Good question. I sat through a rather opaque and intellectually arid hour-and-a-half presentation by three leading practitioners of the theory and remained baffled, as did, I'd wager, many of the librarians in the hall. If you distill it down to essentials, a Threshold Concept seems very similar to what we used to call in philosophy seminars on the intractable (ahem) theories of Wittgenstein "getting a friggin' clue." But clarity is not the surest path to tenure.

The philosophy propelling this new trend in "knowledge management" is even more ominous than its mystifying nomenclature. In an age of Google, Edward Snowden and Wikipedia, some academic librarians feel that their tenuous position as gatekeepers of knowledge is under siege. The theory of Threshold Concepts seems to provide a last desperate shot for librarians to reassert their role as information power-brokers, herding naïve students and guileless library patrons toward "authoritative" and "credible" sources of news (such as the *New York Times*, naturally.) It's the latest reactionary counter-attack on the man who swung a wrecking ball through the brittle pretensions of the profession's old-guard: Michel Foucault. In *The Order of Things*, Foucault exposed the repressive political engines driving the classification and regulation of knowledge and the arbiters of "worthy" texts have been on the run ever since. (More on this at a later date.)

Many of the 12,000 or so librarians who converged here during a week of pitiless summer sun seem displaced, wandering aimlessly down De Chirico-like corridors, looking at Google maps on their smartphones. Perhaps they are scanning the dreamscape for a bookstore. They will search in vain. Here the only books are kept by sports bookies, those exacting archivists of accounts that must be paid.

Kimberly and I set up camp in the Riviera, a bum choice on my part. I wanted to stay in the old Vegas, the sand-blasted city of mobsters and show girls, Howard Hughes and the honorable Dr. Thompson.

That Vegas is long gone and the Riviera is a decaying relic of its passing. The crumbling hotel is wedged between vast parking lots on the north end of the Strip, across Las Vegas Boulevard from the even more decrepit Circus Circus, which resembles a sinister abandoned set from a slasher film.

Behind the Riviera looms a stout white warehouse. On the side of the building in large red block lettering is writ: Indoor Skydiving. Think about it. Just another tantalizing episode of the Vegas alt reality show. Of course, most of the indoor skydiving in this city is done on the floors of the casinos.

The traffic on the Strip is dominated by a dizzying circuit of cabs and trucks hauling advertisements for shows by unknown magicians, and fading stars like Celine Dion, Olivia Newton-John and Rod Stewart, who seems intent on completing his 30-year-long arc of descent by becoming the town's new Engelbert Humperdinck. But the most frequent mobile ads were for "Direct to You" prostitutes, "girls who really want to meet you." These emaciated blondes all sport immaculately redesigned breasts and exquisitely polished nails on delicate feet that apparently leave behind quite heavy carbon footprints.

Nevada is fast becoming a Tea Party sanctuary, but Vegas remains a solidly union town of culinary, hotel and casino workers. But even this is beginning to change. You can see the future on the gaming floors of the Bellagio and the Venetian, where more and more operations are becoming automated. The real surprise for me was the number of virtual black jack tables, where dealer avatars with distracting cleavage run the games on widescreen monitors. The human players, perhaps visually sedated by years of video gaming, sit silently at the tables, clinging to a desperate faith in the fairness of the casino's poker algorithms. Call it an Homage to Catatonia.

On the plane from Portland, I sat next to an engineer who has been working for the last decade at Lake Mead. The reservoir is shriveling, drying up before our eyes. The water level drops each year, leaving a baleful white stain on the walls of Black Canyon. His company's job is to paint the freshly exposed bone-white walls of the canyon back to their accustomed color, so as not to frighten the tourists.

Of course, it's not the tourists who should be petrified by the dwindling of Lake Mead, but the moguls of the Strip. They are the retailers of illusion. The biggest Mirage in town isn't the shimmering gilt-colored casino, with its topless poolside bar ($40 entry fee) and ghastly aquarium, but the illusion of water. Slotted on the desiccated basin floor of the Mojave, Las Vegas is moistened by less than four inches of rain a year. That's the old average. The future looks even drier. Yet there is water everywhere on the strip: the vast pools of Caesar's Palace, the waterfalls at the Wynn, the gondola-festooned lagoons of the Venetian, the dancing fountain at the Bellagio. The biggest illusion, the one that must be maintained at all costs, is that in Vegas there are no limits.

Over the course of the last 30 years, Vegas has been transformed from Sin City to a family theme park to an unapologetic advertisement for boundless gluttony. You can thank Steve Wynn for this grotesque metamorphosis, the man who punched his elbow through Picasso's "Le Rêve" while showing off his most celebrated possession to friends. Wynn later unloaded the re-stitched painting of a masturbating woman for $154 million on his noxious pal Stephen A. Cohen, the billionaire hedge funder whose SAC firm is perennially under investigation for insider trading.

Wynn made his mark running bingo parlors in Maryland. In the early 1970s, he came to Vegas and made a speculative land deal with Howard Hughes, which netted him a few million and controlling interest in the Golden Sands, where he lured Frank Sinatra and his entourage. The game changer occurred in 1989 when Wynne opened the first mega-resort casino on the new Strip, the Mirage, a 3,000 room Polynesian-themed gilded palace of sin with an erupting volcano. The construction of the Mirage was financed by another master of illusion, junk bond king Michael Milken. Treasure Island and the Bellagio, at the time the most expensive hotel ever built, soon followed.

In 2005, when Wynn opened his towering 650-foot tall luxury resort hotel and casino on the north side of the Strip he said he had wanted to call it Le Rêve. In the end, he opted for something a little less exotic: the Wynn. The décor of the Wynn (and it's twin curving bronze tower the Encore) is a wispy simulacrum of oriental opulence, designed to excite the sensibilities of Saudi princes on the prowl, Russian oligarchs with millions to burn in a weekend, and the Kardashian brood. In elegant harmony with this theme, the resort boasts two iridescent sculptures (Popeye and Tulips) by the con artist of tasteless triviality: Jeff Koons. It struck me that basement of the Wynn is the perfect tomb for Koons' moronic confections.

In the end, Wynn lent the name of the Picasso painting to a popular permanent show at his resort. Le Rêve (curiously translated as 'A' Dream) is a kind of aquatic Tempest, featuring bald men making dare-devil dives in Speedos, frisky Flappers splashing in platinum blond wigs, and synchronized swimmers flashing red stilettos. In other words, yes, a wet dream.

But the dream is coming to an end. A reckoning is coming. The water is running out. Today 90 percent of the city's water is sucked from Lake Mead and Lake Mead is drying up. The latest forecasts predict the once vast reservoir may be completely tapped out by 2021. Count 'em: That's seven years. After that, all bets are off. No water tunnels or emergency pipelines can possibly compensate for the shortage. Vegas's days are numbered. Deal with it, baby.

Sitting at a bar inside the Luxor's dark pyramid, watching a feisty Algerian team push the haughty German squad to the brink of elimination in the World Cup, I struck up a conversation with a Mexican-American man who works down in the canyon. His company performs a macabre service. They fish out the bodies of the jumpers, Vegas's losers, the victims of the gaming tables, the aging strippers and hookers, the dead-enders, those who have maxed out, those who have reached their last threshold and take a leap off the new Pat Tillman Memorial Bridge, sky diving into the Colorado River, 840 feet below.

"We snag four or five bodies a month," he tells me, as he tosses back his third Jack and Coke of the afternoon. "Vegas is still a hard town. Eventually your luck is going to run dry. Know what I mean?"

– July 4, 2014

CHRONICLE OF A FLOOD FORETOLD

By Jeffrey St. Clair

Houston didn't need to be warned. The city had already been sunk by four major hurricanes, each less powerful than Harvey, in the last 80 years. Generational storms. But boomtowns have short memories. After each epochal deluge, Houston rebuilt on the ruins. Rebuilt in a Texas way: Bigger. Brasher. Gaudier. Rebuilt on the very same vulnerable grounds. In the same pathway of destruction.

After each inundation, Houston got larger, as if to defy the mutating atmosphere gathering against it. It grew, it bulged and it sprawled. Into bayous. Into swamps. Into brownfields and floodplains. Into coastal prairies. Ripping up the last natural defenses between the city and the well-beaten storm track. Houston absorbed oil men, ex-presidents and immigrants, retirees, hedge funders and refugees from Katrina. Forty thousand new residents stream into the city every year. Houston grew and grew until it swelled into the second largest city in the nation in terms of land area it consumed and the fourth in terms of population. Bigger than Dallas, bigger than Boston, bigger than Phoenix, bigger than Philly.

Houston got bigger, but so did the hurricanes. Now the only barrier between Houston and the storms is the toxic crescent of oil refineries and chemical plants that spike up along the Gulf Coast from Beaumont to Corpus Christi. There would be no escape from Harvey. There will be no escape from the next storm or the ones following that. Storms which will be wetter, fiercer and more poisonous. Storms fueled by a Gulf that is warming inexorably, whose waters are rising inch by inch, year by year. Storms envenomed by the deadly detritus of the very industry which has super-charged them.

Tropical Storm Harvey entered the cauldron Gulf of Mexico on August 23, rapidly intensified, formed an eye and was declared a Hurricane the following day. Fed by the sun-seared waters of the Gulf, Harvey roared into a Category 3 storm in a matter of days, swirling with 100 mph winds as it bared down on the Texas coast. In the early morning hours of August 26, Harvey slammed into Rockport as a Category 4 storm, lashing the town with a ferocious storm surge propelled by 130 mph winds. Boats were torn from their moorings, trees were uprooted and sent flying, entire blocks of buildings were obliterated. Three hours later the storm had traversed Capano Bay before smashing into the town of Holiday Beach, where suddenly it began to slow, edging closer and closer to Houston, until the storm finally stalled for two days, a hovering cyclone of destruction, as it unleashed 50 inches of rain on the most densely populated swath of land on the Gulf. Then it backed out onto open water again, reorganized itself, and crawled north making landfall again near the oil port of Beaufort, then tearing up into Louisiana, where it swamped hundreds of homes in Lake Charles under four feet of water.

As the waters surged into Houston's bayous, streets and neighborhoods, more than 30,000 people fled their homes looking for shelter. Bay City was evacuated, as the downtown submerged under 10-feet of water. The town of Conroe was cleared on August 28, after the local dam began to overflow. The next day a levee along the Columbia Lakes breached and with the waters rising more than 6 inches an hour the Army Corps of Engineers began spilling water out of the dams at both Barker and Addison Reservoirs, flooding Buffalo Bayou. In a scene that resembled the fleet of Little Ships in the film Dunkirk, the so-called Cajun Navy of volunteer boaters deployed into the floodwaters to rescue people trapped on the roofs of houses, cars and buildings and clinging to overpasses, trees, and floating telephone poles.

At least 60 people perished in the floods and the death count is still rising. According to the Texas Department of Safety, 185,000 homes were damaged by the floodwaters, at least 10,000 of them rendered uninhabitable. Thousands remained in shelters two weeks after the storm dissipated with nowhere to go.

Along the petro-chemical zone, refineries flooded, pipelines ruptured, chemical plants exploded, and toxic waste sites were swamped. An early estimate, almost certainly low, calculated that two million pounds of hazardous chemicals had been released into the air during the flood by the big oil companies alone. Two oil tanks ruptured spilling 30,000 gallons of crude into the floodwaters. Another storage tank released 9,500 gallons of highly toxic wastewater. These were only the highlights in a state where regulators are charged with concealing not exposing such incidents.

In the spirit of American exceptionalism, Trump called the flooding "unprecedented." Wrong. It wasn't even unprecedented for that very same week, as more than 2500 people perished in flooding from monster storms in Sierra Leone and Bangladesh. With the even more potent Hurricane Irma charging across the Caribbean toward Florida, these super-storms are beginning to look like the new normal. We hear the boosters and politicians reassuringly describe Harvey as a "1000-year event." The term itself suggests that the hurricane was the product of some vast celestial cycle for beyond human influence. Nonsense. This was Houston's third "500-year flood" in the last three years! Time must be moving much faster now.

The liberal response to all of this is to demand that Trump make a public act of contrition by acknowledging the existence of climate change in some primetime speech. How quaint. I don't care what Trump believes or what he says. What difference could it possibly make at this point? Climate change is a fact. The sea levels are rising. The polar ice caps are melting. The forests of the West are burning. The Colorado River is dwindling. The snowpack in the Rockies, Sierras and Cascade Mountains is shrinking. Bird migration patterns are changing. Coral Reefs are bleaching out. Salmon and grizzlies are being driven toward extinction. All of this is happening whether Donald Trump and Scott Pruitt believe it or not. And there's little they could do to change the dynamic, even if they were willing to try.

Barack Obama prattled poetic platitudes about global warming week after week for eight years and over that time atmospheric carbon levels rose from 392 PPM in 2008 to 412 PPM this summer. Since Obama took office, the average water temperature of the Gulf of Mexico rose by 1 degree Fahrenheit and the sea level of the Gulf is now six inches higher than it was when Rita hit the coast of Texas in 2005. I tend to see Harvey as the latest aftershock of the political mentality that led to Deepwater Horizon. The Obama mentality, if you will. The pious mentality that signs the toothless Paris Accords, while authorizing deepwater drilling, fracking, coal liquidification, mountaintop removal mining, LNG terminals and offshore drilling.

At root, Trump and Obama share the same lethal ideology of endless growth and consumption that has served as a death warrant on the planet and millions of new solar panels and wind turbines won't bring us back from the brink. Trump may believe his own bullshit. Obama knew better and didn't have the guts to speak the truth. What is that truth? That unchained capitalism is the invisible hand driving the destruction left by Katrina, Sandy and Harvey. Here I'm not referring only to the manufactured power of the new breed of hurricanes themselves, but to the moral blindness that stalks the aftermath, an omnivorous economic machine that learns nothing from so much tragedy, privation and death.

In a few months, amnesia will once again begin to grip Houston and the Gulf Coast. The reconstruction will begin. Bridges, roads and levees will be repaired. The refineries will fire back up. The chemical plants will resume their dark operations. New buildings will be built on the old, financed by federal and state subsidies and loans. Houston, which brands itself "the city without limits," will continue its ceaseless expansion. The displaced will quietly move on, desperately looking for shelter and work in San Antonio, Memphis, Biloxi. But what's misery for many is a business opportunity for the few. The most malign kind of looting is done by the post-disaster speculators, bankers and real estate magnates who will pilfer the wreckage for profit. Five years from now Houston will look shiny and new again, as it blindly awaits the flood next time.

– September 2017

A CRISIS WITH NO END: WHY FLINT IS STILL THE ISSUE

By Joshua Frank

Last year the water crisis in Flint, Michigan made headlines for weeks, even though by the time it finally did the damage was done. The water that residents of Flint were forced to drink, over 100,000 of them, was tainted with lead, lots of it. Upwards of 12,000 children, most from minority, impoverished neighborhoods, had elevated levels of the metal in their blood. Today, the lead in Flint's water has taken a physical, as well as a mental toll on those impacted and the water is still tainted.

"I get really emotional about it, because I have no idea about the effects it will have," Sarah Conn recently told CBC. "[My son] could have cognitive problems and behavioral problems when he gets older and I won't know for sure if the lead is why, or not, and it makes me really sad."

Federal regulators announced on March 7 that 90 percent of water samples taken in Flint were now below federal levels for lead content. But these tests are very misleading, if not outright bogus. The official federal level for lead contamination is 15 ppb and Flint's water is coming in at around 12 ppb in most cases. However, this is still not as low as levels ought to be, especially for growing children. The American Academy of Pediatrics' Council on Environmental Health recommends that drinking water for kids should not exceed 1 ppb of lead and the new proposed state standard in Michigan is 10 ppb. To top it off, nearly 28,000 residences in Flint still need to have their old pipes replaced. Thus far the city has only completed 800 homes.

"There have been constant improvements [in water quality], there's no question about that, but I don't consider that an all clear," retired Brig. Gen. Michael C. McDaniel told reporters at a recent national water infrastructure conference in Flint.

That's not all that comforting to those living in Flint who've been dependent on bottled water for daily needs like brushing and drinking for the past year. Adding insult to injury, water bills in Flint have also skyrocketed. The state's subsidy on water in the city, which cut bills by 65 percent, ended last month. So as of March people in Flint are paying a lot more, in most cases double their previous bill, for water that still doesn't meet the state's proposed levels.

"We can't keep living this. It's killing us. It's literally killing us to live this and it's going on its second year now … I'm living a low standard life," says Flint resident and activist Gladyes Williamson. "This is not a third world country. This is the United States of America. This is Michigan."

Flint, of course, is just the tip of the lead-laden iceberg. Across the United States an estimated 10 million underground lead pipes must be replaced, with only a few cities actively addressing the issue. In the Bronx, for example, two public schools, P.S.41 and I.S.158, had staggering lead readings in February ranging from 63.8 ppb to 442 ppb. The nation's aging water infrastructure, if it isn't tackled immediately, could harm an untold number of people, primarily children who are most susceptible to lead's various impacts, like poor cognitive development.

"And in the aftermath of Flint, what we now realize is … that probably we're never going to be able to say that it's safe to drink water from a lead pipe—not only in Flint but in fact, all around the United States," Marc Edwards, an engineer at Virginia Tech, told PRI. "What we discovered in Flint is that some of the worst houses actually had a lead pipe followed by a galvanized iron pipe. And what had happened over the almost a century some of these pipes had been in the ground is, the iron rust on the galvanized iron pipe sponged up lead at very, very high levels."

The scenario Professor Edwards lays out is occurring across the country. With weak federal drinking water standards, an understaffed EPA and a Trump administration hell-bent on slashing agency funds, the problem of lead-polluted water will only get worse. Sadly, the ultimate toll this catastrophe has on all those vulnerable children in Flint and elsewhere won't be known for decades to come.

– March 10, 2017

MARIA'S MISSING DEAD

By Jeffrey St. Clair

They knew it was coming. They knew when it would hit. They knew how strong the winds would be and how much rain the storm bands would unleash. They knew how high the surf might surge. They knew it would take out Puerto Rico's decrepit power grid. They knew the island's archaic water system would fail. They knew there would be landslides, burying roads, cutting off towns and isolating villages. They knew bridges and small dams would collapse. They knew backup generators would run out of gas. They knew hospitals and clinics would lose power. They knew tens of thousands of house would be destroyed, leaving families homeless for months. They knew there would be deaths and thousands of injuries. They knew children would be separated from parents, the elderly and infirm left alone. They knew there would be shortages of food, water, and medicine. They knew that Puerto Rico, struggling under crushing debt, imposed austerity and the cruel legacy of colonialism, was even less capable of dealing with the immediate aftermath of a super-storm than was Houston or New Orleans or Miami. They knew and yet they did nothing.

Hurricane Maria gave plenty of warning. Despite being under siege from Trump's budget cuts, NOAA had meticulously tracked the storm since it first formed as an ominous wrinkle in the broiling waters of the eastern Atlantic off the coast of West Africa. They tracked it as it migrated across the Atlantic, incubating in 85-degree waters until it coalesced into a tropical depression near the Lesser Antilles. Then within 24 hours, Maria morphed from a tropical storm into a powerful hurricane, fueled by the most "explosive intensification" ever documented in the Atlantic Basin. On September 19, Maria entered in the Caribbean Sea, after smashing across the island of Dominica packing 165 mile per hour winds, the fiercest ever to hit the island.

The first tentacles of Maria lashed Puerto Rico on September 20th. Over the next 24 hours, some parts of the island were drenched by 40 inches of rain, eight inches more than Houston received over three days during Hurricane Harvey. The power went out within a few hours, plunging the island into the largest blackout in US history and the second largest in the history of the world. For months, people in rural villages were forced to drink water contaminated by toxic waste, rotting animal corpses and raw sewage.

George W. Bush was swiftly vilified for his callously lethargic response to the swamping of New Orleans after Hurricane Katrina. Yet within a mere two weeks, Congress had appropriated $60 billion in emergency funding for Katrina survivors. In the wake of Maria, the government of Puerto Rico pleaded with the Trump administration for $94 billion disaster relief. It took the Ryan/McConnell-led Congress six months to act on Puerto Rico's urgent request for help and then they only allocated a mere $16 billion in federal aid. In those six months, more than 5,700 Puerto Ricans may have died, according to a mortality analysis by public health researchers at Harvard University. These weren't victims of the storm itself, but of government indifference and incompetence in the days, weeks and months that followed.

In the months after the storm, Puerto Ricans died from lack of basic medical care. They died because they ran out of crucial medicines. They died because they couldn't get to dialysis treatments. They died because their breathing machines stopped working. They died of chronic conditions and acute disorders. They died of stress and heart attacks. they died of dehydration, exposure and starvation. They died from despair and suicides. They died from the criminal neglect of their own government.

Trump should thank Roseanne Barr, whose racist Twitter-spasm knocked the Harvard Report on post-Maria deaths in

Puerto Rico off the Sunday morning news talk shows, none of which even mentioned the staggering mortality rate, which was 90 times the government's own total. The press, which largely left the island after Trump's paper-towel tossing photo op in San Juan, is nearly as complicit as the president.

For weeks, the official death toll in Puerto Rico stood at 16, an absurd figure that Trump repeatedly invoked in a running advertisement for how his administration should have rated a "10 out of 10" for its response to the Hurricane. This number eventually climbed to 64 deaths, and there it stood for 8 months, rarely questioned by the media despite the ongoing carnage of the island. The devastating Harvard Report, released on the eve of the new Atlantic hurricane season, came and went, a brief interlude in the national psychodrama.

"It took too long to understand the need for an appropriate response was not about politics but about saying lives," said Carmen Yulín Cruz, San Juan's feisty mayor. "Now will the government believe it?" There's no sign that the government even read it, nevermind absorbed its urgent lessons.

Now there is no excuse. We all know what Puerto Ricans have suspected all along. Still, they do nothing. Instead, FEMA and its crony-contractors are leaving the island, where tens of thousands of Puerto Ricans remain without safe drinking water and reliable electrical power. Fields remain fallow. Food is scarce. And people are dying every day. But who's counting?

– June 2018

DOWN THE RIVER WITH VLADIMIR PUTIN

By Jeffrey St. Clair

You don't see the Grand River coming. It sneaks in from the northeast, down a vaulted corridor of rock. You feel its muscular pulse first, sucker-punching you with a new surge to the current. The river runs a vibrant reddish-brown, the color of native America.

Here at the marriage of the Grand and the Green is where the real Colorado River is born. It flows freely for 18 miles, then dies beneath the chill waters of Lake Powell. These 18 miles are the only free-flowing stretch of the Colorado River from here to the Sea of Cortez, turbulent, tepid, freighted with silt.

The river that runs through Grand Canyon is not free. It bears no resemblance to the natural Colorado. Its flow is minutely fine-tuned by the hydro-engineers that operation Glen Canyon Dam. The water emerges from the spillways at 47 degrees, 50 degrees cooler than the Colorado on an average summer day. Cold enough for rainbow trout. Frigid and blue. Cataract Canyon is all that remains of the river John Wesley Powell encountered. And half of it has been drowned.

Our guide, John Weisheit, motions us over to a beach on river right where several other rafts are anchored. This is the famous Spanish Bottom. One of the guides is leading a group of jolly Germans, who look almost as Aryan as the suburban saints of Provo. He gestures at our rafts and kayaks and tells his clients with a smirk and a theatrical shake of his head, "Those are self-bailing boats."

Then the rival guide pushes his raft (a non-bailing bucket boat) off the beach and heads off down Cataract Canyon. On the bucket boat's stern, the icon of authenticity wears a propeller. I guess that's how you run Fast Food Rapids. Get 'em in, get em out. Slam, bam, thank you mam. The whitewater quickie.

But who is bailing the hydrocarbons?

***

The river clientele are becoming increasingly international, as younger Americans opt for extreme sports, such as base jumping, or root themselves in front of online gaming monitors and swell to such obese proportions that they can no longer squeeze through security screens at airports, never mind stuff themselves into a kayak.

Moab is a favored destination for Germans, obsessed with John Wayne, who urge their guides to haul them off to places where they can get their photos snapped in front of locations from John Ford films.

Australians come to the river to tempt death, badgering their guides to take the most dangerous course through the biggest rapids. One Aussie offered Weisheit $1,000 to intentionally flip his raft in the cauldron of Big Drop One. "I'm not going to do that," Weisheit told him. "But will you still pay me $1,000 if the river flips us anyway?"

The English, as a group, tend to be prissy. They refuse to swim naked, make odd, animal-like noises in the Groover, wear dress shoes in the raft and, according to the late river-runner and writer Ellen Meloy, insist on referring to each river eddy as, yes, an Edward.

It will surprise no one that the French come to dispute.

They complain about the lack of standing room in their tents, the omnipresence of bugs, the paucity of rapids prior to Cataract, the soaking from the rapids themselves, and, most viciously, they bitch about the quality of riverside meals, prepared by the river guides following a hard day rowing in sweltering heat. After being offered a plate with Indiana-grown corn-on-the-cob lathered in garlic butter, a French tourist shoved the fare back at the guide and exclaimed, "Why do you serve me this pig food?" These are the clients you send for firewood near the scorpion's nest and the faded midget rattlesnake's den.

But the consensus of the guides is clear. The crudest, cheapest and most demeaning patrons are Russian men, led by their President Vladimir Putin.

A couple of years ago Vladimir Putin journeyed to the American Southwest to take his son on an initiation ritual. The boy's mother is now an American citizen. First stop was a big game ranch in Texas, where Putin and Jr blasted zebras, antelopes and bison. Apparently, Putin, reenacting a scene out of Mailer's *Why Are We In Vietnam*, marked his son's forehead in the blood of one of these hapless creatures.

Then it was on to Moab, Utah, for a raft trip down Cataract Canyon on the Colorado River. The Moab river guide community is still shaking its head from its close encounter with the Russian president and former KGB man. "We get a lot of whacked-out people coming down the river, but Putin really is a dangerous guy, a real mobster," a guide told me.

"His packs were loaded with guns, vodka and tens of thousands of dollars in cash," the guide said. "He seemed to be a little on edge. He was a real bully. He was drunk much of the time and bossed people around as if they were his personal slaves. They refused to use the Groover. They pissed and shat wherever they wanted. They fired off their guns. They caught channel catfish and bashed their heads in with rocks."

Putin and his son were soon bored with the redbrick canyons and Class five rapids. "By the third day, Putin demanded that the guides call in a helicopter to have his party picked up and flown out. Then he got drunk and began to threaten the guides. He started bragging about how many people he had personally killed. 'More than 40', he said."

The rafts finally exited Cataract and motored across 30 miles of Lake Powell's flat water to the marina complex at Hite. The next step on the Putties' tour was supposed to be a four-wheeler excursion tearing up the desert in the bizarre Needles District of Canyonlands. But Putin opted for a more traditional form of initiation for his son, straight out of *Notes from the Underground*. From the Hite marina, he placed a call to Las Vegas.

"Get us some whores," Putin shouted into his cellphone. "Price is no object."

***

As Weisheit deals with some administrative matters and checks the rigging of the rafts for the first rapids, I take a short walk through the meadows of Spanish Bottom, following a trail that winds up into the Maze to the Chocolate Drops, the surrealistic Harvest Panel pictograph and a group of strange multi-colored rock spires called the Doll House, which could pass for Utah's version of Antonio Gaudi's Sagrada Familia Cathedral.

Cairns mark the way, even though the way is obvious. Everyone wants to leave their testimonial to treading the wilderness. I leave my own by toppling the cairns as I pass them, scattering the stones among the yellow beeplants and Indian ricegrass.

I stumble across a lithified mound of cowshit. Cows haven't grazed here in at least forty-five years, since Canyonlands became a national park and all the bovine marauders were finally evicted. Even the most mundane scars take decades to heal in this desert. Putin's shit is probably out there too, slowly turning to stone.

– Mar 17, 2014

SECTION 3
POLITISCAPES

PAPER TRAILS: BIG TIMBER, THE CLINTONS AND THE ORIGINS OF THE WHITEWATER SCANDAL

By Jeffrey St. Clair

Of the thousands of stories written about the Whitewater scandal, some 90 percent have concerned themselves with the cover-up question: if or how the Clinton White House suppressed evidence in the wake of Vince Foster's suicide. Almost all the remaining stories deal with the efforts of Governor Bill and the First Lady of Arkansas to keep their friend James McDougal's Madison Guaranty Savings & Loan afloat. Meanwhile, one of the great untold stories of Whitewater is the chummy nexus of the Clintons and big timber, which may have played a role in the original Whitewater Estates deal and certainly was evidenced in a subsequent transaction that amounted to a last-ditch effort to save the Whitewater Development Corporation from bankruptcy.

The WDC began its ventures with a land deal designed to channel fast money to Bill and Hillary. In 1978, state Attorney General Clinton was in the midst of his first campaign for the governorship when he and Hillary, along with Jim and Susan McDougal, bought 230 acres of riverfront land in the Ozark Mountains of northern Arkansas. Though title to the land was in the Clintons' name, the couple put down no money. McDougal did not yet have the S&L and was a financial fixer and property dealer. He fronted the money for the down payment on the loan.

And where did the land come from? Its previous owner-of-record was a partnership, 101 River Development, whose role appears to be strictly that of a conduit. 101 River Development held the property for only three days, and folded its tent within a couple of weeks of the sale. The previous owner had been a group of local businessmen. And prior to them, the last owner had been International Paper, Arkansas's largest landholder—a $16 billion a year timber giant with 7 million acres of land across the United States, and 800,000 acres in Arkansas. It had logged off the best timber on the site and then sold the riverfront acres cheap to the local partnership of Arkansas bankers and businessmen.

How long the local partners held the land, or the terms on which it passed from IP to them to 101 River Development to the Clintons and McDougals, is unclear. But it is evident that the Whitewater sale came at a time when the timber giant was holding a keen ear to the pronouncements of candidate Clinton. The young attorney general vowed that as governor he would restrict clearcutting on land held by companies such as International Paper, Georgia-Pacific, and Weyerhaeuser. These paper and timber companies had gone on a logging binge in the mid-1970s, clearcutting 1,000-acre chunks of forest at a time. Clinton promised to introduce legislation banning the practice as soon as he entered the governor's office.

Clinton won the governorship in November of 1979. Environmentalists eagerly awaited action from the new governor to stop clearcutting and to stem the flow of industrial poisons that suffused the state's water and air. But the promises of the campaign trail soon lost their fire. Clinton's commitment was pallid from the start; his two predecessors as governor, Dale Bumpers and David Pryor, had both tangled with the timber companies on the issue of clearcutting with far more vigor.

When the newly elected governor formed a task force on clear-cutting stocked with conservationists, the panel swiftly took heat from loggers and from the boardrooms of Weyerhaeuser and Georgia-Pacific. A startled Clinton kicked off the conservation-ists, installed industry hacks in their place, and recommended voluntary compliance with soft regulations.

The Arkansas voters turned out Clinton at the end of his two-year term in 1980. He left the governor's mansion and went to work at the Little Rock law firm of Wright, Lindsey and Jennings. His office was in the Worthen Bank, controlled by the powerful Stephens family. Hillary was at the Rose law firm. Both firms represented the timber giants of Arkansas before state regulatory bodies such as the Pollution Control Board and the Department of Ecology. Meanwhile, Clinton was refashioning himself as a New Democrat, sensitive to the concerns of business and zealous to purge himself of all "progressive" taint.

Clinton recaptured the governor's office in 1982, the same year that McDougal bought Madison Guaranty Savings & Loan. Among those contributing to candidate Clinton's campaign treasury were International Paper, Georgia-Pacific, and Tyson Foods. Their investment was swiftly rewarded. Clinton redux was now equipped with a philosophical approach to regulation highly congenial to the resource industries and to the poultry factories.

Tyson in particular became a key ally of Clinton's after the latter learned his lesson from the trucking dispute. Tyson planes ferried the First Family on its travels and Tyson funds poured into Clinton's campaign coffers. In return, the poultry magnate received roughly $12 million worth of tax breaks during Clinton's years as governor. Nor was Clinton diligent in monitoring the environmental record of Tyson Foods or of the poultry industry in general.

But if the disastrous impact of Tyson's chicken farms on the Arkansas River is fairly well known, the pulp plants of International Paper, Georgia-Pacific, and James River were more toxic still. International Paper's mill at Pine Bluff is one of the most virulent in the nation, venting nearly 2 million tons of chemicals a year into the air and water.

From 1982 forward, Clinton argued that compliance to environmental standards could best be achieved on a voluntary basis, rather than by the imposition of exigent (and politically perilous) rules and regulations. To this end Governor Clinton stacked his pollution control board with members friendly to industry. In 1985 he promoted and then signed into law a huge tax break for industrial corporations of his state, including the big timber companies. This easing of the corporate fiscal burden was offset by a regressive sales tax on the citizenry.

Clinton's big offering to the timber companies was the Manufacturers' Investment Sales and Use Tax Credit, known by critics as the "IP bailout law" in honor of International Paper. Under this program state tax breaks were approved for more than $400 million in projects by International Paper and three other paper mills that then-state Senator Ben Allen of Little Rock called "the worst corporate citizens in Arkansas"—all this in a state with one of the lowest per capita incomes in the nation and where 29 percent of the children and half the state's black residents lived in poverty.

A few years later state officials tried to keep International Paper and two Georgia-Pacific mills off a toxic waterways list, despite evidence they were contaminating rivers with dioxin. Meanwhile, International Paper, while taking repeated advantage of the manufacturers' sales tax credit, was ladling out money to candidate Clinton.

It was around this time that Clinton supervised another land deal highly favorable to the timber giants. In later years, taunted with the fact that his state ranked 48th in environmental quality, Clinton would make much of the fact that as governor he had acquired thousands of acres for state-owned forests. Two types of deals were involved here. In one, Clinton swapped state-owned lands mantled with valuable trees for corporate parcels which had been recently cut over. In the other type, the state simply acquired at inflated prices land which the timber companies had recently logged.

Nourished by these benefices, the timber companies, along with Tyson, began to urge Governor Clinton—now nearing the end of his third term—to consider challenging Dale Bumpers for the Senate seat he had held since the early 1970s. The companies had no love for Bumpers. He had led the charge to reform forest policies on federal lands, culminating in the passage of the National Forest Management Act. Bumpers was also, as already noted, a spirited critic of the clearcutting and pesticide practices of the big timber companies in Arkansas. But Clinton was then contemplating a run for the White House. And so the timber companies, along with other corporate interests, funded the Democratic Leadership Council—Clinton's launching pad.

The kindly deeds President Clinton has performed for the timber giants are well known. But for International Paper in particular, Clinton wrought two spectacular favors. First, he refused to take any action to stem the flow of raw log exports from the Pacific Northwest, where International Paper holds about half a million acres. Second, the generous Habitat Conservation Plans tirelessly promoted by Interior Secretary and fellow DLC member Bruce Babbitt allowed International Paper and Georgia-Pacific to continue to cut trees on land occupied by endangered species such as the red-cockaded woodpecker.

But the funds that helped to establish the DLC may not have been IP's only big favor to Clinton. In the mid-1980s, when the Whitewater Development Corporation was foundering on the verge of bankruptcy, it was International Paper that sold 500 acres to McDougal and Clinton at the generous price of $1,000 an acre. WDC put little money down and later defaulted on the loan. Finally, when the McDougal/Clinton partnership defaulted on their land purchase from International Paper in 1987, the timber company kept the Clintons off the ensuing lawsuit.

Incidentally, the 500-acre parcel, known as Lowrance Heights, was located near the Castle Grande development to which Hillary devoted the notorious "missing" 60 hours of billed time on behalf of Madison Guaranty. And therein lies yet another possible accommodation between the Clintons and the paper companies: According to Arkansas press accounts, when the Castle Grande deal began to fall apart and threaten Madison's financial health, McDougal and Clinton pressured timber executive Dean Paul into taking out an $825,000 loan to rescue Castle Grande. Nearly $100,000 of that "loan" ended up in Whitewater accounts, and some of it may also have found its way into Clinton's campaign chest. Yet another Clinton/timber thread: Although Hillary's incredible success in commodities trading has been widely advertised as an exercise in cattle futures, in fact part of her conversion of $1,000 into $98,000 came in trades on timber futures.

The Clintons never so much as visited Whitewater Estates or the International Paper land. But the only person who appears to have made any money in any of the Whitewater real estate deals (aside from the sellers) was Hillary. She "bought"—there's no evidence she put any of her own money down—a model home on a lot that promptly sold, netting her $30,000.

The linkages between the Clintons and the paper companies actually do not end there. When the Whitewater scandal finally exploded, Attorney General Janet Reno hired as special prosecutor Robert Fiske of Davis, Polk and Wardwell—the New York law firm that also represented International Paper.

The timber companies are not the most familiar pillars of the Arkansas power structure—that status falls to Tyson, Wal-Mart, and the Stephens family—but they are probably the most potent of the lot. All told, International Paper, Weyerhaeuser, Georgia-Pacific, and Potlatch control more than 2.5 million acres of land in Arkansas and operate more than 30 mills. It is scarcely surprising that it crossed the corporate mind of International Paper that a pleasant offering of real estate to the Clintons, via McDougal, would not be such a bad idea.

– December, 2000

HOW MUCH HAS CHANGED? OBAMA ADMINISTRATION DEALS SERIES OF ANTI-ENVIRONMENTAL BLOWS

By Jeffrey St. Clair and Joshua Frank

With little more than 100 days in office, the Democrats, under the leadership of President Barack Obama, have unleashed a slew of anti-environmental policies that would have enraged any reasonable conservationist during the Bush years.

Take the delisting of the gray wolf in the western Great Lakes and parts of the northern Rockies, which was announced during the waning days of the Bush era and upheld by Obama earlier this spring.

About 200 packs of wolves live in the northern Rocky Mountains today. But only 95 of these packs are led by breeding pairs, which is significantly less than half of what most biologists consider to be a healthy number in order to fend off imminent decline and long-term genetic problems for the species.

In Idaho, free-roaming wolves have been radio-collared, allowing their human killers to track and gun them down by helicopter. Freed from the protections of the Endangered Species Act, the state plans to permit hundreds of these wolves to be slaughtered this coming winter. Only a few environmental groups have stepped up in the wolves' defense, with the Center for Biological Diversity, based in Tucson, Arizona, leading the charge.

It's not just the wolf that's been hung out to dry. Shortly after Obama's inauguration, Interior Secretary Ken Salazar and Commerce Secretary Gary Locke announced they were revoking an 11th-hour Bush directive that weakened the ESA listing process.

However, shortly thereafter the Department of the Interior refused to repeal a special rule that would have granted the polar bear protection from the impacts of global warming. Salazar said his agency does not believe the law was intended to address climate change, even though many policy analysts believe the ESA could be used to limit the issuing of permits for development projects that would potentially threaten the polar bear by emitting additional greenhouse gases.

"The Endangered Species Act is not the proper tool to deal with a global issue—global warming," Salazar said. "We need to move forward with a comprehensive climate change and energy plan we can be proud of." Apparently federal protection should not be granted if the industry's emissions happen outside the polar bear's natural habitat. The Obama administration, under Salazar's watch, is refusing to lead the way in protecting the bear's dwindling populations. Of course, the oil and gas cartels were unabashedly pleased with the decision. So much for thinking globally and acting locally.

"We welcome the administration's decision because we, like Secretary Ken Salazar, recognize that the Endangered Species Act is not the proper mechanism for controlling our nation's carbon emissions," said American Petroleum Institute President Jack Gerard. "Instead, we need a comprehensive, integrated energy-and-climate strategy to address this complex, global challenge."

That's not the only recent victory for Big Oil provided by Salazar's office. During one of the most ridiculous episodes of the 2008 presidential campaign, the strange tag-team of Sen. John McCain, R-Ariz., and Alaska Gov. Sarah Palin led their diminutive crowds in spastics of "Drill, baby, drill." Offshore oil drilling and a new generation of nuclear power plants represented the sum total of the McCain/Palin energy plan.

Although it seemed like political comedy at the time, this strategy has now been at least partially embraced by the Obama administration. As the clock approached midnight for the Bush administration, his Interior Department put forward a rule opening 300 million acres of coastal waters to oil drilling.

According to the hastily prepared decree, the leasing was to begin by March 23, 2007.

Enter Salazar with a maneuver that is typical of the Obama approach to environmental politics: Instead of killing the drilling plan outright, Salazar merely extended the analysis period for six months. The environmental lobby was given a procedural crumb, while the oil hounds still had its long-sought prize on the table for the taking.

Although offshore drilling is so intensely unpopular in coastal states that even former Florida Gov. Jeb Bush stood up to his brother's attempts to expand drilling in the Gulf of Mexico, Salazar, accompanied by a consort of oil lobbyists, held four town hall forums this spring on offshore drilling and left the distinct impression that he was leaning toward what he called a "comprehensive approach" to energy development, in which the oceans will be mined for offshore wind, wave power and, yes, oil.

This is proving to be an administration that doesn't know the meaning of the word "no."

Down in Appalachia, things are not much better, where the coal-extraction industry was recently given the green light to proceed with 42 of its 48 pending mountaintop-removal permits. While Obama speaks out about the negative impact of the aptly named process, where mountains are blown apart to expose thin lines of coal, he is not willing to take on an industry that continually pollutes rivers and threatens public health.

"If you still have an Obama sticker on your car, maybe think about scraping it off and sending it to the White House with your objections," says Mike Roselle of Climate Ground Zero, who is working hard to stop mountaintop removal in West Virginia and elsewhere. "Blowing mountains to pieces is a crime."

When it comes to CO_2 emissions, the EPA has also been more bark than bite. While admitting that greenhouse gases are a threat to human health, the agency will not necessarily move to regulate industry emissions.

White House climate czar Carol Browner and EPA administrator Lisa Jackson initially said that such a declaration would "indeed trigger the beginning of regulation of CO_2," but only weeks later, Jackson reversed her belief that industry would be affected by the White House's admission.

Speaking before the U.S. Senate Environment and Public Works Committee, Jackson said on May 12: "The endangerment finding is a scientific finding mandated by law. … It does not mean regulation."

In fact, instead of implementing real regulatory oversight to combat the alleged culprits of global warming, the Obama administration has held its campaign promise to tackle CO_2 emissions by embracing free-market environmentalism, i.e. cap-and-trade.

Obama proposes reducing U.S. emissions 83 percent by 2050 by essentially allowing industry to regulate itself by putting a price on carbon. But many say there is a reason industry isn't frightened.

"[Cap-and-trade] programs have so many leaks, trap doors and perverse side effects that they'll probably do more harm than good," says Ted Nace, director of CoalSwarm, an environmental project of the Earth Island Institute that seeks to shut down coal plants in the U.S.

"The illusion that a solution is in place will then prevent simpler, more focused solutions from being implemented. An example of this phenomenon is the sulfur trading system. Proponents of cap-and-trade point to it as proof that pollution markets work, but decades after the program went into place, I can show you a big database of coal plants that continue to spew inordinate amounts of sulfur dioxide," says Nace. "A simpler solution to the global-warming problem would be to mandate that all the existing coal plants be phased out in an orderly, phased manner."

Not surprisingly, Obama refuses to consider strict regulation, let alone a carbon tax to address the country's big CO_2 emitters. Instead, after intense pressure from the pollution lobby, Obama's approach to attacking climate change has been whittled down to nothing more than weak market-driven economics that can too easily be manipulated politically. Polluters will be let off the hook because they can simply relocate or build new infrastructure in places where there are few or no carbon regulations.

But by far the boldest stroke of this spring was Obama's courageous decision to zero out funding for the planned nuclear-waste repository at the sacred Yucca Mountain. This vault on earthquake-prone lands of the Western Shoshone near Las Vegas was long meant to be the escape hatch for the nuclear industry's most aggravating problem: where to hide the accumulating piles of radioactive material from the nation's 104 commercial nuclear reactors.

Sen. Harry Reid, D-Nev., says Yucca Mountain is dead. So does Energy Secretary Stephen Chu. But Yucca Mountain has been buried before only to rise up from the grave. If indeed Obama has succeeded in killing it off, this alone will eclipse all of the vaporous achievements of the Clinton era.

Still, appraisal of the true meaning of the Yucca Mountain decision must be countered by the administration's ongoing promotion of nuclear power as corrective to climate change. Chu and Obama's chief science advisor, John Holdren, are pushing for federal subsidies for a new generation of nuclear power plants—even though Obama has admitted there's no safe place to store nuclear waste. Even more disturbing, Holdren continues to hawk the fool's gold of the nuclear lobby: fusion energy.

In an interview with *Science*, Holdren said: "We need to develop and deploy approaches to nuclear energy that can minimize the liabilities that have inhibited expansion of that carbon-free energy source up until now. We need to see if we can make fusion work. This is a quest in which I've been engaged since 1965. Again, I started [my work at MIT] in that domain. At that time, people thought fusion was 15 years away. Now people think it's 40 or 50 years away. We need to shrink that time scale again by increasing the investment for making that domain."

This means billions more for the nuclear lobby under the guise of research and development, the pipeline of federal subsidies that has kept the industry alive since Three Mile Island.

In May, Obama announced a sweeping overhaul of the car-fuel-efficiency and exhaust-emissions standards, which have languished unmodified for more than a decade. These long-overdue upgrades will force car makers (if there are any left five years from now, when the rules are slated to finally kick in) to curb carbon-dioxide emissions by 35 percent and hike fuel efficiency standards from 30 to 35 miles per gallon. While the proposal has been hailed as historic, it has plenty of drawbacks.

For starters, the plan capitulated to automakers by endorsing a national emissions standard, which will likely pre-empt states, such as California, from adopting even more stringent clean air rules. Obama also gave the auto industry a few more years to come into compliance with these rather modest requirements. No wonder the move was hailed by traditional Motor City defenders such as Sen. Carl Levin, D-Mich., and Rep. John Dingell, D-Mich.

Less endearing is the Obama administration's relentless push to replace oil with biofuels, which will push marginal agriculture lands into production of genetically engineered and pesticide-saturated monocrops, scalping topsoil and draining dwindling water supplies across the Great Plains and Midwest. Overseeing this misguided scheme is Obama's Agriculture Secretary Tom Vilsack, the former governor of Iowa, who has long been a servant of industrial agriculture and the bioengineering industry.

Under Vilsack, the biofuels project is poised to move far beyond burning corn and soybeans for fuel. They want to chop down national forests and burn the public's trees inside a new generation of biomass power generators.

This insidious and little-noticed program will be marshaled by biomass booster Homer Lee Wilkes, a little-known urban planner from Madison, Miss. Wilkes was Vilsack's surprise pick for the powerful slot of Undersecretary of Agriculture for Natural Resources and the Environment, a position that, among other responsibilities, places Wilkes in control of the U.S. Forest Service.

So look for a new wave of timber sales on federal lands, sanctified in the name of fighting climate change, categorically excluded from full environmental analysis and enthusiastically supported by so-called collaborative groups who will be first in line to cash in on the lucrative logging contracts. Greens with chainsaws.

– May 28, 2009

OBAMA'S NUCLEAR DREAMS: RESURRECTING A NOXIOUS INDUSTRY

By Jeffrey St. Clair and Joshua Frank

He may soon be called the nuclear industry's Golden Child. No president in the last three decades has put more taxpayer dollars behind atom power than Barack Obama. And there may be good reason why the president is salivating over the prospect of building new nuclear power plants around the country.

It was one of the most important issues of the 2008 presidential campaign. The perceived threat of global warming began to make even the most skeptical of politicians a bit nervous. Both the Democrats and Republicans proposed searching for more domestic oil supplies, promising to drill up and down the spine of the Rocky Mountains and even off the fragile coastlines of Florida and California. The future of planet Earth, they claimed, is more perilous than ever.

Al Gore made his impact.

Too bad the Gore effect is like a bad hangover: all headache and no buzz. The purported solution the Obama administration has heaved at the imminent warming crisis, nuclear technology, is just as hazardous as our current methods of energy procurement. Yet, Obama isn't the first Democrat in recent years to tout nuclear virtues.

Al Gore, who wrote of the potential green merits of nuclear power in his book *Earth in the Balance*, earned his stripes as a Congressman protecting the interests of two of the nuclear industry's most problematic enterprises, the TVA and the Oak Ridge Labs. And, of course, Bill Clinton backed the Entergy Corporation's outrageous plan to soak Arkansas ratepayers with the cost overruns on the company's Grand Gulf reactor, which provided power to electricity consumers in Louisiana.

The Clinton years indeed saw an all-out expansion of nuclear power around the globe. First came the deal to begin selling nuclear reactors to China, announced during Jiang Zemin's 1997 visit to Washington, even though Zemin brazenly vowed at the time not to abide by the so-called "full scope safeguards" spelled out in the International Atomic Energy Act.

The move was apparently made over the objections of Clinton's National Security Adviser Sandy Berger, who cited repeated exports by China of "dual use" technologies to Iran, Pakistan and Iraq. The CIA also weighed in against the deal, pointing out in a report to the president, "China was the single most important supplier of equipment and technology for weapons of mass destruction" worldwide. In a press conference on the deal, Mike McCurry said these nuclear reactors will be "a lot better for the planet than a bunch of dirty coal-fired plants" and will be "a great opportunity for American vendors"—that is, Westinghouse.

A day later, Clinton signed an agreement to begin selling nuclear technology to Brazil and Argentina for the first time since 1978, when Jimmy Carter canceled a previous deal after repeated violations of safety guidelines and nonproliferation agreements.

In a letter to Congress, Clinton vouched for the South American countries, saying they had made "a definitive break with earlier ambivalent nuclear policies." Deputy National Security Adviser Jim Steinberg justified the nuclear pact with Brazil and Argentina as "a partnership in developing clean and reliable energy supplies for the future." Steinberg noted that both countries had opposed binding limits on greenhouse emissions and that new nuclear plants would be one way "to take advantage of the fact that today we have technologies available for energy use which were not available at the time that the United States and other developed countries were going through their periods of development."

The atom lobby during the 1990s had a stranglehold on the Clinton administration and now they seem to have the same suffocating grip around the neck of Barack Obama.

In 2006 Obama took up the cause of Illinois residents who were angry with Exelon, the nation's largest nuclear power plant operator, for not having disclosed a leak at one of their nuclear plants in the state. Obama responded by quickly introducing a bill that would require nuclear facilities to immediately notify state and federal agencies of all leaks, large or small.

At first it seemed Obama was intent on making a decent change in the reporting protocol, even demonizing Exelon's inaction in the press. But Obama could only go so far, as Exelon executives, including Chairman John W. Rowe, who serves as a key lobbyist for the nuclear energy lobby, have long been campaign backers, raising hundreds of thousands of dollars dating back to Obama's days in the Illinois State Legislature.

Despite his initial push to advance the legislation, Obama's office eventually rewrote the bill, producing a version that was palatable to Exelon and the rest of the nuclear industry. "Senator Obama's staff was sending us copies of the bill to review, we could see it weakening with each successive draft," said Joe Cosgrove, a park district director in Will County, Illinois, where the nuclear leaks had polluted local ground water. "The teeth were just taken out of it."

Inevitably, the bill died a slow death in the Senate. And like an experienced political operative, Obama came out of the battle as a martyr for both sides of the cause. His constituents back in Illinois thought he fought a good fight, while industry insiders knew the Obama machine was worth investing in.

Obama's campaign wallet during the 2008 election, while rich with millions from small online donations, was also bulging in contributions given by employees of Exelon, his firth largest bloc of campaign contributors. Two of Obama's largest campaign fundraisers include Frank M. Clark and John W. Rogers Jr., both top Exelon officials. Even Obama's chief strategist in 2008, David Axelrod, has done consulting work for the company.

During a Senate Committee on Environment and Public Works hearing in 2005, Obama, who served on the committee, asserted that since Congress was debating the negative impact of CO_2 emissions "on the global ecosystem, it is reasonable—and realistic—for nuclear power to remain on the table for consideration." Shortly thereafter, *Nuclear Notes*, the industry's leading trade publication, praised the senator. "Back during his campaign for the U.S. Senate in 2004, [Obama] said that he rejected both liberal and conservative labels in favor of 'common sense solutions'. And when it comes to nuclear energy, it seems like the Senator is keeping an open mind."

Obama's Department of Energy also committed a total of $8.33 billion in loan guarantees for the construction and operation of two new nuclear reactors at a plant in Georgia. It was the administration's first move to throw taxpayers' dollars at new nuclear power operations.

"When the new nuclear reactors come on line, they will provide reliable, base-load electricity capable of serving about 550,000 residences or 1.4 million people," the Energy Department said in a press release.

Carol Browner, director of the White House Office of Energy and Climate Change Policy said, "[reactors are] just the first of what we hope will be many new nuclear projects."

Sadly for the credibility of the atom lobby, some of their more eye-grabbing numbers don't check out. For example, as noted in a report by the Nuclear Energy Institute, the nuclear industry claims that the world's 447 nuclear plants reduce CO_2 emissions by 30 percent. But existing nuclear plants save only about 5 percent of total CO_2 emissions, hardly a bargain given the costs and risks associated with nuclear power.

As you go up the nuclear fuel chain, you have carbon dioxide emissions at every single step—from uranium mining, milling, enrichment, fuel fabrication, reactor construction to the transportation of the radioactive waste.

Moreover, the nuclear lobby likes to compare its record to polluting coal-fired plants, rather than renewables such as solar, wind and geothermal. Even when compared to coal, atomic power fails the test if investments are made to increase the efficient use of the existing energy supply instead. One recent study by the Rocky Mountain Institute found that "even under the most optimistic cost projections for future nuclear electricity, efficiency is found to be 2.5 to 10 times more cost effective for CO_2-abatement. Thus, to the extent that investments in nuclear power divert funds away from efficiency, the pursuit of a nuclear response to global warming would effectively exacerbate the problem."

Clearly, Obama recognizes the inherent dangers of nuclear technology and knows of the disastrous failures that plagued Chernobyl, Mayak and Three Mile Island. Yet, despite his attempts to alert the public of future toxic nuclear leaks, Obama still considers nuclear power a viable alternative to coal-fired plants. The atom lobby must certainly be pleased.

– March 10, 2010

BP'S INSIDE GAME

By Jeffrey St. Clair

By the morning of May 24, the tide had turned against President Barack Obama in the Gulf. Weeks of indecision at the White House and the Interior Department had shifted the balance of blame. BP was no longer seen as the lone culprit. Now, the Obama administration was viewed by many—including some senior members of their own party—as being fully culpable for the ongoing disaster off the coast of Louisiana. The political situation was so dire that Rahm Emmanuel called an emergency meeting in the Oval Office to regroup. Huddling with Obama and Rahm that bleak morning were Homeland Security Secretary Janet Napolitano, Interior Secretary Ken Salazar, Coast Guard Commandant Thad Allen, climate czar Carol Browner and, most cynical of all, economic advisor Lawrence Summers, author of an infamous 1991 memo at World Bank calling "the economic logic behind dumping a load of toxic waste in the lowest wage country [...] impeccable and we should face up to that."

The president was pissed. In a rare display of emotion, Obama ranted for 20 straight minutes. The target of his anger wasn't BP but the press. He fumed that he was being unfairly portrayed as being remote and indifferent to the mounting crisis in the Gulf. "Hell, this isn't our mess," Obama railed. The president expressed particular contempt for Louisianan James Carville, whose nightly barbs on CNN seemed to have found their mark. After two hours of debate, Obama's Gulf supposed dream team arrived at the dubious conclusion that the main problem was that there were simply too many public voices speaking for the administration. No one seemed to be in control. There were discordant accounts of the severity of the spill between the EPA and the Interior Department. Agencies were intruding on each other's terrain.

So, it was decided that the administration would speak with one voice, and that voice would be Thad Allen's, the portly Coast Guard Commandant who had been lauded in the press as a heroic figure in the aftermath of Katrina. It was the wrong lesson to draw after a month of false moves. The problem wasn't message control, but a profound bureaucratic lethargy that ceded almost absolute control over the response to the spill to BP. This fatal misstep came courtesy of yet more bad advice from Ken Salazar, who told Obama that under the terms of the Oil Pollution Control Act of 1990, passed in the wake of the wreck of the Exxon Valdez, BP was legally responsible for the cleanup of the Gulf.

Salazar's logic was perverse. He reasoned that, by giving free rein to BP under the cover of the Oil Pollution Control Act, the administration could keep its hands clean and blame any failures in the Gulf on the oil company. This strategy blew up in the face of the administration. It was all over once Rep. Ed Markey pressured BP into releasing the live video feeds from the remote-controlled submersibles, showing the brown geyser of crude erupting from the remains of the failed blowout preventer.

But then the administration was boxed into an untenable position. Instead of distancing itself from BP, the Obama team, thanks to Salazar, found itself shackled to the company. Two weeks after the blowout, a top Coast Guard official went so far as to praise "BP's professionalism" during a nationally televised press briefing.

It should have been different. Within hours of the explosion, the federal government should have seized control of both the well and the cleanup operations. The only responsibility that should have been left to BP was to sign checks for billions of dollars. The authority for such a takeover derives from an administrative rule called the National Contingency Plan, which calls for the federal government to take authority over hazardous waste releases and oil spills that pose "a substantial threat to the public health or welfare of the United States based on several factors, including the size and character of the discharge and its proximity to human populations and sensitive environments. In such cases, the On-Scene Coordinator is authorized to direct all federal, state, or private response and recovery actions. The OSC may enlist the support of other federal agencies or special teams."

The National Contingency Plan calls for the On-Site Coordinator "to direct all federal, state and private response activities at the site of discharge." The Plan, written in 1968, came in response to one of the world's first major oil spills and cleanup debacles. On March 18, 1967, the Liberian-flagged supertanker Torrey Canyon, taking a dangerous shortcut near Seven Stones reef, struck Pollard's Rock off the coast of Cornwall, gouging a deep hole into the holds of the ship. Over the course of the next few days, oil drained into the Atlantic. Then, on Easter the ship itself broke in two, releasing all 35 million gallons of crude oil, owned by, yes, British Petroleum into sea. The wreck plunged the government of Harold Wilson into crisis mode. The government allowed BP to pour millions of gallons of an unproven but toxic dispersant on dark-stained waters—the chemical had been manufactured by a subsidiary of the oil company. When that proved to have little effect, the Wilson government called upon the Royal Air Force to conduct a bombing raid on the Torrey Canyon. The planes dropped 42 bombs in effort to sink the ship and burn off the oil slick. The sea burned for two weeks, but the incendiary raids did little to staunch the oily tides. In the end, more than 120 miles of the Cornish Coast were coated in oil and the spill took a heavy toll on fish, birds and sea mammals. The crude spoiled beaches from Guernsey to Brittany.

In order to avoid a similar cleanup folly in the U.S., the National Contingency Plan called for a single agency to take swift control over big oil spills. That agency was the newly created EPA.

But when Rahm Emmanuel summoned the administration's oil response team to the strategy session in the Oval Office, he didn't send an invitation to Lisa Jackson, the spunky head of the Environmental Protection Agency. Why was Jackson missing? Because she had reportedly incurred the wrath of BP executives for pressing the company to curtail its controversial use of the toxic dispersant Corexit. Also noticeably absent from the Obama brain trust were two other officials who might have contributed a more realistic appraisal of the deteriorating situation in the Gulf: Jane Lubchenko, director of the National Oceanic and Atmospheric Administration NOAA, and Energy Secretary Stephen Chu, owner of the Nobel Prize, so often invoked by White House press secretary Robert Gibbs as a public assurance that the administration was on top of the situation. Each had been inexplicably exiled from Obama's inner circle.

It didn't help, of course, that in the early days of the disaster Obama's officials opted to downplay the severity of the oil gusher erupting out of the crumpled riser pipe 5,000 feet below the surface of the Gulf. In the first official remarks from the administration after the explosion of the Deepwater Horizon rig, Coast Guard rear admiral told the press that the spill was expected to be very minor, amounting to only the few thousands gallons of crude present in the mile-long pipe at the time of the accident. This false information flowed directly from BP. A few days later, after the incinerated rig had toppled and sank to the bottom of the Gulf, this specious number was revised upward to a total of no more than 1,000 gallons a day. So said Admiral Thad Allen, head of the Coast Guard and Incident Commander for the Gulf. Again, Allen had made this optimistic assessment based solely on information coming from BP. Two weeks later, the upper limit for the leak was raised to 5,000 barrels a day.

But NOAA knew better. In fact, in the hours after the spill, top NOAA officials gathered in Seattle for an emergency session that was streamed live on the agency's website. The video feed, which was later removed from the website, captured the agency's top scientists at work. Their initial survey of the scope of the spill proved prescient. One scientist warned that the agency needed "to be prepared for the spill of the decade." Another NOAA scientist charted out the worst-case scenario on a whiteboard: "Est. 64k–100k barrels a day." Right on the money, even though it took the Obama administration more than 50 days to admit that the oil was flowing at a rate of more than 14,000 barrels a day.

Of course, the administration could have simply subpoenaed BP's own records, as Congressman Ed Markey eventually did. On June 20, Markey released an internal memo from BP that estimated that as much as 100,000 barrels a day might be surging out of the broken wellhead. Far from fact-checking BP's information, some members of the Obama administration were acting as conduits for the company's lowballing. None played a more important role than Sylvia Baca, whose facility with moving seamlessly between the government and the corporations she was meant to regulate should had won her frequent flyer points for trips through the revolving door. Last summer, Ken Salazar appointed Baca to serve as assistant administrator for lands and minerals of the scandal-rife Minerals Management Service (MMS). This powerful but shadowy post did not require Senate confirmation. Thus, Baca's previous career did not become the subject of public inquiry.

Salazar had plucked Baca right from the ranks of BP's executive suites, where, according to her CV, she served "as general manager for Social Investment Programs and Strategic Partnerships at BP America Inc. in Houston, and had held several senior management positions with the company since 2001, focusing on environmental initiatives, overseeing cooperative projects with private and public organizations, developing health, safety, and emergency response programs and working on climate change, biodiversity and sustainability objectives." Prior to joining BP, Baca spent six years at the right hand of Bruce

Babbitt, serving as assistant secretary of the Interior for Lands and Minerals Management.

Baca's years in the Clinton administration proved very productive for the oil industry as a whole and her future employer in particular, a period when oil production on federal lands soared far above the levels of the first Bush administration. An internal Interior Department memo from April 2000 spelled out the achievement for Big Oil:

"We have supported efforts to increase oil and gas recovery in the deep waters of the Gulf of Mexico; we have conducted a number of extremely successful, environmentally sound offshore oil and gas lease sales; and we have opened a portion of the National Petroleum Reserve in Alaska to environmentally responsible oil and gas development, where an estimated 10 trillion cubic feet of recoverable gas resources lie in the northeast section of the reserve."

The memo goes on to highlight the feats in the Gulf of Mexico, which saw a tenfold increase in oil leasing during the Clinton years.

"From 1993 to 1999, 6,538 new leases were issued covering approximately 35 million acres of the Outer Continental Shelf.... Lease Sale 175 in the Central Gulf of Mexico, held on March 15, 2000, offered 4,203 blocks (22.29 million acres) for lease. The Interior Department received 469 bids on 344 blocks. There were 334 leases awarded....More than 40 million acres of federal OCS blocks are currently under lease. Approximately 94 per of the existing OCS leases (7,900) are in the Gulf, and about 1,500 of these leases are producing.... Issued over 28,000 leases and approved over 15,000 permits to drill...Implemented legislation changing the competitive lease term from five years to ten years, allowing lessees greater flexibility in exploration without endangering the lease."

Thus had the table been set for the depredations of the George W. Bush administration.

Mission accomplished, Baca settled into her high-paying gig as a BP executive. One of Baca's roles was to recruit Hollywood celebrities to help greenwash the oil giant as environmentally enlightened corporation, which was engaged in a mighty war against the evil forces of climate change. When Baca left BP to join the Obama administration, they weren't left in the lurch. As the curtains closed on the Bush administration, BP recruited one of the Interior Department's top guns to join its team. As the chief of staff for the MMS in the Gulf Region, James Grant had worked to make sure that deepwater leases moved forward with, as he put it in one memo, "few or no regulations or standards."

Having succeeded in this endeavor, BP enticed Grant to join their team as their "regulatory and environmental compliance manager" for the Gulf of Mexico, an assignment that included shepherding the Deepwater Horizon through the regulatory maze at MMS. Grant began lobbying his former colleagues in the Interior Department to open currently protected areas to oil leasing, particularly in the eastern Gulf of Mexico near the coast of Florida. Grant also warned the Obama administration, including his former corporate colleague Sylvia Baca, not to cave to demands by environmentalists for "policies that may establish exclusionary zones, disrupt MMS leasing or affect opportunities for economic growth." He needn't have worried.

***

It's clear that Sylvia Baca should never have been eligible to resume her job at the Interior Department. Obama had piously pledged to close the revolving door and bar corporate lobbyists from taking posts in agencies that regulated the activities of their former employers. Several environmental lobbyists were denied positions in the Interior Department and EPA under these supposedly ironclad ethics rules. However, Baca slipped through at the behest of Salazar who made a special appeal to Attorney General Eric Holder. Salazar told Holder that Baca was an "indispensable" member of his team, emphasizing her "detailed knowledge of Interior's land and energy responsibilities."

According to Deputy Interior Secretary David Hayes, Baca recused herself from all leasing decisions regarding BP. However, sources inside the Interior Department tell me that Baca played a key role in a procedural decision in the early days of the Obama administration that allowed the Deepwater Horizon project and Big Oil operations on federal lands to move forward with scant environmental review. The National Environmental Policy Act (NEPA) is a federal law passed during the glory days of environmental legislation, otherwise known as the Nixon administration. It requires a full-scale environmental impact statement (EIS) for any federal project that might pose a "significant impact on the quality of the human environment."

These EISs often run to more than a 1,000 pages in length and evaluate the possible ecological, social and economic consequences of the proposal, including worst-case scenarios. These documents are prepared by the permitting agency with consultation from the Fish and Wildlife Service and the EPA. But an administrative order during the second Bush administration ordered the Minerals Management Service to issue "categorical exclusions" from NEPA compliance to Big Oil projects in the Gulf and Alaska. In addition, the Bush administration allowed the oil companies to prepare their own safety and environmental plans, which would then be rubber-stamped by officials at MMS. From 2001 through 2008, more than 2,400 oil leases had been allowed to go forward in the Gulf without any serious environmental review.

When the Obama administration came into power, this policy was under furious legal and political assault by environmental groups. But Salazar was zealous that there would be no interruption in the pace of oil leasing in the Gulf. In fact, he wanted it speeded up. Restoring NEPA compliance to the oil industry, Salazar's enforcer, Baca warned, would slow down the approval process for leases by a year or more and, even worse, make the projects vulnerable to protracted litigation by environmentalists. She counseled that it would be better to stick with the Bush era rules. Salazar agreed.

So, it came to pass that on April 6, 2009, the Interior Department granted BP a categorical exemption for Lease 206, the Deepwater Horizon well. The BP exploration plan included a skimpy 13-page environmental review, which called the prospect of a major spill "unlikely." The company told the Interior Department that in the event of a spill "no mitigation measures other than those required by regulation and BP policy will be employed to avoid, diminish or eliminate potential impacts on environmental resources." The request was approved in a one-page letter that imposed no special restrictions on the oil company, warning only that BP "exercise caution while drilling due to indications of shallow gas."

Famous last words.

– November 26, 2010

A PALER SHADE OF GREEN: OBAMA AND THE ENVIRONMENT

By Jeffrey St. Clair and Joshua Frank

Although America's greatest Interior Secretary, Harold Ickes, who had the post for nearly a decade under FDR, was from Chicago, the playbook for presidential transitions calls for picking a Westerner for Interior, as long as the nominee isn't a Californian. Pick someone from Arizona or New Mexico or Colorado. Of course, Colorado has produced two of the worst recent Interior Secretaries: James Watt and Gale Norton. Ken Salazar may make it three.

And why not? After all, Salazar was one of the first to endorse Gale Norton's nomination as Bush's Interior Secretary. By almost any standard, it's hard to imagine a more uninspired or uninspiring choice for the job than professional middle-of-the-roader Ken Salazar, the conservative Democrat from Colorado. This pal of Alberto Gonzalez is a meek politician, who has never demonstrated the stomach for confronting the corporate bullies of the West: the mining, timber and oil companies who have been feasting on Interior Department handouts for the past eight years. Even as attorney general of Colorado, Salazar built a record of timidity when it came to going after renegade mining companies.

The editorial pages of Western papers largely hailed Salazar's nomination. The common theme portrayed Salazar as "an honest broker." But broker of what? Mining claims and oil leases, most likely.

Less defensible were the dial-o-matic press releases faxed out by the mainstream groups, greenwashing Salazar's dismal record. Here's Carl Pope, CEO of the Sierra Club, who fine-tuned this kind of rhetorical airbrushing during the many traumas of the Clinton years:

"The Sierra Club is very pleased with the nomination of Ken Salazar to head the Interior Department. As a Westerner and a rancher, he understands the value of our public lands, parks, and wildlife and has been a vocal critic of the Bush Administration's reckless efforts to sell-off our public lands to Big Oil and other special interests. Senator Salazar has been a leader in protecting places like the Roan Plateau and he has stood up against the Bush's administration's dangerous rush to develop oil shale in Colorado and across the West.

"Senator Salazar has also been a leading voice in calling for the development of the West's vast solar, wind, and geothermal resources. He will make sure that we create the good-paying green jobs that will fuel our economic recovery without harming the public lands he will be charged with protecting."

Who knew that strip-mining for coal, an industry Salazar resolutely promoted, was a green job? Hold on tight, here we go once more down the rabbit hole.

The Sierra Club had thrown its organizational heft behind Mike Thompson, the hook-and-rifle Democratic congressman from northern California. Obama stiffed them and got away with it without enduring even a whimper of disappointment.

In the exhaust-stream, not far beyond Pope, came an organization (you can't call them a group, since they don't really have any members) called the Campaign for American Wilderness, lavishly endowed by the centrist Pew Charitable Trusts, to fete Salazar. According to Mike Matz, the Campaign's executive director, Salazar "has been a strong proponent of protecting federal lands as wilderness...As a farmer, a rancher, and a conservationist, Sen. Salazar understands the importance of balancing traditional uses of our public lands with the need to protect them. His knowledge of land management issues in the West, coupled with his ability to work with diverse groups and coalitions to find common ground, will serve him well at the Department of the Interior."

Whenever seasoned greens see the word "common ground" invoked as a solution for thorny land use issues in the Interior West it sets off an early warning alarm. "Common ground" is another flex-phrase like, "win-win" solution that indicates greens will be handed a few low-calorie crumbs while business will proceed to gorge as usual.

In Salazar's case, these morsels have been a few measly wilderness areas inside non-contentious areas, such as Rocky Mountain National Park. Designating a wilderness inside a National Park is about as risky as placing the National Mall off-limits to oil drilling.

But Salazar's green gifts haven't come without a cost. In the calculus of common ground politics, trade-offs come with the territory. For example, Salazar, under intense pressure from Coloradoans, issued a tepid remonstrance against the Bush administration's maniacal plan to open up the Roan Plateau in western Colorado to oil drilling. But he voted to authorize oil drilling off the coast of Florida, voted against increased fuel-efficiency standards for cars and trucks and voted against the repeal of tax breaks for Exxon-Mobil when the company was shattering records for quarterly profits.

On the very day that Salazar's nomination was leaked to the press, the Inspector General for the Interior Department released a devastating report on the demolition of the Endangered Species Act under the Bush administration, largely at the hands of the disgraced Julie MacDonald, former Deputy Secretary of Interior for Fish and Wildlife. The IG report, written by Earl Devaney, detailed how MacDonald personally interfered with 13 different endangered species rulings, bullying agency scientists and rewriting biological opinions. "MacDonald injected herself personally and profoundly in a number of ESA decisions," Devaney wrote in a letter to Oregon Senator Ron Wyden. "We determined that MacDonald's management style was abrupt and abrasive, if not abusive, and that her conduct demoralized and frustrated her staff as well as her subordinate managers."

What MacDonald did covertly, Salazar attempted openly in the name of, yes, common ground. Take the case of the white-tailed prairie dog, one of the declining species that MacDonald went to nefarious lengths to keep from enjoying the protections of the Endangered Species Act. Prairie dogs are viewed as pests by ranchers and their populations have been remorselessly targeted for elimination on rangelands across the Interior West.

Ken Salazar, former rancher, once threatened to sue the Fish and Wildlife Service to keep the similarly imperiled black-tailed prairie dog off the endangered species list. As a US senator, Salazar also fiercely opposed efforts to inscribe stronger protections for endangered species in the 2008 Farm Bill.

"The Department of the Interior desperately needs a strong, forward looking, reform-minded Secretary," says Kieran Suckling, executive director of the Tucson-based Center for Biological Diversity. "Unfortunately, Ken Salazar is not that man. He endorsed George Bush's selection of Gale Norton as Secretary of Interior, the very woman who initiated and encouraged the scandals that have rocked the Department of the Interior. Virtually all of the misdeeds described in the Inspector General's expose occurred during the tenure of the person Ken Salazar advocated for the position he is now seeking."

As a leading indicator of just how bad Salazar may turn out to be, an environmentalist need only bushwhack through the few remaining daily papers to the stock market pages, where energy speculators, cheered at the Salazar pick, drove up the share price of coal companies, such as Peabody, Massey Energy and Arch Coal. The battered S&P Coal Index rose by three per cent on the day Obama introduced the coal-friendly Salazar as his choice to head Interior.

Say this much for Salazar: he's not a Clinton retread. In fact, he makes Clinton Interior Secretary Bruce Babbitt look like Ed Abbey.

As Hot Rod Blajogevich demonstrated in his earthy vernacular, politics is a pay-to-play sport. Like Ken Salazar, Barack Obama's political underwriters included oil-and-gas companies, utilities, financial houses, agribusiness giants, such as Archer Daniels Midlands, and coal companies. These bundled campaign contributions dwarfed the money given to Obama by environmentalists, many of whom backed Hillary in the Democratic Party primaries.

Environmentalists made no demands of Obama during the election and sat silently as he promoted off-shore oil drilling, pledged to build new nuclear plants and sang the virtues of the oxymoron known as clean-coal technology. Obama probably felt he owed them no favors. And he gave them none. The environmental establishment cheered never-the-less.

***

Of all of Barack Obama's airy platitudes about change, none were more vaporous than his platitudes about the environment and within that category Obama had little at all to say about matters concerning public lands and endangered species.

As Interior Secretary, Ken Salazar wasted no time in turning the department into a hive of his homeboys. This clique of lawyers and former colleagues earned the nickname the Colorado Mafia, Version Three. It's Version Three because Colorado Mafia Version One belonged to James Watt (a Colorado transplant) and his Loot-the-West zealots from the Mountain States Legal Fund. The Version Two update came in the form of Gale Norton and her own band of fanatics, some of whom remain embedded in the Department's HQ, just down the hall from Salazar's office.

Beyond a perverse obsession with Stetson hats, Salazar and Watt share some eerie resemblances. For starters, they look alike.

There's a certain fleshy smugness to their facial features. Who knows if Salazar shares Watt's apocalyptic eschatology (Why save nature, Watt once quipped, when the end of the world is nigh.), but both men are arrogant, my-way-or-the-highway types. Watt's insolent demeanor put him to the right even of his patron Ronald Reagan and ultimately proved his downfall. (Salazar may well meet the same fate.) Most troubling, however, is the fact that both Watt and Salazar hold similar views on the purpose of the public estate, treating the national forests and Bureau of Land Management lands not as ecosystems but as living warehouses for the manufacture of stuff: lumber, paper, wedding rings, meat, energy.

With this stark profile in mind, it probably came as no big shock that the man Salazar nominated to head the Fish and Wildlife Service, the agency charged with protecting native wildlife and enforcing the Endangered Species Act, viewed those responsibilities with indifference if not hostility. For the previous twelve years, Sam Hamilton ran the Southeast Region of the Fish and Wildlife Service, a swath of the country that has the dubious distinction of driving more species of wildlife to the brink of extinction than any other.

From Florida to Louisiana, the encroaching threats on native wildlife are manifest and relentless: chemical pollution, oil drilling, coastal development, clearcutting, wetland destruction and a political animus toward environmental laws (and environmentalists). And Sam Hamilton was not one to stand up against this grim state of affairs.

A detailed examination of Hamilton's tenure by Public Employees for Environmental Responsibility revealed his bleak record. During the period from 2004 through 2006, Hamilton's office performed 5,974 consultations on development projects (clearcuts, oil wells, golf courses, roads, housing developments and the like) in endangered species habitat. But Hamilton gave the green light to all of these projects, except one. By contrast, during the same period the Rocky Mountain Office of the Fish and Wildlife Service officially consulted on 586 planned projects and issued 100 objections or so-called jeopardy opinions. Hamilton has by far the weakest record of any of his colleagues on endangered species protection.

There's plenty of evidence to show that Hamilton routinely placed political considerations ahead of enforcing the wildlife protection laws. For example, in the agency's Vero Beach, Florida office Fish and Wildlife Service biologists wrote a joint letter in 2005 complaining that their supervisors had ordered them not to object to any project in endangered species habitat—no matter how ruinous.

Take the case of the highly endangered Florida panther. One of Hamilton's top lieutenants in Florida has been quoted as telling his subordinates that the big cat was a "zoo species" doomed to extinction and that to halt any developments projects in the panther's habitat would be a waste of time and political capital.

"Under Sam Hamilton, the Endangered Species Act has become a dead letter," says PEER's Executive Director Jeff Ruch, noting that the White House announcement on Hamilton touted his "innovative conservation" work. "Apparently, the word 'no' is not part of 'innovative' in Mr. Hamilton's lexicon. To end the cycle of Endangered Species Act lawsuits, the Fish and Wildlife Service needs a director who is willing to follow the law and actually implement the Act. Hamilton's record suggests that he will extend the policies of Bush era rather than bring needed change."

Obama and Salazar put the fate of the jaguar, grizzly and northern spotted owl in his compromised hands. Feel the chill?

Over at the Agriculture Department Obama made a similarly cynical pick when he chose former Iowa governor Tom Vilsak to head the agency that oversees the national forests. Vilsak resides to the right of Salazar and not just in the sitting arrangement at Cabinet meetings. He is a post-Harken Iowa Democrat, which means he's essentially a Republican who believes in evolution six days a week. (He leaves such Midwestern heresies at the door on Sundays.) Think Earl Butz—minus the racist sense of humor (as far as we know).

Vilsak is a creature of industrial agriculture, a brusque advocate for the corporate titans that have lain waste to the farm belt: Monsanto, Archer Daniels Midland and Cargill. As administrations come and go, these companies only tighten their stranglehold, poisoning the prairies, spreading their clones and frankencrops, sucking up the Oglalla aquifer, scalping topsoil and driving the small farmers under. It could have been different. Obama might have opted for change by selecting Wes Jackson of the Land Institute, food historian Michael Pollan or Roger Johnson, president of the National Farmers Union. Instead he tapped the old guard, a man with a test tube in one hand and Stihl chainsaw in the other.

Through a quirk of bureaucratic categorization, the Department of Agriculture is also in charge of the national forests. At 190 million acres, the national forests constitute the largest block of public lands and serve as the principal reservoir of biotic diversity and wilderness on the continent. They have also been under a near constant state of siege since the Reagan era: from clearcuts, mining operations, ORV morons, ski resorts and cattle and sheep grazing.

Since 1910, when public outrage erupted after President William Taft fired Gifford Pinchot for speaking out against the corrupt policies of Interior Secretary Richard Ballinger, the chief of the Forest Service had been treated as a civil service employee and, much like the director of the FBI and CIA, was considered immune from changes in presidential administrations. This all changed when Bill Clinton imperiously dismissed Dale Robertson as chief in 1994 and replaced him with Jack Ward Thomas, the former wildlife biologist who drafted Clinton's plan to resume logging in the ancient forests of the Pacific Northwest. Thomas' tenure at the agency proved disastrous for the environment. In eight years of Clinton time, the Forest Service cut six times as much timber as the agency did under the Reagan and Bush I administrations combined. The pace of logging set by Thomas continued unabated during the Bush the Younger's administration.

So Vilsak soon gave the boot to Gail Kimbell, Bush's compliant chief, and replaced her with a 32-year veteran of the agency named Tom Tidwell. Those were 32 of the darkest years in the Forest Service's long history, years darkened by a perpetual blizzard of sawdust. You will search Google in vain for any evidence that during the forest-banging years of the Bush administration, when Tidwell served as Regional Forester for the Northern Rockies, this man ever once stood up to Kimbell or her puppetmaster Mark Rey, who went from being the timber industry's top lobbyist to Bush's Undersecretary of Agriculture in charge of the national forests. No, Tidwell was no whistleblower. He was, in fact, a facilitator of forest destruction, eagerly implementing the Kimbell-Rey agenda to push clearcuts, mines, oil wells and roads into the heart of the big wild of Montana and Idaho.

Despite this dismal resumé, Tidwell's appointment received near unanimous plaudits, from timber companies, ORV user groups, mining firms and, yes, the Wilderness Society. Here's the assessment of Cliff Roady director the Montana Forest Products Association, a timber industry lobby outfit: "His appointment keeps things on a fairly steady course. He reported to Gail Kimbell, and they worked together really well. He's somebody we'd look forward to working with."

And here, singing harmony, were the tweets of Bob Eckey, a spokesman for the Wilderness Society, which some seasoned observers of environmental politics consider to be yet another timber industry lobby group: "Tidwell understands the American public's vision for a national forest has been changing."

During his tenure in Montana, Tidwell specialized in the art of coercive collaboration, a social manipulation technique that involves getting environmental groups to endorse destructive projects they would normally litigate to stop. Yet, when copiously lubricated with the magic words "collaboration" or "climate change" most environmentalists can be enticed to swallow even the most ghastly of clearcuts in the most ecologically sensitive sites, such as the Bitterroot Mountains in Montana to the fast-dwindling ponderosa pine forests of Oregon's Blue Mountains.

One of Tidwell's highest priorities is turn the national forests into industrial biomass farms, all in the name of green energy. Under this destructive scheme, forests, young and old alike, will be clearcut, not for lumber, but as fuel to be burned in biomass power generators. Already officials in the big timber states of Oregon and Washington are crowing that they will soon be able to become the "Saudi Arabia" of biomass production. Did they run this past Smokey the Bear?

Of course, Smokey, that global icon of wildfire suppression, and Tidwell found common ground on another ecological dubious project: thinning and post-fire salvage logging. We've reached the point where old-fashioned timber sales are a thing of the past. Now every logging operation comes with an ecological justification—specious though they all certainly turn out to be.

The Alliance for the Wild Rockies, one of the few green outfits to consistently stand up against Democratic Party-sponsored depredations on the environment, sued Tidwell at least 20 times during his time as regional forester in Missoula. There's no record of Tidwell being sued even once by Boise-Cascade, Plum Creek Timber or the Noranda Gold Mining Company.

Yet by and large, the mainstream environmental movement muzzled itself while the Obama administration stocked the Interior Department with corporate lawyers, extraction-minded bureaucrats and Clinton-era retreads. This strategy of a self-imposed gag order only served to enable Salazar and Vilsak to pursue even more rapacious schemes without any fear of accountability.

The pattern of political conditioning has been honed to perfection. Every few weeks the Obama administration drops the Beltway Greens a few meaningless crumbs—such as the reinstitution of the Clinton Roadless Area rule—which greedily gobble them up one after the other until, like Hansel and Gretel with groupthink, they find themselves hopelessly lost in a vast maze of Obama-sanctioned clearcuts. After that, they won't even get a crumb.

On the environment, the transition between Bush and Obama was disturbingly smooth when it should have been decisively abrupt.

– March 11, 2011

DEATH BY POLLUTION: HOW THE OBAMA ADMINISTRATION JUST PUT THOUSANDS OF LIVES AT RISK

By Joshua Frank

It must be election season. Like other prominent Democrats, Environmental Protection Agency Administrator Lisa Jackson has been making the rounds. Two weeks ago she popped up on Jon Stewart's "Daily Show" and explained that regulating toxins like mercury from coal burners across the country would prevent thousands of deaths and create jobs. She even rallied people to action.

"Environmentalism is not a spectator sport," Jackson told Stewart, as if she was encouraging viewers to turn off their televisions and get busy. "You actually have to stand up and demand that we be vigilant in protecting our air and water."

It was certainly a boisterous display of support for stronger environmental statues, something Jackson happens to know a little bit about. However, just one week after Jackson's Comedy Central performance the EPA indefinitely delayed essential health protections designed to reduce public exposure to airborne toxins such as mercury, arsenic, lead, and acid gases by thousands of tons per year.

It was back in 1990 when President H.W. Bush signed Clean Air Act Amendments into law, requiring the EPA to establish emission standards limiting toxins like mercury from the largest pollution sources. One of these laws, called Boiler MACT, covers emissions from boilers that produce power, like those from large to small coal plants. In February 2011, under court order, the EPA was forced to finally issue these rules. But the EPA moved to indefinitely delayed the law from going into effect.

"Two years ago the Obama administration took office vowing to protect public health and respect the law," said Earthjustice attorney James Pew shortly after the EPA's announcement. "Today's action disserves both of these principles. By the EPA's own calculations, the health protections it has elected to delay would save up to 6,500 lives each year."

In fact, according to the EPA itself, more than 4,000 non-fatal heart attacks, 1,600 cases of acute bronchitis and 313,000 missed work and school days would be avoided if the law was enacted—not to mention upwards of 6,600 premature deaths. All these benefits, despite the fact that the proposal had been dramatically watered down after industry pushed the EPA to weaken its original draft of the rule early last summer.

"It appears that EPA has addressed many of the industry complaints while still putting out standards that would bring significant public health benefits," Frank O'Donnell of Clean Air Watch told *Greenwire*. "Let's hope that EPA stands its ground when industries argue for further changes."

But the EPA didn't stand its ground. It soon backed off and has now delayed the rule indefinitely.

By all accounts the action to protect human health by regulating toxic emissions is long overdue. While there are several major air pollutants at play, mercury may be the most significant. One the largest producers of airborne mercury happens to be coal plants. This pollution ends up in water, poisoning fish and the humans that eat them. And the poisoning is rampant.

In August 2009, the U.S. Geological Survey released a study of mercury contamination in fish in 291 streams around the country. The study, which is the most comprehensive to date, was conducted from 1998 to 2005 and tested over 1,000 fish. Every fish tested, including those from isolated rural waterways, contained at least trace amounts of toxic mercury. According to the researchers, the majority of mercury in the streams tested came from coal plants.

This pollution has a direct impact on human health. According to the Centers for Disease Control and Prevention, 8 percent of American women of childbearing age have unsafe levels of mercury in their blood, putting approximately 322,000 newborns at risk of neurological deficits. Mercury exposure can also lead to increased cardiovascular risk in adults.

In response to the USGS study, Interior Secretary Ken Salazar said, "This science sends a clear message that our country must continue to confront pollution, restore our nation's waterways, and protect the public from potential health dangers."

Nonetheless, industry is no doubt pleased with the EPA's announcement to delay regulating emissions from power plants. Since 2006 the EPA has been under court order to complete its boiler emissions ruling. The agency extended deadlines a number of times. Finally, after years or procrastination, the final issuing was set for January 2011. House Republicans weren't pleased and a month before the law went into effect the EPA caved and sought to extend its deadline for another 15 long months. However, the U.S. District Court denied the EPA's request, stating it had had plenty of time to iron out any wrinkles in the proposed boiler rule.

Since the District Court decided not to back the EPA, Lisa Jackson's trusted agency went about creating a new so-called reconsideration process for these specific boiler emissions rules. This reconsideration, though, didn't buy the EPA a lot of time, only 90 days per the guidelines outlined by the Clean Air Act.

Through some pretty imaginative legal maneuvering, the EPA then managed to take the 90-day stay and extend it into an indefinite one. At that point, Lisa Jackson threw the Clean Air Act and all those people who would benefit from this particular boiler ruling under the proverbial bus. "[The] agency has elected to stay the effective date pursuant to the Administrative Procedure Act (APA), rather than to section 307(d)(7)(B) of the Clean Air Act," explains the Center for Progressive Reform. "Section 705 of the APA, the EPA explains, provides that 'an agency … may postpone the effective date of [an] action taken by it pending judicial review'—provided that the agency finds that 'justice' requires staying the effectiveness of the rule until judicial review has been completed. Thus, the EPA set about cobbling together a weak explanation of why 'justice' requires an indefinite stay of the Boiler MACT rule's effective date."

It is difficult to understand how delaying a ruling that will save thousands of lives could be halted over concerns of "justice." But then again, the delay is not about justice, it's about politics. With the 2012 elections fast approaching, the Obama administration and their go-to gal Lisa Jackson at the EPA are putting reelection aspirations ahead of public and environmental health.

By sidelining the ruling indefinitely, even with court challenges that are likely to come because of the EPA's blatant disregard for the Clean Air Act, any decision on the Boiler MACT rule will not happen until after election 2012. Obama clearly feared the polluters' retaliation far more than any backlash from eco-minded voters. As such, he and the EPA have pandered to the Tea Party and its mantra that regulation intrudes on the free market and the will of the people.

In the meantime, what are the people living near toxic coal plants supposed to do? According to CoalSwarm, 126 coal burning plants are located near residential areas, accounting for 17.5 percent of total U.S. coal power capacity. A total of 6.11 million people live within three miles of these plants and have an average per capita income of just over $18,500, which is 14 percent lower than the average American. Not surprisingly, 43.7 percebt of these folks are people of color.

With Lisa Jackson's and the EPA's delay on the boiler emissions ruling, the Democrats and President Obama have turned their backs on the most disenfranchised and vulnerable among us. This action is not only unforgivable, it is a death sentence for thousands of people who could be spared.

– June 3, 2011

HOW OBAMA DEFANGED THE EPA

By Joshua Frank

It was a tumultuous tenure, productive by some accounts, lackluster by most, but one thing is for certain, Lisa Jackson's short time as administrator at the Environmental Protection Agency was anything but dull. On December 27, 2012 the often-fiery Jackson announced she was not going to return for a second term, and it is surely not difficult to see why she's fleeing her post.

Since President Obama was ushered into office in 2008, the EPA has consistently faced ridicule and criticism from corporate polluters and their greedy allies in Washington, DC. On virtually every occasion Obama refused to side with Jackson's more rationale, often science-based positions, whether it was cleaning up the air or forcing the natural resource industries to abide by existing regulations.

Ultimately, the EPA is only as formidable as the White House allows it to be, and on Obama's watch the agency has not received the support it has desired or deserved.

Take the case of the Deepwater Horizon oil spill. Even though those three horrible months watching oil spew into the Gulf have seeped out of our collective memory, the BP disaster is one of the largest stains on Jackson's four-year stint at EPA. Soon after the underwater blowout, Jackson, a New Orleans native, demanded BP halt their use of the toxic dispersant Corexit 9500 to clean up their gushing mess. She took a tough line against a company that had gotten away with far too much for too long.

It could have been Obama's iron-fist moment, where the young president stood up to the oil industry and permitted the EPA to run the operation instead of letting BP's inept management have full control of the cleanup process.

Of course, after eight indulgent years of President Bush, BP executives weren't used to being bullied into submission by some bureaucrat, especially a surly woman at the EPA, so they dialed up their friendly White House staff and complained that Jackson had overstepped her boundaries. Obama quickly obliged and forced the EPA to bite its tongue. Then Obama's Chief of Staff Rahm Emmanuel discreetly assembled the administration's oil response team. Lisa Jackson was conspicuously absent from the list.

Even though it was the largest oil spill the US had experienced in decades, Obama prevented the agency in charge of overseeing the country's environmental regulations from being involved in any meaningful way. Could it have been that Obama surrendered to BP because he had two years earlier accepted more campaign cash from the company—a mix of cash from employees and political action committees—than any politician over the last twenty years? Not many in the environmental community were asking.

***

Following an EPA report on greenhouse gas emissions in 2009, Lisa Jackson appeared ready for a fight. In a written statement, Jackson declared carbon dioxide and five other greenhouse gases a threat to public health. No EPA administrator had ever made such bold comments.

"These long-overdue findings cement 2009's place in history as the year when the United States Government began addressing the challenge of greenhouse-gas pollution and seizing the opportunity of clean-energy reform," said Jackson.

It was her first major initiative at the EPA. This so-called "endangerment finding" was the necessary prerequisite that allowed the agency to enforce new fuel economy and greenhouse gas standards for motor vehicles and power plants. Jackson also moved to set stronger standards for mercury and toxic emissions and permitted California to implement its own set of greenhouse gas standards for vehicles, a reversal of a Bush-era policy.

This isn't to say that Jackson enjoyed Obama's support along the way. In fact, in some cases the administration outright opposed her efforts. In 2011 the White House moved to block the EPA from updating national clean air standards for smog. The episode echoed Bush tactics, where political expediency often trumped hard science. Sadly, Obama's team was successful at stopping Jackson and the courts have stalled the EPA's efforts to limit power plant pollution that blows across state lines.

"Disheartened would be a mild way to describe how clean air advocates felt when that happened," said Frank O'Donnell of DC-based Clean Air Watch. "Rather than rewarding Jackson for doing the right thing, the White House shoved her aside and literally adopted the polluter-friendly policy of … [President Bush] … and then proceeded to defend that flawed Bush policy in court."

The message from the White House to clean-air advocates was clear: "Because the Republicans are so rotten on environmental issues, you're stuck with whatever we do. If you don't like it, tough luck. We don't really care what you think. You have nowhere else to go."

"I don't recall any of the traditional clean-air champions in Congress raising hell over this. Party loyalty trumped substance," recalls O'Donnell, who has spent decades working for better clean air standards in Washington. "William Faulkner once wrote, 'Hollywood is a place where a man can get stabbed in the back while climbing a ladder.' Lisa Jackson's experience with ozone showed that an EPA administrator can get stabbed in the back by her boss just for doing her job."

Jackson faced a similar uphill battle when it came to the issue of coal ash. In 2009 the EPA began the process to regulate coal ash, a byproduct of coal incineration, which contains toxic metals like mercury, arsenic, beryllium, cadmium, chromium and nickel. The United States produces over 70 million tons of coal ash annually. After numerous incidents where ash from power plants has made its way into groundwater supplies, environmentalists and concerned citizens have called for such coal waste to be regulated.

"The time has come for common sense national protections to ensure the safe disposal of these materials," said Jackson when the EPA moved to first regulate coal ash, only to be halted by the White House. "Today, we are proposing measures to address the serious risk of groundwater contamination and threats to drinking water, as well as stronger safeguards against structural failures of coal ash impoundments."

In 2008 a coal slurry impoundment at the Tennessee Valley Authority's Kingston coal-fired power plant in Harriman, Tennessee, collapsed and more than 500 million gallons of toxic coal ash to enter the Tennessee River. Approximately 525 million gallons of black coal ash flowed into tributaries of the Tennessee River—the water supply for Chattanooga and millions of people living downstream in Alabama and Kentucky.

Obama wasn't pleased with Jackson's move to regulate filthy coal ash. In fact, he forced the EPA to delay its rules on multiple occasions. Despite lawsuits waged by environmental groups, on January 2013 the EPA announced it "cannot provide a 'definitive time' for promulgating final regulations on the management of coal ash from power plants."

No doubt it has been instances like these that prompted Lisa Jackson to leave the EPA and turn her back on Obama's White House—a conflict adverse administration that more often than not made it difficult for Jackson to do her job. While she was no environmental crusader, as she defended fracking practices as well as nuclear energy, Jaskson did believe in regulatory enforcement. Her replacement, expected to be Gina McCarthy, will likely find the Obama White House as equally challenging in upholding these laws.

– November 12, 2013

PESTICIDES, NEOLIBERALISM AND THE POLITICS OF ACCEPTABLE DEATH

By Jeffrey St. Clair

In 1900, cancer killed three people in America out of every hundred. Today, it's 33 out of every 100—more than one-in-four Americans die from cancer. These figures come from Dr. Joseph Weissman, a professor of medicine at UCLA. Weissman reckons that a fair slice of this explosion in cancer mortality can be laid at the door of petro-chemicals, particularly those used by the food industry.

On August 1, 1996, the same day Bill Clinton announced his decision to sign the welfare bill, Congress passed—with the White House's glowing approval—the Food Quality Protection Act. In the House, the vote was unanimous. In the Senate, only one voice was raised against its passage. In consequence, a few years down the road, Dr. Weissman or his co-researchers will have to recalibrate their numbers, for the worse. You wouldn't know it from the papers, from the radio, or from TV, but this Food Quality Protection Act signals a retreat as momentous as the one on welfare, and once again, children will be paying much of the price.

The purpose of this bill, which was cosponsored by Rep. Thomas Bliley and Rep. Tom DeLay, respectively a mortician from Virginia and pest exterminator from Texas, was to overturn the Delaney Clause, in force since the 1950s and the only absolute prohibition against carcinogens in processed foods. This clause has been the target of the food industry since it became law. It was finally done in by the usual coalition: business lobbyists, the White House, PR firms, big green organizations, and the elite media.

Immediately after the Congress passed the bill, Clinton took to the airwaves on his Saturday radio show to commend the Republican Congress for rejecting "extremism on both sides" and finding the "common ground." "I call this the Peace of Mind Act," Clinton went on, "because parents will know that the fruits, grains, and vegetables children eat are safe. Chemicals can go a long way in a small body."

But by throwing out the Delaney Clause, the federal government simply abandoned any effort to prevent cancer provoked by pesticides and instead goes into the cancer management business by way of "risk assessment." Corporate and governmental statisticians will broker the "acceptable" number of people permitted to contract cancer from pesticide residues, comforted in the knowledge that most of these people will be poor and black or Hispanic. To put it another way, the government regulators are now set to determine how many people may be sacrificed in order for the food and chemical industries to make more money with fewer liabilities.

Amid all the talk about returning decision-making to the states, the new law explicitly prohibits states from adopting tougher safety standards than those required by the federal government. With the Delaney Clause dead on the floor of Congress, some 80 pesticides that were about to be outlawed as carcinogens now remain in use. Call it the Dow-Monsanto bail-out bill, since these two companies make most of the chemical killers that were on the list to be banned.

The present calculation by the National Academy of Sciences is that between 30,000 and 60,000 people die each year from exposure to cancer-causing chemicals. Those at highest risk are children. The Academy's study found that for some children, "exposures to just five pesticides found on eight foods could be sufficiently high enough to produce symptoms of acute organophosphate pesticide poisoning." Another report cautions that by an average child's first birthday, the infant has been exposed to more than eight carcinogenic pesticides in amounts that exceed the previous standards set for a lifetime of exposure.

The post-Delaney standards for "acceptable risk" are set by the EPA, operating on recommendations of the food industry lobbyists, based on research from chemical industry scientists. "The new law brazenly codifies how many people the food industry can kill with pesticides," said Patty Clary, director of Californians for Alternatives to Toxics. "About as many a year as went down on Flight 800, per chemical." Clary adds that the Food Quality Protection Act doesn't even address the topic of synergy, the toxic multiplier effect that occurs when more than one pesticide is involved.

Scientific research has shown that a cocktail mix of pesticides such as dieldrin, chlordane, and endosulfan is 1,600 times more toxic than the discrete chemicals administered separately. Dieldrin and chlordane are banned chemicals that persist in the environment at dramatic levels. Endosulfan remains in wide use. All are known to be endocrine disrupters and are linked to breast and uterine cancers, birth defects, and infertility.

This chemical soup is what children will now go on eating everyday in products like raisins that are marketed directly at kids. "Chemicals go a long way in a small body," Clinton said. He could have been more specific. The new law now ensures that when children eat strawberries, they will also be ingesting the deadly chemical residue left by benamyl, captan, and methyl bromide. The average apple and peach has eight different pesticides embedded in it. Grapes have six and celery five. Children get as much as 35 percent of their likely lifetime dose of such toxins by the time they are five. Thus, something intrinsically bad is happening at the worst possible time, when DNA transcription is still going on.

With the new pesticide law giving agribusiness the green light—within the flexible parameters of risk assessment—there's now scant incentive to transfer to other methods of ensuring high productivity in fields and orchards. But pesticides become less effective the more they are used. American farmers sprayed 33 percent more pesticides per acre in 1990 than they did in 1945. Over the same 45-year period, crop losses from pests increased from 31 to 37 percent. The response has been ever-greater dosings with pesticides. Addiction to chemical-intensive agriculture has become so acute that bio-engineers at the Monsanto Corporation have concocted "Round-Up Ready" soybeans. It is a deadly circle of poisons.

The risks from chemical-intensive agriculture come not only in the food, but also in the application of the pesticides, mostly in the form of aerial spraying. The federal Office of Technology Assessment reckons that more than 40 percent of the pesticides dumped by planes drifts off the target area, ending up in streams, schoolyards, and neighborhoods. Fluorescent tracers have shown that it takes only a moderate breeze to carry poisons such as 2,4-D and paraquat 20 to 50 miles. One study found poisons such as toxaphene, furan, and dioxin in the mud on the bottom of Lake Siskiwit, on Isle Royale—a wilderness island in the middle of Lake Superior. The pesticides had been wind-carried there over more than 200 miles.

Workers are always the first to pay the price. In central Washington in 1995, 55 workers in an apple orchard became seriously ill after the wind shifted and they became exposed to the pesticide carbaryl. The EPA and the chemical industry claim that the regulations for the use of such pesticides will prevent any adverse health consequences. In their idyllic scheme, harvesting spraying takes place in perfect windless weather, with workers decked out in the latest protective gear and with detailed warning labels emblazoned on the poison brews. Real life in the fields means planes dumping clouds of pesticide in the wrong place at the wrong time, no protective clothing, poisons mixed with bare hands, workers uninformed about the dangers of the chemicals they are told to handle. The instructions for the use of pesticides are usually printed only in English, while most field workers are Spanish-speaking.

This Food Quality Protection Act is the consummation of a campaign by the food and chemical industries that has stretched over decades, ever since Rachel Carson's *Silent Spring* alerted the public to chemical poisoning back in the 1950s. The Delaney Clause found its defenders in the National Coalition for Alternatives to Pesticides, Food & Water, Environmental Research Foundation, Mothers and Others for a Livable Planet, Cancer Prevention Coalition, and dozens of grassroots groups across the country such as Californians for Alternatives to Toxics.

In the end, they were no match for the forces arrayed against them. As Clinton signd the fatal bill into law, with a youngster (one-in-four chances of croaking from cancer) at his elbow, Katie McGinty, head of the White House Council on Environmental Quality, hailed the act as the dawning of a new age of environmentalism. "I truly believe that the president will go down in history for having put in place a new generation of environmentalism, based on cooperation, not confrontation; defining and securing the common ground, defining the common interest, not the special interest." McGinty should know all about special interests. At an earlier stage of her career, before she began ministering to Al Gore, McGinty was a lobbyist for the American Chemical Association.

But why wasn't there a fight from the big green groups inside the Beltway over Delaney? Kurt Davies, of the DC-based Environmental Working Group, which backed the awful bill, says it was about political realism. "An idealist would interpret the loss of Delaney as a retreat from environmental protection," Davies said. "But realistically, Delaney was going and keeping it just wasn't a tenable battle. We just didn't have the voice. We weren't getting the thousands of letters needed to the Hill. Without that, it was just bending to the enemy."

Of course, the reason those letters weren't coming in to congressional offices was that the big green organizations had long since decided to give in on Delaney, trade it off in the interests of "realism." Organizations such as the unabashedly pro-corporate Environmental Defense Fund even attacked Delaney as an inefficient barrier to flexible environmental regulation. Groups like the Natural Resources Defense Council and National Wildlife Federation actually joined with lobbyists from Dow and Monsanto in testimony supporting the bill as a "sensible solution that goes a long way toward protecting the health of consumers."

Michael Colby, at the Vermont-based Food & Water group, pithily called this surrender "a classic case of activist malpractice. These organizations back legislation that gives corporations the right to pollute at the expense of the public health, while promoting the law as an improvement. Meanwhile, citizens are left to face the onslaught of more cancer risks, states are held hostage to weaker federal health standards, and the chemical companies and big environmental groups are laughing all the way to the bank."

– October 2, 2015

THE PORTER RANCH GAS LEAK: BLAME GOV. JERRY BROWN

By Joshua Frank

News came earlier this week that the horrific gas leak spewing methane at a natural gas storage facility in Porter Ranch, just outside Los Angeles, will be capped and contained by the end of February. Of course, it's a promise that has come far too late. If you think Donald Trump is a national disgrace, you haven't been paying much attention to what's been happening here in California. Not that you can be blamed for not knowing how bad the atmosphere-warming leak actually is, nobody that has the power to do anything about it seems to care all that much, certainly not California's governor-for-life Jerry Brown.

While the leak was first discovered in late October, it took Brown two full months to declare a state of emergency. This, after UC Davis scientist Stephen Conley in early November determined that 100,000 pounds of methane was leaking per hour at the site, or 1,200 tons per day. Of course, this inaction is par for the course for Brown, who has long ignored the perils of oil and gas production in the state, especially when it comes to fracking, which may have played a role in the Porter Ranch rupture. In the short term, scientists estimate the leaking methane is more than 80 times more potent than CO_2 when it comes warming of our atmosphere.

"To put this into perspective, the leak effectively doubles the emission rate for the entire Los Angeles Basin," attested Conley. "On a global scale, this is big."

For what it's worth, the Obama administration, longtime boosters of natural gas, hasn't been much help either. While activists have called on the White House to declare the Porter Ranch leak a natural disaster so residents can seek tax and mortgage relief, Obama has ignored their pleas. As of early January, 6,500 families had applied for relocation assistance—the stench of methane is simply too unbearable to live with. All of this could have been prevented of course, because the Aliso Canyon storage facility, which is owned by SoCalGas, a subsidiary of Sempra Energy, did not have a safety valve in place that would have helped to avert such a catastrophe.

SoCalGas also doesn't appear to be too concerned with the welfare of those living in and around Porter Ranch. They won't release air quality data and were seeking to expand the gas facility before they even dealt with their leak.

"At this rate, in just one month, the leak will have accounted for one-quarter of the total estimated methane emissions in the state of California. So it is no surprise that residents here feel sick," writes Erin Brockovich, who has called the Porter Ranch leak the BP oil spill on land. "While I can escape to my home to recover from my symptoms, this community wakes up to conditions that cause vomiting, nosebleeds and serious respiratory issues daily. And no one really knows the potential long-term side effects of benzene and radon, the carcinogens that are commonly found in natural gas. This dangerous environment is why the Los Angeles Unified School District unanimously voted last week to close two Porter Ranch schools and relocate their nearly 1,900 students and staff to protect their safety."

A sane approach to the situation would be to be to immediately put a halt to all oil and gas production in Aliso Canyon (an outright ban on all fracking in California wouldn't be a bad idea either). Currently there is legislation slogging its way through Sacramento to this effect, but it's likely to die a slow death in committee hearings before it ever makes it to Brown's desk. To top things off, the Southern California Air Quality District has repeatedly refused to close down the Aliso facility.

"The Air District doesn't need to stall any longer because it has all the information it needs to make the right decision right now: shut down the Aliso facility once and for all. We appreciate the Board hearing from the public, but this decision needs to be made fast," says Matt Pakucko of Save Porter Ranch, a group seeking to stop the methane leak. "[This is an] insult to all of us who have been displaced from our homes, and [to] our kids who have been forced out of their schools because the air is too toxic to breathe."

So why is Brown essentially sitting this one out, even though the Porter Ranch leak is by far the worst environmental disaster California has experienced in years? The answer may have a lot to do with his cozy ties to the oil and gas industry. Brown has pocketed over $2,014,570.22 from the oil and gas cartel since his 2006 race for California Attorney General. The industry has also poured lavish amounts of cash, nearly $1.2 million, into the coffers of Brown's favorite ballot initiatives, such as Prop 30, which passed a temporary tax in 2012 to fund state schools. It's pay-to-play politics, and the California's governor knows the game well.

Brown's sister, Kathleen Brown, also enjoys quite a few intimate connections to California gas producers. She sits on the board of Sempra Energy, the company that owns SoCalGas, and is richly compensated for her role—$267,865 in 2013 and $188,380 in 2014. Additionally, Kathleen Brown is a partner at Manatt Phelps, a law firm that often represents the fracking industry. Jerry and Kathleen are close. She was a delegate to Brown's 2014 trade and investment mission to Mexico and Governor Brown appointed her husband Van Gordon Sauter to the California State Athletic Commission.

Sure, Jerry Brown proclaims to be a warrior in the fight against climate change, but his resumé is stained with industry cash. The mammoth methane leak in Porter Ranch is just one example of Brown's bureaucratic negligence and there is certainly more where that came from. Want to stop another devastating disaster like the Porter Ranch methane leak? The first order of business is to clean house and get rid of Brown and the rest of his oil and gas cronies. Only then will state regulators and legislators begin to play hardball with California's powerful fossil fuel polluters. Until then, don't expect much accountability.

– January 22, 2016

THE MAN IN THE SOUNDPROOF BOOTH

By Jeffrey St. Clair

At last the war is over. Scott Pruitt was ushered out to unfurl the white flag and announce the surrender. In the latest humiliating defeat, the United States went to war against coal and lost, the first national offensive to be routed by an inanimate object.

Pruitt declared the unconditional surrender in his home state of Kentucky, one of the bloodiest battlegrounds, indeed a veritable bituminous Gettysburg, of the war. In Kentucky and neighboring West Virginia, the fighting had come to be known as the War of Green Aggression.

The plans for the ceasefire were apparently hatched in a soundproof booth inside Pruitt's bunker at the headquarters of the Environmental Protection Agency in Washington, DC, quietly constructed for $25,000 using the agency's black budget. Why the secrecy? To keep the dire news from leaking to the troops on the frontlines. After all, to paraphrase John Kerry, who would want to be the last EPA case officer to fall in a failed assault on coal?

From his soundproof booth, Pruitt made his secret entreaties with the emissaries of coal, negotiating the terms of surrender, the fine details of the armistice and the reparations that would be made to the enemy. There were talks of subsidies, gutted regulations, bailouts, government support of exports. The capitulation would be complete.

Trump campaigned for more than a year to end Obama's martial entanglements. The problem was where to find a general, who could find a way to lose with dignity? In Scott Pruitt, Trump discovered his Marshal Pétain. As attorney general of Oklahoma, Scott Pruitt had proved himself one of the most vocal peaceniks in the covert wars on fossil fuels.

A failed baseball player at the University Kentucky, Pruitt fled the Midwest for Oklahoma, where he consoled himself at the University of Tulsa Law School (ranked 82th in the nation) and later a small-time legal practice. But Pruitt soon bored of the law and launched a career in politics, landing a seat in the Oklahoma state senate in 2006. It was here in the oil patch where Scott Pruitt became a fossil fuels pacifist, his conversion facilitated by his close friendship with oil industry tycoon Harold Hamm, CEO of Continental Resources.

Pruitt was skillfully trained in anti-war organizing techniques at numerous retreats hosted by the American Legislative Exchange Council (ALEC), the rightwing "model bill" factory, that successfully pushed through energy deregulation bills in the late 1990s which many war historians now consider to be one of the hidden casus belliof the War on Coal, which would erupt in fury 15 years later.

ALEC, which functions as a kind of Highlander Center for training the Coal War resistance, tutored the eager young pacifist on such matters as the scientific flaws in climate change theory, drilling into Pruitt's mind the notion that the consequences of global warming, if indeed the planet is warming, might well prove to be "neutral or beneficial." And, more crucially, ALEC taught Pruitt that any attempts to regulate the emission of greenhouse gasses might create "great economic dislocation."

Pruitt used his ALEC training manuals to spot infiltrators and saboteurs, none more dangerous to the cause of peace than suburban homeowners who secretly affixed solar panels to their roofs and then nefariously tried to sell their energy back to the grid. These unassuming citizens, Pruitt learned, were really dangerous "freeriders" and "redistributionists" whose seemingly innocuous actions imperiled the future of Coal. They should be hunted down, punished and fined before the contagion spread.

By 2014, Scott Pruitt had been fully trained and was ready for action on the frontlines. Even though he ran unopposed for reelection as Attorney General, his campaign, co-chaired by Harold Hamm, raked in more than $300,000 from the anti-war movement across the country. And the money came not just from the embattled coal region, but also from its fossil fuel allies, the frackers and oil drillers, who feared they might fall next. Even non-aligned industries, such as nuclear power, often a rival to coal, pitched in for the struggle. Pruitt summed up his version of the Coal War Domino Theory this way: "I think that the progression from coal to natural gas is rather small. I think the attitude with the EPA is that fossil fuels are bad—period. And they're doing everything they can to use the rule-making process to attack both."

As the Ramsey Clark of the anti-Coal War Movement, Pruitt tried to peacefully end the hostilities against coal through a string of lawsuits. Pruitt sued to stop the cross-state pollution rule, rules limiting mercury emissions and air toxins, regulations on regional haze, and, of course, Obama's Clean Power Plan, known in Coal Country as the Final Solution. In little more than three years, Pruitt filed 13 lawsuits against the agency he now leads. Pruitt even sued the EPA over Oklahoma being battered by frivolous litigation filed by environmental groups. He lost them all. But, like a good anti-war activist, he wasn't chastened by defeat. "You know, this is coerced conservation, in effect," Pruitt said. "This is the administration saying 'we're going to penalize fossil fuels. We're going to emphasize renewables, cause energy costs to skyrocket.'"

Pruitt also proved himself a crafty organizer with a Yippie-like facility for anti-war pranksterism. During his term as Attorney General, Pruitt bombarded the EPA, Interior Department, and Office of Management and Budget with dozens of letters on state stationary decrying the barbarous War on Coal. But the recipients had no idea that the letters were actually written by executives and lobbyists from the besieged fossil fuel industry itself.

Pruitt, by this time a seasoned activist, brushed off the criticism of his plagiarized missives with the exuberant delinquency of Jerry Rubin. "Those kinds of questions arise from the environment we are in—a very dysfunctional, distrustful political environment," Pruitt courageously told the *New York Times*. "I can say to you that is not who we are or have ever been, and despite those criticisms we sit around and make decisions about what is right, and what represents adherence to the rule of law, and we seek to advance that and try to do the best we can to educate people about our viewpoint."

This is, of course, the kind of gallantry under fire which caught Trump's attention. Pruitt had the kind of guts that it would take to finally bring to an end the noxious war on coal.

The retreat began soon after Pruitt's confirmation. Pruitt immediately announced the fake science policies behind the war would be rescinded. War propaganda on the EPA website was struck down. Pruitt himself proclaimed that carbon dioxide had been wrongly implicated as an culprit of climate disruption, declaring that it is not "a primary contributor to the global warming that we see."

A man of his word, Pruitt swiftly pledged to slash the EPA's war budget by 24 percent and to furlough more than 24 percent of the agency's foot-soldiers. Pruitt then drafted an Executive Order for Trump to revoke Obama's authoritarian Clean Power Plan, which Trump duly signed on March 28, 2017. In another move to demilitarize the EPA, Pruitt informed the Justice Department that the agency would no longer pay the legal costs of any lawsuits aimed at inflicting undue hardship and pain on polluters at Superfund sites.

After huddling with other anti-war activists at the Trump hotel in Washington, Pruitt took decisive action to quash the hawks within his own agency. In late April, Pruitt terminated the tenures of members of the EPA's pro-war Board of Scientific

Counselors and pledged to replace the blood-thirsty scientists with dovish representatives from the oil and coal block.

By early summer, coal had advanced on all fronts, until it had Washington nearly encircled. At this point, Pruitt embarked on a desperate gambit of shuttle diplomacy to bring hostilities to a final close. These stealthy flights, many of them on military and private jets at US government expense, enabled Pruitt to receive a kind of checklist from the ambassadors of coal to assure a cessation of conflict across all fronts: pull out of the Paris Accords, block new fuel efficiency standards for cars and trucks, suspend rules mandating higher efficiency standards for household appliances, gut regulations capping methane emissions from oil and gas wells, etc. In all, Pruitt crushed 52 environmental rules that were savaging non-violent industries.

Rarely has Washington witnessed a vocal pacifist accumulate so much power so quickly and prevail in so many victories against an entrenched war machine. Of course, all high-profile peace activists sooner or later become targets themselves and Scott Pruitt was no exception. Sensing his vulnerability to enraged eco-terrorists and other pro-war fanatics, Pruitt reluctantly, but prudently, surrounded himself an 18-person security detail to guard him 24-hours a day. His bodyguards were culled from the elite Criminal Division of the EPA, where they had otherwise been wasting taxpayer dollars harassing corporations for bogus environmental crimes.

Scott Pruitt is one of the few anti-war activists to understand how the tax code itself provides the fuel that drives the war machine. So, even though an armistice was declared ending the War on Coal on October 10, 2017, Pruitt later warned that for the new peace treaty to prosper any lingering militaristic incentives must be eliminated. Pruitt specifically targeted for deletion dangerous provisions that provide tax breaks for wind, geothermal and solar power, so that the US doesn't risk falling prey to the same kind of guerrilla insurgency that swept South Australia, where 48% of the region's electrical power is now generated by rooftop solar panels.

The War on Coal is, of course, unlike most other wars. Now that it is over, the killing will begin. So, sit back and watch the body count rise.

– October 13, 2017

SECTION 4
WARSCAPES

THE WAR ON IRAQ IS ALSO A WAR ON THE ENVIRONMENT

By Jeffrey St. Clair and Joshua Frank

The ecological effects of war, like its horrific toll on human life, are exponential. When the Bush Administration and their Congressional allies sent our troops in to Iraq to topple Saddam's regime, they not only ordered these men and women to commit crimes against humanity, they also commanded them to perpetrate crimes against nature.

The first Gulf War had a horrific effect on the environment, as CNN reported in 1999, "Iraq was responsible for intentionally releasing some 11 million barrels of oil into the Arabian Gulf from January to May 1991, oiling more than 800 miles of Kuwaiti and Saudi Arabian coastline. The amount of oil released was categorized as 20 times larger than the Exxon Valdez spill in Alaska and twice as large as the previous world record oil spill. The cost of cleanup has been estimated at more than $700 million."

During the build up to George W. Bush's invasion of Iraq, Saddam loyalists promised to light oil fields afire, hoping to expose what they claimed were the U.S.'s underlying motives for attacking their country: oil. The U.S. architects of the Iraq war surely knew this was a potential reality once they entered Baghdad in March of 2003. Hostilities in Kuwait resulted in the discharge of an estimated 7 million barrels of oil, culminating in the world's largest oil spill in January of 1991. The United Nations later calculated that of Kuwait's 1,330 active oil wells, half had been set ablaze. The pungent fumes and smoke from those dark billowing flames spread for hundreds of miles and had horrible effects on human and environmental health. Saddam Hussein was rightly denounced as a ferocious villain for ordering his retreating troops to destroy Kuwaiti oil fields.

However, the United States military was also responsible for much of the environmental devastation of the first Gulf War. In the early 1990s the U.S. drowned at least 80 crude oil ships to the bottom of the Persian Gulf, partly to uphold the U.N.'s economic sanctions against Iraq. Vast crude oil slicks formed, killing an unknown quantity of aquatic life and sea birds while wrecking havoc on local fishing and tourist communities.

Months of bombing during the first Gulf War by U.S. and British planes and cruise missiles also left behind an even more deadly and insidious legacy: tons of shell casings, bullets and bomb fragments laced with depleted uranium. In all, the U.S. hit Iraqi targets with more than 970 radioactive bombs and missiles.

More than 15 years later, the health consequences from this radioactive bombing campaign are beginning to come into focus. And they are dire. Iraqi physicians call it "the white death"—leukemia. Since 1990, the incident rate of leukemia in Iraq has grown by more than 600 percent. The situation was compounded by Iraq's forced isolation and the sadistic sanctions regime, once described by former U.N. secretary general Kofi Annan as "a humanitarian crisis", that made detection and treatment of the cancers all the more difficult.

Most of the leukemia and cancer victims aren't soldiers. They are civilians. Depleted uranium is a rather benign sounding name for uranium-238, the trace elements left behind when the fissionable material is extracted from uranium-235 for use in nuclear reactors and weapons. For decades, this waste was a radioactive nuisance, piling up at plutonium processing plants across the country. By the late 1980s there was nearly a billion tons of the material.

Then weapons designers at the Pentagon came up with a use for the tailings. They could be molded into bullets and bombs. The material was free and there was plenty at hand. Also uranium is a heavy metal, denser than lead. This makes it perfect for use in armor-penetrating weapons, designed to destroy tanks, armored-personnel carriers and bunkers.

When the tank-busting bombs explode, the depleted uranium oxidizes into microscopic fragments that float through the air like carcinogenic dust, carried on the desert winds for decades. The lethal bits when inhaled stick to the fibers of the lungs, and eventually begin to wreck havoc on the body in the form of tumors, hemorrhages, ravaged immune systems and leukemias.

It didn't take long for medical teams in the region to detect cancer clusters near the bomb sites. The leukemia rate in Sarajevo, pummeled by American bombs in 1996, tripled in five years following the bombings. But it's not just the Serbs who are ill and dying. NATO and U.N. peacekeepers in the region are also coming down with cancer.

The Pentagon has shuffled through a variety of rationales and excuses. First, the Defense Department shrugged off concerns about Depleted Uranium as wild conspiracy theories by peace activists, environmentalists and Iraqi propagandists. When the U.S.'s NATO allies demanded that the U.S. disclose the chemical and metallic properties of its munitions, the Pentagon refused. Depleted uranium has a half-life of more than 4 billion years, approximately the age of the Earth. Thousand of acres of land in the Balkans, Kuwait and southern Iraq have been contaminated forever.

Speaking of DU and other war-related disasters, former chief U.N. weapons inspector Hans Blix, prior to the 2003 invasion of Iraq, said the environmental consequences of the Iraq war could in fact be more ominous than the issue of war and peace itself. Despite this stark admission, the U.S. made no public attempts to assess the environmental risks that the war would inflict.

Blix was right. On the second day of President Bush's invasion of Iraq it was reported by the *New York Times* and the BBC that Iraqi forces had set fire to several of the country's large oil wells. Five days later in the Rumaila oilfields, six dozen wellheads were set ablaze. The dense black smoke rose high in the southern sky of Iraq, fanning a clear signal that the U.S. invasion had again ignited an environmental tragedy. Shortly after the initial invasion the United Nations Environment Program's (UNEP) satellite data showed that a significant amount of toxic smoke had been emitted from burning oils wells. This smoldering oil was laced with poisonous chemicals such as mercury, sulfur and furans, which can causes serious damage to human as well as ecosystem health.

According to Friends of the Earth, the fallout from burning oil debris, like that of the first Gulf War, has created a toxic sea surface that has affected the health of birds and marine life. One area that has been greatly impacted is the Sea of Oman, which connects the Arabian Sea to the Persian Gulf byway of the Strait of Hormuz. This waterway is one of the most productive marine habitats in the world. In fact the Global Environment Fund contends that this region "plays a significant role in sustaining the life cycle of marine turtle populations in the whole North-Western Indo Pacific region." Of the world's seven marine turtles, five are found in the Sea of Oman and four of those five are listed as "endangered" with the other listed as "threatened."

The future indeed looks bleak for the ecosystems and biodiversity of Iraq, but the consequences of the U.S. military invasion will not only be confined to the war stricken country. The Gulf shores, according to BirdLife's Mike Evans, is "one of the top five sites in the world for wader birds, and a key refueling area for hundreds of thousands of migrating water birds." The U.N. Environment Program claims that 33 wetland areas in Iraq are of vital importance to the survival of various bird species. These wetlands, the U.N. claims, are also particularly vulnerable to pollution from munitions fallout as well as oil wells that have been sabotaged.

Mike Evans also maintains that the current Iraq war could destroy what's left of the Mesopotamian marshes on the lower

Tigris and Euphrates rivers. Following the war of 1991 Saddam removed dissenters of his regime who had built homes in the marshes by digging large canals along the two rivers so that they would have access to their waters. Thousands of people were displaced. The communities ruined.

The construction of dams upstream on the once roaring Tigris and Euphrates has dried up more than 90 percent of the marshes and has led to extinction of several animals. Water buffalo, foxes, waterfowl and boar have disappeared. "What remains of the fragile marshes, and the 20,000 people who still live off them, will lie right in the path of forces heading towards Baghdad from the south," wrote Fred Pearce in the *New Scientist* prior to Bush's invasion in 2003. The true effect this war has had on these wetlands and its inhabitants is still not known.

The destruction of Iraqi's infrastructure has had substantial public health implications as well. Bombed out industrial plants and factories have polluted ground water. The damage to sewage-treatment plants, with reports that raw sewage formed massive pools of muck in the streets of Baghdad immediately after Bush's 'Shock and Awe' campaign, is also likely poisoning rivers as well as human life. Cases of typhoid among Iraqi citizens have risen tenfold since 1991, largely due to polluted drinking water.

That number has almost certainly increased more in the past few years following the ousting of Saddam. In fact during the 1990s, while Iraq was under sanctions, U.N. officials in Baghdad agreed that the root cause of child mortality and other health problems was no longer simply lack of food and medicine but the lack of clean water (freely available in all parts of the country prior to the first Gulf War) and of electrical power, which had predictable consequences for hospitals and water-pumping systems. Of the 21.9 percent of contracts vetoed as of mid-1999 by the U.N.'s U.S.-dominated sanctions committee, a high proportion were integral to the efforts to repair the failing water and sewage systems.

The real cumulative impact of U.S. military action in Iraq, past and present, won't be known for years, perhaps decades, to come.

– October 29, 2007

HANFORD'S NUCLEAR OPTION

By Joshua Frank

Razor wire surrounds Hanford's makeshift borders while tattered signs warn of potential contamination and fines for those daring enough to trespass. This vast stretch of eastern Washington, covering more than 580 square miles of high desert plains, is rural Washington at its most serene. But it's inaccessible for good reason: It is, by all accounts, a nuclear wasteland.

During World War II, the Hanford Reservation was chosen by the federal government as a location to carry out the covert Manhattan Project. Later, plutonium produced at Hanford provided fuel for the "Fat Man" bomb that President Truman ordered to be dropped on Nagasaki in 1945, killing upward of 80,000 Japanese. In all, nine nuclear reactors were built at Hanford, the last of which ceased operation in 1987. The U.S. Environmental Protection Agency now estimates that as a result of the nuclear work done at Hanford's facilities, 43 million cubic yards of radioactive waste were produced and more than 130 million cubic yards of soil ultimately were contaminated.

During Hanford's lifespan, 475 billion gallons of radioactive wastewater were released into the ground. Radioactive isotopes have made their way up the food chain in the Hanford ecosystem at an alarming rate. Coyote excrement frequently lights up Geigers, as these scavengers feast on varmints that live beneath the earth's surface. Deer also have nuclear radiation accumulating in their bones as a result of consuming local shrubbery and water. The Washington Department of Ecology has deemed Hanford the most contaminated site in North America—a jarring fact, as the Columbia River, lifeline for more than 10,000 farmers and dozens of commercial fisheries in the Pacific Northwest, surges along Hanford's eastern boundary.

In 1989 Hanford changed from a nuclear-weapons outpost to a massive cleanup project. Since then, the site has become the largest and most costly environmental remediation the world has ever seen.

The U.S. Department of Energy (DOE), the agency that oversees energy and the safety of handling nuclear material, supervises the cleanup efforts, which are currently undertaken by Bechtel National Inc.—infamous for its mishandling of Iraq reconstruction efforts—and a handful of other companies like URS and CH2M HILL. But despite more than two decades of cleanup efforts and billions of dollars spent, only a tiny fraction of Hanford's radioactivity has been safely contained. And the final costs for the Hanford cleanup process could exceed $120 billion—higher even than the $100 billion tab for the International Space Station.

Now outrage is brewing at Hanford. Some prominent employees working on the project are blowing the whistle over what they believe to be dismissals of internal scientific assessments, as well as alleged abuses of managerial power that have been called to the attention of the Obama Administration, to no avail. These staffers point to institutional failures within the DOE and Bechtel as toxic as the nuclear waste they're tasked to clean up, asserting that the DOE lacks critical experts on staff to oversee the project and Bechtel rushed through shoddy design plans in order to pocket some quick cash. The consequences are not only jeopardizing safety and putting the project at risk of failure, they are also likely to cost taxpayers even more money should fatally flawed construction ultimately require a complete overhaul.

"We need alternatives to the current plan right now," Dr. Donald Alexander, a high-level DOE physical chemist working at Hanford, says in distress. "We need a different design and more options on the table. This appears to be a hard thing for [DOE and Bechtel] management to accept. They have spent years of time and money on a bad design, and it will delay the project even more."

***

It's the tail end of summer, and Alexander is about to head off on a weekend camping trip with his son in northern Idaho. While his spirits are high at the thought of his upcoming retreat, Alexander somberly assesses the Hanford situation from his vantage point.

"One of the main problems at Hanford is that DOE is understaffed and overtasked," Alexander explains. "As such, we cannot conduct in-depth reviews of each of the individual systems in the facilities. Therefore there is a high likelihood that several systems will be found to be inoperable or not perform to expectations."

Alexander knows his nuclear disasters well, as he led one of the DOE's first scientific delegations to Russia's Mayak nuclear facility in 1990. Mayak, one of the largest nuclear production plants in the former Soviet Union, suffered a deadly accident in 1957 when a tank containing nuclear materials exploded. The Mayak facilities are comparable to the plutonium production units built at Hanford, which is considered a "sister facility." Since they are so close in design and makeup, Mayak is often seen as an example of what can go wrong with the production of plutonium and the storage of nuclear waste at Hanford. Alexander's team negotiated the transfer of data collected by the Soviets on the health effects of Mayak's radioactive release, establishing a program that allows Russian and U.S. scientists to share nuclear cleanup technologies and research.

Currently, federal employees at DOE headquarters in Washington, D.C., are evaluating whether Bechtel's construction designs at the site have violated federal law under the Price-Anderson Amendments Act (PAAA). An amendment to the Atomic Energy Act of 1954, the PAAA governs liability issues for all non-military nuclear-facility construction in the United States, which includes Hanford.

These concerns are triggering other investigations, some of which have yet to be publicized. In September 2011, the DOE's Office of Health, Safety, and Security headed to Hanford to conduct a follow-up investigation about safety-culture issues. This visit comes on the heels of a June investigation by the Defense Nuclear Facilities Safety Board (DNFSB), an independent organization tasked by the executive branch to oversee public health and safety issues at the DOE's nuclear facilities. In a report addressed to Secretary of Energy Steven Chu, DNFSB investigators wrote that "both DOE and contractor project management behaviors reinforce a subculture ... that deters the timely reporting, acknowledgement, and ultimate resolution of technical safety concerns."

After reviewing 30,000 documents and interviewing 45 staffers, the DNFSB reported that those who went against the grain and raised concerns about safety issues associated with construction design "were discouraged, if not opposed or rejected without review." In fact, according to the DNFSB, one of these scientists, Dr. Walter Tamosaitis, was actually removed from his position as a result of speaking up about design problems.

It's not just the DNFSB that is concerned with the safety culture and management at Hanford. *Seattle Weekly* has obtained official documents revealing that the Government Accountability Office (GAO), the Congressional arm in charge of investigating matters relating to contractors and other public fund recipients, visited the Hanford site last month. In an outline sent to DOE personnel in advance of their visit, the GAO wrote that it will look into how contractors are addressing concerns over what they call "relatively lax attitudes toward safety procedures," "inadequacies in identifying and addressing safety problems," and a "weak safety culture, including employees' reluctance to report problems." Their findings likely will be made public in early 2012.

This wasn't the first time the GAO investigated DOE contracts with Bechtel. In 2004, the agency released a report critical of the DOE and Bechtel's clean-up plans, warning of faulty design and construction of the Tank Waste Treatment and Immobilization Plant (WTP), a structure at the heart of the clean-up effort. The WTP building was not designed to withstand a strong earthquake, but only after prodding from the DNFSB did the DOE force Bechtel to go back to the drawing board to ensure the plant could withstand one. As a result, Bechtel's design and cost estimates to finish construction skyrocketed from $4.3 billion to more than $10 billion. And in 2006, GAO released another paper critical of Bechtel's timeline and cost estimates, which seemed to change annually, saying that they have "continuing concerns about the current strategy for going forward on the project."

These flawed plans flew under the radar because the DOE does not have enough staff to thoroughly review every design piece put forth by Bechtel, says Alexander. As a result, expensive mistakes like these could occur again. The lack of key staff to oversee Bechtel's work continues to plague the WTP project to this day.

The concerns of the GAO, the DNFSB, and Alexander all point to a flawed relationship between the DOE and Bechtel, which is both the design and construction authority on WTP. Once operable, the plant will turn the millions of gallons of radioactive sediment currently in the site's waste tanks into glass rods by combining the toxic gunk with glass-forming material at a blistering 2,100 degrees Fahrenheit—a process called vitrification. The rods will then be shipped to an offsite location to be stored indefinitely.

Bechtel's contract is what is known in contractor parlance as "cost and schedule performance based." Such contracts, standard in the defense world, reward contractors like Bechtel for "meeting milestones" within their proposed budget—in some instances, even if plans and construction turn out to be critically flawed. Despite certain mistakes, including those made during the first three years of building the WTP with seismic deficiencies, Bechtel boasted in 2004 that they had received 100 percent of the available milestone fees available to the company through their Hanford contract with DOE.

The DOE is tasked with overseeing the project and signing off on their recommended procedures, but Alexander argues that the agency is incapable of proper oversight. "In the past 45 years, about 400,000 people ... have been irradiated [because of the Mayak disaster]," reflects Alexander. "It's quite possible that a similar accident could happen here. That's why it is so important that we get the Hanford cleanup facilities up and running properly, as soon as possible."

***

There is something ominous about Hanford, and it's not just the radioactivity.

The Wanapum Tribe, which survived here for centuries, feasting on the once-mighty Columbia River salmon runs, was evicted less than 70 years ago by the federal government so the feds could manufacture fuel for the A-bomb. It was certainly a marvelous scientific achievement when the first plutonium rolled out of Hanford's B Reactor, which is now just one of the many structures that haunt this dry landscape. But cleaning up Hanford's aftermath may prove even more of an accomplishment than it took to create the nuclear reservation in the first place.

Richland, population 48,000, is the city closest to Hanford. Local bars on the weekends overflow with Hanford contractors, and the cash they put down for shots and rounds of cold beer is abundant. The local watering hole, aptly named the Atomic Ale Brewpub, is decorated with Hanford artifacts and memorabilia, and serves beer like Plutonium Porter and Jim's Radioactive Rye. Richland High School's mascot is the Bombers. Despite its toxicity, locals have evidently embraced Richland's nuclear lore.

Richland's economy has long been sustained by the nuclear industry. Before the current cleanup of Hanford began to bring money into the community, the development of nuclear technologies ruled the town for decades. Just outside a more upscale neighborhood is a sprawling industrial park that serves as the district office for Hanford contractors and DOE employees. Without Hanford contracts employing thousands, Richland certainly would be struggling.

During the Cold War, while Hanford was operating at full capacity, Richland received the brunt of the site's radioactive pollution. As plutonium production reached its peak in the mid-1950s through the mid-1960s, plant operators at Hanford were told to ignore wind patterns, and released toxic debris into the air throughout the day. As a result, the cities of Richland, Pasco, Kennewick, and Benton City all exceeded acceptable levels of radioactive contamination.

During a more devastating period, such as the December 1949 "Green Run" when raw uranium fuel was being processed, a winter storm struck the region, causing heavy radioactive deposits to snow down on Richland and other rural farm communities. Samples of radioactivity taken during the Green Run incident were 1,000 times the government's recommended level, potentially impacting tens of thousands of people.

For years, the government kept documentation of potentially lethal amounts of radiation in the area classified. Not until 1986, after public demand mounted, did it release almost 20,000 pages of historical data showing how much nuclear pollution had plagued the entire region, affecting literally millions of people. As a result, a class-action suit was filed in 1991 by 2,400 individuals—"downwinders"—who claimed they had developed thyroid cancer after being exposed to radioactive iodine-131 emissions from Hanford. A jury deadlocked on the issue, which led to a 2005 mistrial. The plaintiffs appealed in 2006, and in 2008 the 9th Circuit Court of Appeals ruled that downwinders are now allowed to sue the contractors that operated Hanford at the time. In July, 139 of these downwinders settled for a meager $5,683 per victim.

Yet the majority of people affected by Hanford pollution have not received compensation of any kind.

***

Today there are a total of 177 underground storage waste tanks at Hanford, 149 of which are single-shelled and considered leak-prone by the EPA. All together, these holding containers house 53 million gallons of scorching-hot radioactive goop—nearly two-thirds of the country's high-level, defense-related radioactive waste.

Many of these tanks are already leaking, and have been for some time; according to the Washington Department of Ecology's estimate, one million gallons of nuclear waste have already poisoned groundwater as it continues to seep toward the Columbia River. However, it is not only leaks that haunt Hanford's scientists and engineers. The longer the waste stays put, the more dangerous it becomes.

"In the extreme," says Alexander, "this could lead to a serious condition that remains undiscovered until it is too late and another Mayak-scale incident occurs."

Alexander is openly concerned that such an event could release dangerous amounts of radioactive material into the atmosphere, contaminating nearby towns and destroying much of Washington's vital agricultural economy. And despite Hanford's already seething radioactivity, the DOE is eyeing the site as a potential waste repository for additional radioactive garbage produced from medical procedures, including cancer treatments, as well as waste associated with oil and gas exploration.

Bechtel has held the rights to build WTP since 2000. The plant, like Bechtel's Hanford contract, is gargantuan. The equivalent of constructing two full-scale nuclear power plants, WTP is to one day span 65 acres and include four major nuclear facilities: Pretreatment, Low-Activity Waste Vitrification, High-Level Waste Vitrification, and an Analytical Laboratory. It's currently the largest single construction operation taking place anywhere in the United States. Not only is the proposed WTP immense, it also comes with a staggering price tag of $12.2 billion, funded solely by the public trust, part of which comes out of the annual DOE budget.

Before Bechtel, the DOE's WTP contract was with British Nuclear Fuel Ltd. (BNFL). But in May 2000, after the company estimated they would spend more than $14 billion—despite an earlier cost estimate of $7 billion—the DOE ended the contract. Bechtel was then awarded the job through a competitive contract bid, receiving a $4.3 billion deal when it assured the DOE it could do the work for less than British Nuclear Fuel's price.

Since then, however, the company's cost estimates, start dates, and deadlines have changed on numerous occasions. Bechtel has also swapped project presidents on four separate occasions, most recently installing Frank Russo as director in January 2010.

Originally, WTP was to begin turning Hanford's radioactive materials into glass by 2011, with all vitrification to be completed by 2028. But in 2007 Bechtel pushed up their original cost estimates to $12.2 billion and their deadlines to start the vitrification process to 2019. Even if they meet this goal, the job will not be finished until 2047. The timeline and cost projections have constantly changed because of poor management decisions and a rush to fast-track completion, say critics, as was the case with the redesign of WTP based on its seismic preparedness.

"Bechtel, by all accounts and purposes, has done an absolutely miserable job," says Tom Carpenter, the professorial executive director of Hanford Challenge, a Seattle-based nonprofit watchdog group that keeps a close eye on all things Hanford. "They [the DOE] simply don't have enough [personnel] to deal with all the technical challenges, so Bechtel is getting away with whatever they want out there."

In fact, Bechtel has hundreds of engineers and scientists on the project, compared to less than a dozen for the DOE at Hanford.

"There are only a few [technical staff] in the Engineering Division," Alexander says. "And there are about seven of us in the Nuclear Safety Division where I work."

Furthermore, an internal DOE document published in August by the Construction Project Review (CPR) states that the current $12.2 billion estimate, which increased in 2007 after the DOE revised their WTP goals, is likely to climb yet again. "Funding uncertainty is the major project risk," the document notes. These increases, says Carpenter, are directly related to the DOE's inability to manage Bechtel.

Rick McNulty, who has worked at Hanford for 17 years and currently holds the position of Organizational Property Management Officer, adds that running out of money is but one of many risks.

On August 4, McNulty—also a lawyer and president of Local 788 of the American Federation of Government Employees, largely made up of Hanford scientists and engineers—requested a dual stop-work order to Bechtel and the DOE to force them to halt immediately the welding of tops on so-called "non-Newtonian vessels" at WTP. These five large containers hold "pulse jet mixers" designed to mix radioactive waste within the vessels when the plant becomes operable. Alexander explains that if these materials cannot stay consistently mixed, WTP will not be able to turn the radioactive waste into glass rods.

McNulty is concerned that Bechtel and DOE management are ignoring sound science, moving forward with a project that has failed small-scale testing on numerous occasions. These tests have shown that solids end up accumulating into small piles, causing the mixers to malfunction. The substances that build up during the mixing process, these studies note, are far more dense and cohesive than originally thought. Consequently, the mixers will likely fail. If these small-scale studies are correct, and the pulse jet mixers start mixing waste, this could cause a radioactive accident.

Perhaps even more frightening, as Alexander points out, is that these same tests show that erosion will likely occur in the so-called "black cells"—the areas around the vessels that house the pulse jet mixers. These areas will become off-limits to maintenance crews once the vessels begin to operate.

"[A] significant risk [is] that the vessel bottoms could be eroded through," says Alexander. "If the [pulse jet mixers] erode the vessel floor, then the [radioactive] contents of the vessel will drain into the black cell that they are entombed in. Because there is no access for men or equipment into black cells, there is no way of providing maintenance within them. The black cell itself would likely have to be abandoned."

Like Alexander, McNulty is worried that there will be no turning back once the vessels become operable because the radioactivity within them will be too high for workers to enter the black cells—meaning that all mechanisms' interiors, from the vessels to the piping, will have to last the lifetime of the machine. Any malfunction of any part would end the vessel operation altogether, creating a potentially deadly nuclear accident.

"We're talking about dealing with nuclear waste here, so we have to make sure everything is functioning properly," adds McNulty. "This whole thing will be shot if these well heads are sealed with a faulty design inside. We need this thing to work; it's not worth rushing."

McNulty's complaint and subsequent request to halt construction came as a result of the aforementioned small-scale studies conducted by Alexander. In an internal "differing opinion" report circulated among DOE management and contractor staff, which challenged Bechtel's notion that the pulse jet mixers would work, Alexander wrote in June 2011: "The Contractor Reports [which are submitted to DOE for review] are neither conservative nor do they provide a realistic portrayal of vessel physics and therefore there is no justification for continued design, procurement, and installation. Contractor Decision Papers are not technically sound and therefore do not Support a Decision to Weld Heads … The Design is not Licensable and management should STOP WORK."

***

Alexander's tests of the pulse jet mixer design plans showed that the model was faulty, yet his pleas to stop construction have gone unheeded by his DOE Project Director, Dale Knutson. In early August, the DOE announced that it was moving forward with welding the tops on the vessels, much to Alexander's dismay.

"We took Dr. Alexander's report into consideration and determined there was no imminent risk to safety if the heads were welded on [the non-Newtonian vessels]," says DOE spokesperson Carrie Meyer. "In the end we looked at the bottom line of the project, and it was a business decision to move forward."

In an internal e-mail obtained by *Seattle Weekly*, dated August 4, Alexander addressed his concerns directly to the DOE's Chief of Nuclear Safety, Richard Lagdon, writing: "Unfortunately the Decision to Weld the Non-Newtonian Vessels was made a day too soon. Based on the testing yesterday evening and the recent testing results it is clear that the Decision to Weld will require rework and place unacceptable liability upon the government … I was the only scientist present to observe these tests. I guess the project doesn't really care about the test results. Testing over the last two weeks demonstrates that we are now at the point where a very expensive contingency option will have to be exercised. This involves either the implementation of design and fabrication of a new vessel or significant modification of the existing vessel. Either option will be extremely costly … This could have been avoided if the DOE technical staff recommendations and those of the DNFSB (among numerous others) had been fairly considered."

On September 1, Knutson and Bechtel WTP Project Director Russo released a joint statement asserting they would sidestep further small-scale testing and instead conduct large-scale analysis in the future, once the units are sealed with the pulse jet mixers inside. "Testing is performed to validate the safety and quality of design and construction," Russo said. "We are confident, based on the results of our small-scale testing, that the mixing design of the vessels meets the safety design basis."

"It's a classic case of management overriding technical staff," says McNulty, who speaks from years of experience at Hanford. "The DOE is in a state of absolute denial about this whole thing. They need to rein [Russo] in. They can't allow him to continue to misrepresent all the internal studies that show [the pulse jet mixers] are simply not going to work."

Last fall, the pulse jet mixers were welded inside the non-Newtonian vessels, but the tops were not sealed shut. Despite opposition from Alexander and other scientists, this portion of the project was pushed forward by Bechtel and DOE management. "I raised issues within DOE, but Bechtel was convinced these pulse jet mixers would work," Alexander says. "The result was that Bechtel was able to get DOE management to sign off on welding the mixers within the vessels."

Once the weld heads encapsulate what studies show to be defective pulse jet mixers, years of research and development will be wasted and billions more will have to be spent to fix what could have been prevented, contends McNulty.

Russo would not submit to an interview with *Seattle Weekly*. Instead, Bechtel spokesperson Suzanne Heaston sent the following statement via e-mail: "Assuming the vessel mixing systems work as designed, welding the heads on now will save taxpayers significant cost and avoid delays in treatment of the waste in the tank farm ... If further testing associated with the mitigation actions determines that they will not perform adequately and operational controls are not adequate, design changes could be required. The timing of the welding of the heads on the vessels is a management decision to proceed … The potential costs of potential rework are less than the known costs of delay."

In other words, even though no small-scale tests have ever shown that the pulse jet mixers will work properly, Bechtel, with the DOE's blessing, will still move forward with welding the heads to the tops of the vessels.

Such illogic mystifies Tamosaitis, a systems engineer who has been employed for more than 40 years by Bechtel subcontractor URS. "So Bechtel charges ahead, welds the heads on [the non-Newtonian vessels], and then waits for the answers that will tell how the tanks need to be changed," he says in response to Bechtel's statement. "What then? Cut the heads off the tanks? Start over building new tanks? Wow. That sounds like a low-cost approach."

In an additional e-mail sent August 2, Alexander writes of how Bechtel management disregarded his early report that their design for the pulse jet mixers was flawed: "In the spring I raised a series of concerns with respect to the performance of the non-Newtonian vessels. Because I raised the issue, Frank Russo directed me to write my issues in a paper over the Easter weekend and deliver the paper on Monday April 5, 2010 … As a consequence the [Bechtel] manager labeled my issues as the 'non- Newtonian curve-ball.' Since when are DOE staff supposed to take direction from Contractor management? … Mr. Russo also directed Dr. Walter Tamosaitis to gather as many top flight PhDs as possible together to discredit my paper. I requested that my paper receive appropriate peer review but that request was denied. Walt had trouble even assembling a team. Walt knew that my issues were technically correct and he never submitted a counter paper."

Shortly after he refused to counter Alexander's internal paper warning about the problems with the pulse jet mixer design, Tamosaitis blew his own whistle, exposing what he saw as safety failures at WTP and citing concerns that the pulse jet mixer design issues would prohibit the plant from operating correctly. As a result, Tamosaitis says he was removed from the project; Bechtel and URS both deny that they removed Tamosaitis because he raised safety concerns.

"The drive to stay on schedule is putting the whole [WTP] project at risk," Tamosaitis contends. "'Not on my watch' is a standard mantra among [DOE and Contract] management who like to intimidate naysayers like me. These guys would rather deal with major issues down the road than fix them up front … Cost and schedule performance trump sound science time and again."

On March 31, 2010, Tamosaitis e-mailed Bechtel managers Michael K. Robinson and Russo about concerns about pulse jet mixer failures raised by the DOE's Alexander, to which Russo replied, "Please keep this under control. The science is over." In an internal e-mail string dated April 14, 2010, Robinson writes to Russo that he will "just have to keep [Tamosaitis] in line."

"As soon as Russo came on board, the chain of command was altered," Tamosaitis says. "Before Russo, I had to report directly to Bill Gay, a URS employee, but Russo removed Gay from the command chain and [made me communicate] directly to Mike Robinson [of Bechtel]. I think Russo believed it was easier to drive ahead with his cost and schedule push if he didn't have two URS managers directly under him."

***

In an e-mail dated March 31, 2010, Russo updated President Obama appointee Inés Triay on the situation. Triay, who did not return calls seeking comment, served as Assistant Secretary for

Environmental Management and oversaw the DOE's Hanford work until July, at which time she stepped down.

"It was like herding cats," Russo wrote Triay about a meeting he'd had with senior contract scientists and engineers regarding his quest to stay on schedule. "Scientists ... were in lock step harmony when we told them the science is ending. They all hated it ... I will send anyone on my team home if they demonstrate an unwillingness or inability to fulfill my direction."

"Walt is killing us," Russo later e-mailed Bill Gay of URS on July 1, 2010, who though removed from the chain of command still had to sign off on Tamosaitis' removal.

"Get him in your corporate office today."

"He will be gone tomorrow," Gay replied.

"This action [Tamosaitis' removal from the Hanford project] was initiated by Dale Knutson probably not knowing the sensitivity," Gay e-mailed to another employee in response to the decision to get rid of Tamosaitis.

Knutson would not respond to interview requests from *Seattle Weekly*. However, in a sworn statement sent to the Department of Labor, Knutson denied that he was in any way involved in the decision to demote Tamosaitis.

While no longer working on Hanford and WTP, Tamosaitis is still employed by URS, but is confined to a windowless basement office in Richland, where he says no management has spoken to him in over a year. His daily work routine isn't that of a normal URS scientist, and he is not even sure what official title he presently has. URS has recently shipped him around the country to work on various company projects as a sort of in-house consultant.

Tamosaitis is suing Bechtel in Washington state, as well as URS and the DOE at the federal level, over his ousting at Hanford. "It is my opinion that [Dale] Knutson and Frank Russo are in lockstep," he asserts. "Due to the constant managerial turnover [on the WTP project], these guys won't likely be there in a few years, so they'd rather have these problems happen on someone else's clock, even though it is always more expensive to fix something later then to do it right the first time."

Three sources working on the DOE's and Bechtel's Hanford vitrification project tell *Seattle Weekly* that "the WTP project is in total jeopardy" because of their employers' refusal to address technical and safety concerns raised by staffers like Tamosaitis and Alexander. These sources, who asked to remain anonymous for fear of retribution by their employers, believe congressional hearings in front of the House Energy and Commerce Committee about the issue are imminent. They also contend that the project could be temporarily shut down any day due to safety concerns.

If it comes to rebuilding these hundred-million-dollar vessels, the costs will skyrocket. As a result, Hanford Challenge's Carpenter and others note, the entire project could fall apart. That means taxpayers will again have to foot the bill for WTP's redesign and construction, postponing its operation indefinitely.

"Clearly, the management system or 'safety culture' is broken," writes Alexander in an August 2 e-mail to McNulty. "I have been under tremendous stress for more than a year. It seems to me that this is beyond a purely technical issue and is a whistleblower issue."

Research support for this story was provided by the Investigative Fund of the Nation Institute and was first published by Seattle Weekly.

– October 18, 2011

A SHORT HISTORY OF ZYKLON B ON THE US-MEXICAN BORDER (PLEASE DON'T SHARE WITH DONALD TRUMP)

By Jeffrey St. Clair and Alexander Cockburn

Zyklon B came to El Paso in the 1920s. In 1929, for example, a U.S. Public Health Service officer, J.R. Hurley, ordered $25 worth of the material—hydrocyanic acid in pellet form—as a fumigating agent for use at the El Paso delousing station, where Mexicans crossed the border from Juárez. Zyklon, developed by DEGESCH (the German Vermin-combating Corporation) was made in varying strengths, with Zyklon C, D and E representing gradations in potency and price.

As Raul Hilberg describes it in *The Destruction of the European Jews*,"strength E was required for the eradication of specially resistant vermin, such as cockroaches, or for gassings in wooden barracks. The 'normal' preparation, D, was used to exterminate lice, mice, or rats in large, well-built structures containing furniture. Human organisms in gas chambers were killed with Zyklon B." In 1929, DEGESCH divided the world market with an American corporation, Cyanamid, so Hurley presumably got his Zyklon B from the latter.

As David Dorado Romo describes it in his marvelous *Ringside Seat to a Revolution: An underground history of El Paso and Juárez: 1893–1923* (available from Cinco Puntos Press, El Paso), Zyklon B had become available in the U.S.A. in the early 1920s when fears of alien infection had been inflamed by the alarums of the eugenicists, most of them from the "progressive" end of the political spectrum. In 1917, the U.S. Congress passed and Woodrow Wilson—an ardent eugenicist—signed the Immigration Law.

The United States Public Health Service simultaneously published its *Manual for the Physical Inspection of Aliens*.

The Manual had its list of excludables from the U.S. of A., a ripe representation for the obsessions of the eugenicists: "imbeciles, idiots, feeble-minded person, persons of constitutional psychopathic inferiority (homosexuals), vagrants, physical defectives, chronic alcoholics, polygamists, anarchists, persons afflicted with loathsome or dangerous contagious diseases, prostitutes, contracts laborers, all aliens over 16 who cannot read." In that same year U.S. Public Health Service Agents "bathed and deloused" 127,123 Mexicans at the Santa Fe International Bridge between Juárez and El Paso.

The mayor of El Paso at the time, Tom Lea Sr., represented, in Romo's words, "the new type of Anglo politician in the 'Progressive Era'. Progressive didn't necessarily mean liberal back then. In Lea's case, 'progress' meant he would clean up the city." As part of his cleansing operations, Lea made his city the first in the U.S. to ban hemp, aka marijuana, as an alien Mexican substance. He had a visceral fear of contamination and, so his son later disclosed, wore silk underwear because his friend, Dr. Kluttz, had told him typhus lice didn't stick to silk. His loins thus protected, Lea battered the U.S. government with demands for a full quarantine camp on the border where all immigrants could be held for up to 14 days. Local health officer B.J. Lloyd thought this outlandish, telling the U.S. surgeon general that Typhus fever "is not now, and probably never will be, a serious menace to our civilian population."

Lloyd was right about this. Lea forced health inspectors to descend on Chihuahuita, the Mexican quarter of El Paso, forcing inhabitants suspected of harboring lice to take kerosene and vinegar baths, have their heads shaved and clothes incinerated. Inspection of 5,000 rooms did not stigmatize Chihuahuita as a plague zone. The inspectors found two cases of typhus, one of rheumatism, one of TB, and one of chicken pox. Ironically,

Kluttz, presumably wearing silk underwear, contracted typhus while supervising these operations and died.

But Lloyd did recommend delousing plants, saying he was willing to "bathe and disinfect all the dirty, lousy people coming into this country from Mexico." The plant was ready for business right when the Immigration Act became law. Soon Mexicans were having their bodies checked, daubed with kerosene where deemed necessary and their clothes fumigated with gasoline, kerosene, sodium cyanide, cyanogens, sulfuric acid and Zyklon B. The *El Paso Herald* wrote respectfully in 1920, "hydrocyanic acid gas, the most poisonous known, more deadly even than that used on the battlefields of Europe, is employed in the fumigation process."

The delousing operations provoked fury and resistance among Mexicans still boiling with indignation after a lethal 1916 gasoline blaze in the El Paso City jail. As part of Mayor Lea's citywide disinfection campaign, prisoners in the jail were ordered to strip naked. Their clothes were dumped in one bath filled with a mixture of gasoline, creosote and formaldehyde. Then they were forced to step into a second bath filled with "a bucket of gasoline, a bucket of coal oil and a bucket of vinegar." At around 3:30 p.m., March 5, 1916, someone struck a match. The jail went up like a torch. The *El Paso Herald* reported that about 50 "naked prisoners from whose bodies the fumes of gasoline were arising", many of them locked in their cells, caught fire. 27 prisoners died. In late January 1917, 200 Mexican women rebelled at the border and prompted a major riot, putting to flight both police and troops on both sides of the border.

The use of Zyklon B became habitual. Health officers would spray the immigrants' clothes. Now, Zyklon B, in gaseous form, is fatal when absorbed through the skin in concentrations of over 50 parts ppm. How many Mexicans suffered agonies or died, when they put on those garments? As Romo told the El Paso-based journalist Paul Spike, writing for the online UK daily *The First Post*:

> This is a huge black hole in history. Unfortunately, I only have oral histories and other anecdotal evidence about the harmful effects of the noxious chemicals used to disinfect and delouse the Mexican border crossers–including deaths, birth defects, cancer, etc. It may well go into the tens of thousands. It's incredible that absolutely no one, after all these years, has ever attempted to document this.

The use of Zyklon B on the U.S.-Mexican border was a matter of keen interest to the firm of DEGESCH. In 1938, Dr. Gerhard Peters called for its use in German Desinfektionskammern. Romo has tracked down an article Peters wrote in a German pest science journal, *Anzeiger für Schädlingskunde*, which featured two photographs of El Paso delousing chambers. Peters went on to become the managing director of DEGESCH, which handled the supply of Zyklon B for the Nazi death camps. He was tried and convicted at Nuremberg. Hilberg reports that he got five years, then won a retrial that netted him six years. He was re-tried in 1955 and found not guilty.

In the U.S.A., the eugenicists rolled on to their great triumph, the Immigration Restriction Act of 1924, which doomed millions in Europe to their final rendezvous with Zyklon B twenty years later. By the 1930s, the eugenicists were mostly discredited, though many—particularly in the environmental movement—remain true to those racists obsessions to this day. The Restriction Act, that monument to bad science married to unscrupulous politicians and zealous public policy for the sake of unborn generations, stayed on the books unchanged for 40 years.

In 1918, disease did indeed strike across the border, as Romo points out. Romo quotes a letter from Dr. John Tappan, who had disinfected thousands Mexicans at the border. "10,000 cases in El Paso and the Mexicans died like sheep. Whole families were exterminated. This was "Spanish" flu, which originated in Haskell County, Kansas.

– *March 18, 2016*

AFGHANISTAN: BOMBING THE LAND OF THE SNOW LEOPARD

By Joshua Frank

> "If we greens don't broaden our thinking to tackle war, we may save some wilderness, but lose the world."
> — David Brower

News alert! Despite what you may have heard, the war in Afghanistan is still raging. Nearly 10,000 US troops remain, and since 2014 the Obama administration has carried out almost 2,000 airstrikes on whatever they damn well please in the country. No question the mounting Afghan death toll and the bombing of hospitals and civilian infrastructure ought to infuriate the few remaining antiwar activists out there; but the toll the Afghanistan war is having on the environment should also force nature lovers into the streets in protest.

Natural habitat in Afghanistan has endured decades of struggle, and the War on Terror has only escalated the destruction. The lands most afflicted by warfare are home to critters that most Westerners only have a chance to observe behind cages in our city zoos: gazelles, cheetahs, hyenas, Turanian tigers and snow leopards among others.

Afghanistan's National Environmental Protection Agency (NEPA), which was formed in 2005 to address environmental issues, has listed a total of 33 species on its Endangered list.

In 2003, the United Nations Environment Program (UNEP) released its evaluation of Afghanistan's environmental issues. Titled "Post-Conflict Environmental Assessment," the UNEP report claimed that war and long-standing drought "have caused serious and widespread land and resource degradation, including lowered water tables, desiccation of wetlands, deforestation and widespread loss of vegetative cover, erosion, and loss of wildlife populations."

Ammunition dumps, cluster bombs, B-52 bombers and land mines, which President Obama refuses to ban, serve as the greatest threat to the country's rugged natural landscape and the biodiversity it cradles.

The increasing number of Afghanis that are being displaced because of military conflict, UNEP's report warned, has compounded all of these problems. It was a sobering estimation. However, it was an analysis that should not come as much of a surprise: warfare kills not only humans, but life in general.

As bombs fall, civilians are not the only ones put at risk, and the lasting environmental impacts of the war may not be known for years, perhaps decades, to come.

For example, birds are killed and sent off their migratory course. Literally tens of thousands of birds leave Siberia and Central Asia to find their winter homes to the south. Many of these winged creatures have traditionally flown through Afghanistan to the southeastern wetlands of Kazakhstan, but their numbers have drastically declined in recent years.

Endangered Siberian cranes and two protected species of pelicans are the most at risk, say Pakistani ornithologists who study the area. The war's true impact on these species is not yet known, but President Obama's continued bombing campaign is not a hopeful sign.

Back in 2001, Dr. Oumed Haneed, who monitors bird migration in Pakistan, told the British Broadcasting Corporation (BBC) that the country had typically witnessed thousands of ducks and other wildfowl migrating through Afghanistan to Pakistan.

Yet, once the US began its air raids, few birds were to be found.

"One impact may be directly the killing of birds through bombing, poisoning of the wetlands or the sites which these birds are using," said Haneed, who works for Pakistan's National Council for Conservation of Wildlife. "Another impact may be these birds are derouted, because their migration is very precise. They migrate in a corridor and if they are disturbed through bombing, they might change their route."

Intense fighting throughout Afghanistan, especially in the White Mountains, where the US hunted bin Laden in the Battle of Tora Bora, has been hit the hardest. While the difficult-to-access ranges may serve as safe havens for alleged al-Qaeda operatives, the Tora Bora caves and steep topography also provide refuge for bears, Marco Polo sheep, gazelles and mountain leopards.

Every missile that is fired into these vulnerable mountains could potentially kill any of these treasured animals, all of which are on the verge of becoming extinct.

"The same terrain that allows fighters to strike and disappear back into the hills has also, historically, enabled wildlife to survive," Peter Zahler of the Wildlife Conservation Society (WCS) told *New Scientist* at the onset of the Afghanistan invasion.

But Zahler, who helped to open a field office for WCS in Kabul in 2006, also warned that not only are these animals at risk from bombing, they are also at risk of being killed by refugees. For instance, a snow leopard, whose endangered population in the country is said to be fewer than 100, can score $2,000 on the black market for snow leopard fur. That money in turn can help these displaced Afghanis pay for safe passage into Pakistan.

Bombings, however, while having an initial direct impact, are really only the beginning of the dilemma. As Zahler told me, "The story in Afghanistan is not the actual fighting—it's the side effects—habitat destruction, uncontrolled poaching, that sort of thing."

Afghanistan has faced nearly 30 years of unfettered resource exploitation, even prior to the most recent war. This has led to a collapse of government systems and has displaced millions of people, all of which has led to the degradation of the country's habitat on a vast scale.

Forests have been ravaged to provide short-term energy and building supplies for refugees. Many of the country's arid grasslands have also been overgrazed and wildlife killed.

"Eventually the land will be unfit for even the most basic form of agriculture," explained Hammad Naqi of the World Wide Fund for Nature in Pakistan. "Refugees—around four million at the last count [in 2001]—are also cutting into forests for firewood."

In early 2001, during the initial attacks, the BBC reported that the United States had been carpet bombing Afghanistan in numerous locations.

John Stufflebeem, deputy director of operations for the US Joint Chiefs of Staff, told reporters at the time that B-52 aircraft were carpet bombing targets "all over the country, including Taliban forces in the north.

"We do use [carpet bombing strategies]," said Stufflebeem. "We have used it and will use it when we need to."

Additionally, Pakistani military experts and others have made allegations that the United States has used depleted uranium (DU) shells to target specific targets inside Afghanistan, most notably against the Taliban frontlines in the northern region of the country.

Using DU explosives is not far-fetched for the United States. The US-led NATO air force used DU shells when it struck Yugoslavia in 1999. Once these deadly bombs strike, they rip through their target and then erupt into a toxic cloud of fire. Many medical studies have shown that DU's radioactive vapors are linked to leukemia, blood cancer, lung cancer and birth defects.

"As US and NATO forces continue pounding Afghanistan with cruise missiles and smart bombs, people acquainted with the aftermaths of two recent previous wars fought by the US fear, following the Gulf and Balkan war syndromes, the Afghan War Syndrome," wrote Dr. Ali Ahmed Rind in the *Baltimore Chronicle* in 2001. "This condition is marked by a state of vague ailments and carcinomas, and is linked with the usage of Depleted Uranium (DU) as part of missiles, projectiles and bombs in the battlefield."

Afghanistan's massive refugee crisis, lack of governmental stability, and extreme poverty, coupled with polluted water supplies, drought, land mines and excessive bombings, all contribute to the country's intense environmental predicament.

Experts unanimously agree, there simply is no such thing as environmentally friendly warfare.

– May 6, 2016

FUKUSHIMA MON AMOUR: THE HUCKSTERS OF THE GREEN ATOM

By Jeffrey St. Clair

Is the crisis in Fukushima over or just beginning? You might be forgiven for scratching your head at that one. Nearly five years after the nuclear meltdown triggered by the Tohoku earthquake and subsequent tsunami, one of the planet's worst radioactive catastrophes has almost completely faded from both the media and public consciousness. Amid that information void, the lethal history of those events has been swamped under pernicious myths being spread by nuclear hucksters.

In brief, the revised story of the Fukushima meltdown goes something like this: the Daiichi facility was struck by an unprecedented event, unlikely to be repeated; the failsafe systems worked; the meltdown was swiftly halted; the spread of radioactive contamination contained and remediated; no lives or illnesses resulted from the crisis. Full-speed ahead!

One of the first to squirm headlong down this rabbit hole of denial was Paddy Reagan, a professor of Nuclear Physics at the University of Surrey: "We had a doomsday earthquake in a country with 55 nuclear power stations and they all shut down perfectly, although three have had problems since. This was a huge earthquake, and as a test of the resilience and robustness of nuclear plants it seems they have withstood the effects very well."

For Reagan and other atomic zealots, the Fukushima meltdown did not represent a cautionary tale, but served as a real time exemplar of the safety, efficiency and durability of nuclear power. Call it Fukushima Mon Amour, or How They Stopped Worrying and Learned to Love the Atom.

Such extreme revisionism is to be expected from the likes of Reagan, and other hired guns for the Big Atom, especially at a moment of grave peril for their economic fortunes. More surreal is the killer compact between the nuclear industry and some high-profile environmentalists, which reached a feverish pitch at the Paris Climate conference this fall. Freelance nuclear shills, such as the odious James Hansen and the clownish George Monbiot, have left carbon footprints that would humble Godzilla by jetting across the world promoting nuclear energy as a kind of technological deus ex machina for the apocalyptic threat of climate change. Hansen has gone so far as to charge that "opposition to nuclear power threatens the future of humanity." Shamefully, many greens now promote nuclear power as a kind ecological lesser-evilism.

Of course, there's nothing new about this kind of rationalization for the doomsday machines. The survival of nuclear power has always depended on the willing suspension of disbelief. In the terrifying post-Hiroshima age, most people intuitively detected the symbiotic linkage between nuclear weapons and nuclear power and those fears had to be doused. As a consequence, the nuclear industrial complex concocted the fairy tale of the peaceful atom, zealously promoted by one of the most devious conmen of our time: Edward "H-Bomb" Teller.

After ratting out Robert Oppenheimer as a peacenik and security risk, Teller set up shop in his lair at the Lawrence Livermore Labs and rapidly began designing uses for nuclear power and bombs as industrial engines to propel the post-World War II economy. One of the first mad schemes to come off of Teller's drafting board was Operation Chariot, a plan to excavate a deep water harbor at Cape Thornton, near the Inuit village of Point Hope, Alaska, by using controlled (sic) detonations of hydrogen bombs.

In 1958, Teller, the real life model for Terry Southern's character Dr. Strangelove, devised a plan for atomic fracking. Working with the Richfield Oil Company, Teller plotted to detonate 100 atomic bombs in northern Alberta to extract oil from the

Athabasca tar sands. The plan, which went by the name Project Oilsands, was only quashed when intelligence agencies got word that Soviet spies had infiltrated the Canadian oil industry.

Frustrated by the Canadians' failure of nerve, Teller soon turned his attentions to the American West. First he tried to sell the water-hungry Californians on a scheme to explode more than 20 nuclear bombs to carve a trench in the western Sacramento Valley to canal more water to San Francisco, the original blueprint for Jerry Brown's Peripheral Canal. This was followed by a plot to blast off 22 peaceful nukes to blow a hole in the Bristol Mountains of southern California for the construction of Interstate 40. Fortunately, neither plan came to fruition.

Teller once again turned to the oil industry, with a scheme to liberate natural gas buried under the Colorado Plateau by setting off 30 kiloton nuclear bombs 6,000 feet below the surface of the earth. Teller vowed that these mantle-cracking explosions, marketed as Project Gasbuggy, would "stimulate" the flow of natural gas. The gas was indeed stimulated, but it also turned out to be highly radioactive.

More crucially, in 1957 at speech before the American Chemical Society Teller, who later helped the Israelis develop their nuclear weapons program, became the first scientist to posit that the burning of fossil fuels would inevitably yield a climate-altering greenhouse effect, which would feature mega-storms, prolonged droughts and melting ice-caps. His solution? Replace the energy created by coal and gas-fired plants with a global network of nuclear power plants.

Edward Teller's deranged ideas of yesteryear have now been dusted off and remarketed by the Nuclear Greens, including James Lovelock, the originator of the Gaia Hypothesis, with no credit given to their heinous progenitor.

There are currently 460 or so operating nukes, some chugging along far past their expiration dates, coughing up 10 percent of global energy demands. Teller's green disciples want to see nuclear power's total share swell to 50 percent, which would mean the construction of roughly 2100 new atomic water-boilers from Mogadishu to Kathmandu. What are the odds of all of those cranking up without a hitch?

Meanwhile, back at Fukushima, unnoticed by the global press corps, the first blood cancers (Myelogenous leukemia) linked to radiation exposure are being detected in children and cleanup workers. And off the coast of Oregon and California every Bluefin tuna caught in the last year has tested positive for radioactive Cesium 137 from the Fukushima meltdown. The era of eco-radiation has arrived. Don't worry. It only has a half-life of 30.7 years.

– February 22, 2017

THE ATOMIC RIVER

By Jeffrey St. Clair

The river is a strong brown god. So declared T. S. Eliot, anyway. Some rivers, perhaps. The Mississippi, the Ohio, the Platte, certainly the Colorado. But not this river. Not Nch'I'Wana. Not the Columbia. Here in the shadow of the Rattlesnake Hills, the river is a clear as a subatomic particle, as cool as the icy hand of death, as fast as coyote sprinting at full stretch.

They call the Reach the last free-flowing run for the Columbia in the United States. The river flows. But it's not entirely free. For 51 miles, from Priest Rapids Dam to the backwaters of McNary Reservoir at Richland, Washington, the waters of the Columbia flow unimpeded by a dam. The flow is regulated by the hydro-engineers upstream at Priest Rapids Dam. The releases of water fluctuate wildly. At peak demand, as the water is rushing through the turbines, the spills can raise the river level of Columbia by as much as 16 feet in a few hours. Still the river has a pulse, a taste of what it once was.

River trips don't need a pretext. But we've got one anyway. Josh is tying the knot—and I'm not talking about a bowline or a clove hitch. He's getting married in a couple of weeks—or some contractual variation of that state of domestic union. This is a bachelor's party of sorts, a final taste of freedom. It's not much of a party. There are only two of us, squeezed into my sockeye-salmon orange inflatable touring kayak. Just the two of us and the whorls and boils of the liberated river. Just us and the river and the monitoring stations, watch towers, patrol boats, warning sirens and razor wire.

Despite its status as a national monument, conferred by Bill Clinton exactly 10 years ago as a morsel to politically-famished greens, the Hanford Reach remains largely a closed and forbidden landscape. Ominous signs warn that entry to the Hanford Nuclear Reservation, the world's most toxic site, on river right will result in arrest and prosecution. Most of the Saddle Mountain Wildlife Refuge on river left is closed. There's no overnight camping allowed anywhere along the Reach. Even the islands are off limits. Only on the river are you really free.

The plan is to kayak as much of the Reach as we can, a forty-mile stretch from below Priest Rapids Dam, once home of Smohallah, the apocalyptic Dreamer of the Wanapum tribe, down to Ringold, site of a strange fish hatchery cordoned off by concertina wire. What dark plot are they protecting the salmon fry from? The Cold War is long gone, but the paranoia persists.

The float will take two days, requiring us to take-out at the old White Bluffs ferry, return to Richland for the night, and then put back in there the next day. That's roughly 200 miles of driving each day to circumvent the sprawling nuclear wasteland of Hanford. But if access to the Reach were easy, the river would be crowded with shitheads on powerboats and jet-skis.

This Saturday morning we have the launch above Vernita Bridge to ourselves. By 9 am, the air is already heating up. The gold slopes of Saddle Mountain to the east blaze in the sun. The sky is cloudless and crystalline. To the Northwest, we can make out the glacier-draped bulge of Mount Rainier, nearly 150 miles away.

The ground at the launch is littered with the corpses of squawfish, large, needle-toothed fish that prey voraciously on steelhead and salmon smolts. The fish are native to the river, but in recent years a bounty has been placed on their heads. Like the sea lions of the lower Columbia, the squawfish, also known as Columbia River pikeminnow, has become a scapegoat for salmon decline. Blame anything but the dams.

We unfold the kayak, inflate its six chambers with a hand pump, clip-in two seats, tuck away our river bags, water and cameras. Despite recent warnings from the Environmental

Working Group about its toxicity, we slather our cavefish-white Oregon flesh in sunscreen. It will do little good. By noon, we will both be sautéed. Our skin will redden and peel. It is a salutary, healing kind of pain, a ritual cleansing—quite unlike the other kind of heat generated by the dark towers on the far side of the river. "Come away, into the Sun" counseled D.H. Lawrence. "It's the Sun you want. You want life."

The rigging of our low-riding craft takes less than five minutes. One last check of essentials.

"Paddles?"

"Check."

"Sunscreen?"

"Check."

"Car keys?"

"Check."

"Obligatory volume of Abbey?"

"Check."

"IED?"

"Check."

"Biodegradable condoms?"

"What?"

"This is a bachelor's party weekend, isn't it?"

We sprinkle some sagebrush into the blue torrent of Nch'I Wana to appease the river gods, push off the gravel-strewn shore and immediately the newly liberated Columbia grabs the bow of the kayak, spins us to the south and hurls us downstream toward the pilings of Vernita Bridge, our portal into the Reach.

The river constricts, flexing its power as the current rips under the bridge. Suckholes swirl on both sides of us. One of them pulls at the bow of the kayak, tilting us toward the whirlpool. I slap the water with a low brace of my paddle and then it playfully releases us and we shoot into the iridescent, writhing surge of the main channel. A few moments later we turn and look back. The bridge is already far behind us.

"Let's have a toast!"

"Absolutely," says Josh. He's from Montana. It's never too early for him.

"Where's the tequila?"

"In the river bag."

Josh fumbles around in the small hold in the bow. Comes up empty-handed.

"Where's the river bag?"

"Uhm, back in Richland?"

"Can we make it down this river sober?"

As if in answer, our kayak is jolted and spins, despite our frantic stroking. We've been gripped by an eddyline, the violent interface between powerful counter-currents, where the river turns back on itself.

Water flows around us, but we are still. Dead calm. Like the movie, but without anyone even remotely resembling Nicole Kidman. The kayak is perpendicular to the current. Not the best position, according to the operations manual. Not by a long shot. There's a movement in the reeds on river right, the nuclear side. It's coyote. He looks our way, ears erect. He sizes us up for a moment as he takes a crap. Then he lopes away toward a low ridge to the west, crowned by two black smokestacks. The twin fangs marking the B and C reactors, the dark towers of Dr. Fermi and Dr. Teller, where the rough nuclear beast came of age.

Reactor B is now a National Historic Landmark inside a National Monument. That's probably not the architectural legacy Enrico Fermi had in mind when he designed the plutonium machine back at his mass atomic death lab at the University of Chicago in 1943. Fermi's schematics to construct a plant to produce fuel for a plutonium bomb by a process of nuclear fission were handed over to the DuPont Corporation, whose engineers had the reactor up and running by September 1944, when Reactor B conducted its first successful nuclear chain-reaction. Ten months later plutonium-239 generated at Hanford would be used for the first nuclear bomb test at the Trinity Site in New Mexico. Three weeks later Hanford fuel would be packed in the "implosion design plutonium device" called Fat Man and detonated over Nagasaki, killing 73,884 people, injuring another 74,000 and exposing another 250,000 to radioactive fallout. That atrocity ended the Pacific War, but Hanford was just gearing up.

Reactor B is not a big building. It only covers about 1,700 square feet, about the size of a suburban house. Last fall, Josh toured the facility with Chelsea. By all accounts, it was such hot date that they soon decided to join together what remains of their half-lives in matrimony. The reactor core is essentially a graphite box about 36 feet tall and 28 feet wide. The core is encased by a 10-inch thick shield of cast iron. Such a tiny little place to generate so much fear, so much death.

The core craves water to keep it cooled down. Lots of water. That's the prime reason the nuclear engineers picked Hanford. It was a remote site with easy access to an almost limitless supply of water. So pumphouses were built to suck up 75,000 gallons of Columbia River water every minute and shoot it through aluminum tubes and around the uranium slugs. The highly contaminated water was then discharged into settling ponds and then flushed back into the river down large sluices. And that's where the trouble started for the river and the fish and the people who ate them.

Coyote pauses on the ridgeline, pisses on a stubby sage and chortles. Always the tricks, the twisted little jokes, with you buddy. Well, here's one on you, coyote. For years, ecologists scouring the Hanford steppe with Geiger counters to chart how the radioactivity at the site is marching its way up the food chain have gotten the loudest pings when sweeping across coyote turds. The Geiger counters almost spasm with excitement. The ecologists have taken to calling the hot coyote scat "hummers."

Here's an object lesson in the upward accumulation of bad isotopes. The deer that graze Hanford's high desert plants are radioactive, too. But their shit doesn't ping like coyote's. That's because deer are vegans. They consume radioactivity from toxic water, willow leaves and forbs. It accumulates in their blood, organs and tissue. But it doesn't bio-magnify. It doesn't increase in toxicity. That only comes with the consumption of radioactive flesh.

There's only one other species at Hanford who's shit sets off coyote-like alarm bells: the deer-hunters of the Hanford Reach. Out here, the Great Chain of Being has gone radioactive.

Through no machination of our own, the river kicks us out of the eddy and sends us twirling downstream, toward the notch in Saddle Mountain, the lovely "alpine view" used to lure workers to the Hanford outback. Boy were they in for a surprise. The austere Saddle Mountain is the tallest range in Washington without trees.

***

The Columbia is the great river of paradoxes. Stroke by stroke, we are paddling deeper and deeper into a conundrum. But the contradictions are mostly ours, not the river's. Let's start with this one. Hanford's corridor of reactors, nine in all, were located here because of the free-flowing river. The river in the Reach remains undammed because of those nukes. The river on both sides of the Reach is dammed up largely to provide power for the Hanford nukes. They call them the Cold War dams: Priest Rapids, McNary, John Day and The Dalles. Each were sold to the public on the promise of cheap power, but much of that energy was secretly re-directed up to Hanford for the production of plutonium for H-bombs. The great salmon-fishing grounds of Celilo were lost largely to satiate Hanford's unquenchable thirst for electric power.

Of course, that didn't stop the Army Corps of Engineers from wanting to inundate the Reach behind a mega-dam to be constructed near Pasco. The plans were first drawn up in 1932, then shelved until the early 1970s, when an unlikely coalition of environmentalists, steelhead fishermen and the Atomic Energy Commission, who were then in charge of Hanford, beat it down.

But dams don't perish so easily and the Pasco project, called the Ben Franklin Dam (at least they didn't appropriate the name of a local chief like Kamiakan), was resurrected by the Carter Administration in 1978. Most dams, like wars, are instigated by Democrats. This time the dam wasn't sold as an engine of cheap hydro-power, but as a mighty facilitator of marine commerce. The idea was to open the entire upper Columbia River to barge traffic and, in the process, make Wenatchee, Washington, nearly 500 river miles from the coast, a deep water port. The Corps sank another $2 million into engineering studies to justify the dam and boosters poured in another $2 million in PR touting how the project would transform the Inland Empire into a glorious engine of commerce.

Alas, it was not to be. This time the dam was killed off by the Reagan administration, which was forced to confront the uncomfortable fact that the waters of the reservoir would have encroached upon the most toxic soil in the world: the radioactive tank farms of Hanford. The sages in the Reagan White House wisely decided that it was better to let the 177 vats of radioactive slop discretely corrode and leak into the groundwater than risk exhuming them and publicly confronting the treacherous mess that had been left behind as an eternal relic of the nation's four-decade long obsession with devices of nuclear annihilation.

So in 1981 the Ben Franklin project was shelved once again. And there it sits, biding its time for a third incarnation. What's the half-life of a dam?

Merrily, merrily we float. Downstream, always downstream. Such a beautiful word. A word with an unimpeachable integrity and authenticity. On this lonely stretch of river, pelicans are our only companions. The big white birds are graceful flyers on 10-foot wingspan, much more so than the ungainly great blue herons that stalk the riverbanks and bark irritably when we paddle by. Both the herons and the pelicans are fish-eaters. The pelicans are voracious feeders, each bird eats as much as 5 pounds of fish each day—more when they are feeding chicks. The white pelicans of the Reach aren't diving birds, like their cousins the brown pelicans of the coast. Instead, they take their prey from the surface of the river while swimming. If ravens are the coyotes of the avian world, pelicans behave more like wolves. They live in highly organized social groups. They hunt together often in coordinated groups of six or ten birds. Sometimes the groups will split, with some pelicans pushing schools of fish into shallow water where the other birds are waiting and a communal and often synchronized feeding frenzy ensues.

The white pelicans will eat almost any fish: chub, perch, bass, carp, rainbow trout. But it's the salmon they love. It's the salmon that have lured them here, decade after decade, in great migrations from their wintering grounds in the Gulf of Mexico.

But it's that passion for fish that has put the pelican, and the herons, eagles and osprey, at risk. For even though the Hanford Reach is home to the last vibrant run of wild Chinook salmon on the Columbia River, those fish, and the others in the Reach, are contaminated with an array of radionuclides and other atomic debris leaching inexorably into the Columbia from the Hanford's 1400 haphazardly-placed waste dumps. By one estimate, these dumps have leaked three-million curies of radiation into the river every year from 1950 through the 1980s. The radiation continues to leak—though leak is perhaps not the right word—largely unabated by the latest techno-fixes.

At Hanford, environmental mitigation is an expensive illusion. How expensive? Back in 2000, the price-tag for cleaning up Hanford was pegged at $100 billion dollars. But in the intervening decade the extent of the contamination has more than tripled. This is delightful news for contractors, such as CHM2 Hill, Westinghouse, Batelle, Bechtel, but a dismal diagnosis for the ecosystem. Just ask any pelican.

On river right we pass the old pumphouse near the sprawling K-Reactor complex. The building is gouged roughly into the river bank. It has a crenellated roofline and dark windows, looking like a ruined castle on the Scottish moors. The pumphouse fed millions of gallons of water into the so-called sister reactors and later into the menacing K-Basins.

When Hanford suddenly stopped producing plutonium in the late 1980s, the atomic engineers were left with a problem. There were more than 100,000 uranium fuel rods and rod fragments that had been irradiated but wouldn't be processed into plutonium. What to do with this hot property? After a few seconds of deliberation, they decided to sink it.

In the 1950s, two vast concrete pools had been constructed less than 400 yards from the Columbia River as temporary storage lagoons. Even though these basins were already 10 years beyond their 20-year life expectancy, the Department of Energy decided to fill them each with a million gallons of water and submerge the deteriorating fuel assemblies.

Out of sight, out of mind. Naturally, it didn't work out that way. Almost immediately, the K-East Basin sprang leaks. Highly radioactive water began to spill onto the ground and leach its way into the river. The irradiate rods began to corrode and decay, dissolving into a lethal sludge.

In 1994, the Energy Department began the dangerously experiment task of fishing out the 2,100 metric tons of fuel rods from the K-East Basin. It took them 10 years to remove the fuel rods and then they hit the sludge. The fuel rods were packed away in another spooky structure at Hanford called the Canister Storage Building, but the thick band of sludge at the bottom of the basin was sucked up in giant vacuums over a four-year period, stuffed in canisters and then submerged into the K-West Basin. The million gallons of water was sucked from the basin, run quickly through a treatment plant and then, somewhat unbelievably, simply sprayed on the ground.

So much for the problematic K-East Basin, right? Wrong. In turns out that the ground beneath the basin is thoroughly saturated with radioactive scum.

What about the K-West Basin, you ask. Good question. It remains filled to the brim with water, fuel rods and sludge. The genial folks at Hanford say not to worry. This radioactive swimming pool is quite impermeable. So far.

But there's no time to dally on such trifles today. The river pulls us away. The current picks up steam. We hit a standing wave, sending a cold spray over the kayak. Then another and another. Suddenly we're drenched. This is Coyote Rapids, a bouncy wave train that is over just as we start to enjoy it. We try to paddle furiously back upstream to ride it again, but the river pushes us back. Exclusive engagement, no replays.

We slide into an eddy below the rapids and nose the kayak toward a gravel bar.

"Look at that," Josh says pointing toward a large bolt in the river. It is bone-white and four-feet long.

"No wonder this place sprang a leak."

We pull the kayak on the bank and step on forbidden ground. Josh heads toward the nearest mutant willow tree to take a piss, while I climb up an old road bed to get a better view of the K-Reactor complex. The road ends at a fence topped with razor wire. There is a large sign featuring stark red letters:

WARNING

You are entering the Hanford Site Emergency Zone. If you hear a steady 3 minute siren leave the area IMMEDIATELY. Turn your radio to KONA 610 AM for emergency information.

"Hey, Josh, where's our damn radio?"

"Back with the Tequila."

***

I am standing next to the perimeter fence, looking across Hanford's secret geography. Behind the K-Reactor complex rises Gable Mountain, a sere ridge of basalt long sacred to the Wanapum people and the birthplace of the Washani Religion, the apocalyptic Dreamer Cult of Smohalla that sparked the great Yakama War of 1855. Now the holy mountain serves as a scenic backdrop for the physics of obliteration.

In the 1940s and 1950s, the Hanford security forces, composed of crack shots from Kennewick and Walla Walla, had the authority to shoot trespassers on sight. In the end, the armed guards chased away a few poachers, some drunken ranch hands from Mattawa and a couple Wanapum elders sneaking into the forbidden land to perform their ancient rituals.

The real atomic spies usually drove right through the front gate, sporting top secret clearance, and drove out again carrying the design schematics for the latest configuration of the H-bomb. The plans were often in Stalin's vault two weeks later. (For more on espionage at Hanford and other sites check out Richard Rhodes' masterful book *Dark Sun: the Making of the Hydrogen Bomb.*)

Hanford's fences, watchtowers and armed guards were an early exercise in perception management, designed to imply that the real threats were external, rather than leaking from the inside-out, day by day, curie by curie, isotope by deadly isotope.

Off the river for only few moments, and, suddenly, the air feels hot, stifling. The Hanford plain sizzles in the unsparing light. The land looks scalded and skinless, like cooked bone.

***

"We're screwed," Josh whispers, urgently pointing down river toward the metallic howl of a jet boat.

"What kind of cyber-sensors does this place have, any way? You've been tip-toeing, haven't you?" I hurl a river-polished rock at the yellow No Entry sign looming above us on the verboten grounds of Hanford's infamous Area 100. Ka-ching!

I stuff a couple of K-Reactor rocks into my pocket. They are oddities from Montana, carried here 20,000 years ago during the mighty Bretz Floods, when the ice dams holding back a vast inland sea cracked, unleashing an 800-foot tall torrent of water that scoured out the coulee country of the Inland Empire and carved the Columbia Gorge. Now they're radioactive. Maybe I'll pack them in my carry-on luggage the next time I fly. Gotta keep those TSA agents on their toes.

The jet boat is the first sign of river traffic we've seen in twelve miles on the Columbia. Human river traffic, that is. The menacing green craft speeds towards us, ripping huge wakes in the surface of the river and startling fifty Canada geese into angry flight.

Someone is standing in the pilot house holding a megaphone. He seems to be pointing it directly at us. Josh takes out his cellphone, for one last talk with Chelsea, before we join the ranks of the disappeared.

"Tell Chelsea to retain Jonathan Turley or that David Cole. Under the Patriot Act, they can keep us incommunicado for months. Years, maybe."

Call fails. No signal. Are they jamming our phones, too? Or, perhaps, it's just another dropped iPhone call. Apple hasn't been the same since Steve Jobs made up with Bill Gates. These damned phones crash more frequently than Windows XP.

"Quick," Josh says. "Hide the contraband."

"We are the contraband."

"Oh, right."

We scramble into the kayak and hurriedly push off. Tragically, the river doesn't abet our getaway. Instead, the current pulls us rapidly toward the approaching assault boat.

"You'll never take us dry!" Josh declares over the roar of the jet boat's engines. Like a true child of Billings, Josh cinches his life-jacket so tightly that he's beginning to sprout cleavage. He's not exactly John Paul Jones up there in the bow.

"Remember to leave room to breathe."

We've both read the accounts of the dead and the brain dead. The drowned and the hypothermic. If you end up in the river out here, the odds of surviving aren't good—and that's not factoring in the radiation exposure.

The water is cold, the current unforgiving, the good Samaritans long since evicted from the premises. So we agreed early on to follow the Apocalypse Now! Rule of Boating Safety: Stay in the boat, even while under furious assault from DoE SEALS, stay in the friggin' boat.

The sun is shining fiercely in our eyes, but it looks like there may be twenty beefy goons crammed into the terrible machine. Surely that's overkill. What kind of a threat do we pose to the priests of Armageddon?

Yes, we're packing a soggy and swollen copy of *The Monkey Wrench Gang* and that might be considered a serious enhancing factor at any secret tribunal. But, hell, Abbey's been dead for twenty years and Doug Peacock's four-hundred miles away, hip-deep in the Yellowstone, draining Tecates and harassing trout.

"Remember Ruby Ridge!" Josh shouts, defiantly shaking his paddle.

"Shssh. Don't antagonize them! They might take it for a weapon."

"But these are our only weapons!"

"What about those water balloons filled with butyric acid we picked up at Captain Paul Watson's wharfside sale?"

"Don't ask."

At last, we can make out the steel-wool voice blaring from the megaphone. It has a strong eastern European accent. Hungarian, perhaps? A voice trying hard to mimic the harsh intonations of the young Edward Teller.

"Zees is verr ve ended zee wahr," the rotund man says, pointing toward the B Reactor. "Und zees is verr ve stopped zee Roozkees," hand sweeping like a mad conductor at the K-Reactor complex. "Und zhat is verr ve kud uf beaten cancer," his stubby finger pointing toward a shadowy complex near Gable Mountain, the mothballed Fast-Flux Breeder Reactor. "If not vor dos damn enfiromentaleezts."

I nudge Josh in the shoulder with my paddle. "Dos damn enFIROmentaleezts? Is he talking about us? You didn't bring any matches, did you? I specifically said, No matches!!"

"Yeah," Josh grins. "But you didn't say anything about my trusty Zippo!"

Click.

"Damn. That could land us another 10 years in the slammer. No vegetarian food, Josh. And the judge might make us write a book report on *Three Cups of Tea*. Just ask that Jonathan Paul."

"What if I remove the flint?"

"Just keep it in open view. Don't conceal that Zippo."

It soon becomes apparent that this is not a Department of Energy Strike Force death-craft racing to defend the nuclear site's vulnerable riparian flank from interlopers in inflatable kayaks, but something much more ominous: a Hanford tour boat, educating plump H-bomb groupies from Moscow (Idaho, that is) and Wenatchee about the archaeological ruins of the Cold War.

Info-sermon complete, the wise-guy pilot revs the engines into an obscene scream. The sharp bow of the big boat rears up into the full-hydroplaning position and bears down on us with malevolent intent, before making an abrupt u-turn that washes us in a curtain of cold spray.

The chunky tourists cheer, flash us ironic waves and speed back to Richland for a box lunch at Gen. Leslie Grove Park, shredding the surface of the river as they disappear behind a funnel of blue smoke.

Our little orange kayak flexes, then scales the violent four-foot wakes and digs out of the deep troughs carved by the absconding jet boat. Wet and battered, we paddle downstream once again, toward the immaculate high cliffs called the White Bluffs.

***

The parapets of the White Bluffs hulk 500-feet above the river. These are not the usual black basalt cliffs that dominate most of the Columbia Plateau. The White Bluffs are the remains of an ancient lake bottom, left by the melted glaciers of the Pleistocene, now being inexorably incised by the steady gnawing of the Columbia.

Geologists categorize the cliffs and nearby hills as part of the Ringold Formation. The people of the river called this eerie landscape the deadlands and it was here that the great healer Smohalla came to pray and mourn when he failed to save his young daughter from one of the plagues introduced by the white people. It was here that Smohalla had his vision of his own death and resurrection and here where he experienced his chilling dream of the end times, when bodies would rise from the earth, and tribal people would once again live as one with the land.

It is possible, even probable, that during his sojourn through these haunted badlands that Smohalla came across the embedded bones of some now extinct Pleistocene creature, a Giant sloth or Wooly Mammoth, which the cliffs frequently disgorge.

The river people called him Starman, as if he could see through deep space into the circulating currents of time. Smohalla could certainly see more clearly than most what was coming from the white invaders, the people he called "red-eyed fools." Dispossession, destruction and death. He had no doubts about the veracity of his vision and counseled sternly against the making of any treaties, any deal that consigned away the sovereign rights of native people to the land, the river, the deer and the fish. Make them take it, if they must, but don't sell it or give it away.

The whites came to White Bluffs in 1855, driven by a frenzy for gold. The creeks were dredged, mines sunk into the strange fluvial soils. No fortunes were made, but people stayed anyway. The small town of White Bluffs sprang up in the valley. Apple, pear and almond trees were planted on the ridges. People squeezed out a hard living from this austere land.

Then in 1943 the government came calling. The people in White Bluff were told that their land was being seized and there could be no appeal. Some residents were given only three days to pack up their belongings and leave. A few months later all of the houses, barns, churches and buildings in White Bluff were bulldozed and torched, the orchards uprooted and burned. And, in a spooky fulfillment of Smohalla's prophecy, nearly 200 bodies from town's cemetery were exhumed from their graves, tossed into Army trucks and hauled off to another graveyard in the town Prosser 30 miles away.

***

On this July day the high desert air will breach the century mark, but the river is cold, probably hypothermic. Once the temperature of the waters rose by more than 2 degrees in less than an hour, when the nuclear engineers at Hanford flushed thousands of gallons of hot water into the great river of the West. Hot as in radioactive.

The consequences of that spill and the others that followed are still being felt and will be for something like eternity. These are the cruel externalities of the atomic age, thyroid cancers for the downwinders and other forms of death for those who live downwater, such as the forty-five babies in the Hanford Region born dead without brains. A cursed landscape? A tormented existence that Smoholla dreamed? Perhaps. But it is a curse we have brought upon ourselves and our descendants until the end of time.

***

Bank swallows buzz our heads. Two trout break the surface of the river in tandem, chasing the same big yellow mayfly. The sun breaches the White Bluffs and burnishes the golden tones of the high desert to the west.

"You know the scenery out here probably hasn't changed all that much since David Thompson floated it in 1811."

"Except for the reactors."

"Except for the them."

"Jeff?"

"Huh?"

"Who's David Thompson?"

"Where did you go to school, Josh?"

"Who says I went to school?"

Therein lies a tale.

Growing up in the cornfields of the Midwest, I had two childhood idols who I couldn't talk about. One was Crazy Horse, who I couldn't bring up at school without getting into a fight with some slick-haired jackass in shit-kicker boots. I went to Shit-Kicker High School. Our mascot was a professional Shit-Kicker, blonde hair, massive biceps, pointy boots. Despite it's name, Indiana was a devoted Custer state. Still is.

The other hero was certain Dafydd ap Thomas (otherwise known as David Thompson) and no one knew who the hell he was. They still don't.

I learned about the life of the great Welsh cartographer one drizzly afternoon in Ely, Minnesota from Sigurd Olson, the Thoreau of the North Woods. Along with Aldo Leopold and Robert Marshall, Olson helped build the political movement to protect wilderness. He was a driving force behind the creation of the Boundary Waters and Voyaguers National Parks, the Reyes Point National Seashore and the Arctic National Wildlife Refuge. He helped write the beautiful authorizing language for the Wilderness Act. Olson was also a gifted historian of the early explorations of Canada and the Pacific Northwest, from Samuel Hearne to Alexander Mackenzie. But ranking above all of these in Olson's estimation was David Thompson, who explored and mapped much of western Canada, as well as Montana, Oregon, Idaho and Washington two hundred years ago.

Olson was in his late-seventies when I met him. But he still spent many solitary weeks in the Quantico-Superior Wilderness, paddling his canoe over those vast windy lakes and humping heavy loads of gear across demanding portages.

"I like to take these trips alone," he told me in his cabin. "The way old Thompson did. Just me and the loons and the stars."

When I was 16 I retraced some of Thompson's travels in Manitoba, from Churchill on Hudson's Bay to the Little Beaver River, two hundred and fifty miles up the Churchill River. Even in the 1970s, this remained a wild region thick with trout, Arctic grayling and bears. Big brown ones. I later wrote a limp novel enmeshing the contours of that trip with Thompson's remarkable life, now consigned to ashes.

Now, on the 200th anniversary of his greatest adventure, a thousand mile-long descent of the Columbia River, from its source in British Columbia to the Pacific Ocean, Thompson remains an obscure figure, eclipsed in the public imagination by Lewis and Clark and John Wesley Powell, who have enjoyed more zealous promoters, from Bernard DeVoto to Wallace Stegner to Ed Abbey. Olson, unfortunately, never got around to writing a book on Thompson.

Of course, in the race for Empire, Thompson ended up on the losing side—that side being the trappers, the fur-traders, voyageurs, the beaver, the otter and, yes, the river tribes themselves. The side of the old ways, living close to the rhythms of land.

Thompson's beautiful and precisely rendered maps were put to a malign purpose. The most malign imaginable, a purpose not different in kind from the complex recipes for brewing a superbomb at Hanford two centuries later. So were his deftly-written journals. They were used first as a guide to western expansion, then as a blueprint for the remorseless exploitation of the natural world and the systematic dispossession and annihilation of the river tribes.

It all must look pretty much the same, as it did in 1811, except for the nuclear plants, barbed wire, sirens, sensors, pumphouses and powerlines. And what is missing. The tribal villages, the bears, the runs of fat summer Chinook salmon. We have entered the world of the seen and the unseen, where we define ourselves more by what we have lost than what we have made.

The sharp eyes of David Thompson would have surely recognized the White Bluffs, the black basalt escarpment of Gable Mountain, the block faults of Rattlesnake and Saddle Mountains and the river itself. This last arc of free-running river, crisp and crystalline and brawny. They ought to rename it Thompson's Reach. Or Smoholla's Reach. Or Sohappy's Reach. Anything but Hanford. Hanford has taken too much already and given nothing back but death, cancer and blank checks for defense contractors.

***

Josh is daydreaming again, hypnotized by white cliffs and blue skies. No one is guiding the boat. We might run into another lost chunk of Hanford, hit an otter, crash a pelican party. Of course, no one needs to navigate. We've slipped into a riparian lethargy. This is the kind of spell cast by desert rivers. Occasionally, a few small cottonwoods and willows on the bank scroll by. But mostly it's rock and sagebrush and sand, bank swallows still circling our heads.

How it came to this is unclear. But we are floating backwards at six river miles an hour. Our paddles are bone dry and hot. They've scarcely touched the water today. Josh is not going to get buffed up for the all-important wedding photographs at this rate. If we're not going to work, there should at least be beer. But once again we've forgotten the Tecate. No one thinks rationally in Richland, Washington. Not at six in the morning. You just want to get out of town and on the river as fast as you can. Maybe those famous headwinds will finally pick up. Maybe they'll blow us all the way back to Coyote Rapids. Out here, on the Atomic River, one is allowed to hope.

"Look at that," Josh says.

"What?"

"Nothing."

"Not Edward Teller's brand of nothing, I hope?"

"No. A beautiful nothing."

"The way it's meant to be."

"Don't tell the Chamber of Commerce. They'll want to fill it with something."

"I'm telling them nothing."

And so we go, floating backwards down the cobalt-blue Columbia, through a beautiful nothingness.

– September 2, 2016

SECTION 5
FRONTLINES

TARGETING EARTH FIRST!

By Jeffrey St. Clair and Joshua Frank

Dave Foreman, co-founder of Earth First!, awoke at five in the morning on May 30, 1989 to the sound of three FBI agents shouting his name in his Tucson, Arizona home. Foreman's wife Nancy answered the door frantically and was shoved aside by brawny FBI agents as they raced toward their master bedroom where her husband was sound asleep, naked under the sheets, with plugs jammed in his ears to drown out the noise of their neighbor's barking Doberman pincher. By the time Foreman came to, the agents were surrounding his bed, touting bulletproof vests and .357 Magnums.

He immediately thought of the murder of Fred Hampton in Chicago, expecting to be shot in cold blood. But as Foreman put it, "Being a nice, middle-class honky male, they can't get away with that stuff quite as easily as they could with Fred, or with all the native people on the Pine Ridge Reservation back in the early 70s."

So instead of firing off a few rounds, they jerked a dazed Foreman from his slumber, let him pull on a pair of shorts, and hauled him outside where they threw him in the back of an unmarked vehicle. It took over six hours before Foreman even knew why he had been accosted by Federal agents.

Foreman's arrest was the culmination of three years and two million tax dollars spent in an attempt to frame a few Earth First! activists for conspiring to damage government and private property. The FBI infiltrated Earth First! groups in several states with informants and undercover agent-provocateurs. Over 500 hours of tape recordings of meetings, events and casual conversation had been amassed. Phones had been tapped and homes broken in to. The FBI was doing their best to intimidate radical environmentalists across the country, marking them as potential threat to national security.

It was the FBI's first case of Green Scare.

The day before Foreman was yanked from bed and lugged in to the warm Arizona morning, two so-called co-conspirators, biologist Marc Baker and antinuclear activist Mark Davis, were arrested by some 50 agents on horseback and on foot, with a helicopter hovering above as the activists stood at the base of a power line tower in the middle of desert country in Wenden, Arizona, 200 miles northwest of Foreman's home. The next day Peg Millet, a self-described "redneck woman for wilderness," was arrested at a nearby Planned Parenthood where she worked. Millet had earlier evaded the FBI's dragnet.

Driven to the site by an undercover FBI agent, the entire episode, as Foreman put it, was the agent's conception. Foreman, described by the bureau as the guru and financier of the operation, was also pegged for having thought up the whole elaborate scheme, despite the fact that their evidence was thin.

Back in the 1970s the FBI issued a memo to their field offices stating that when attempting to break up dissident groups, the most effective route was to forget about hard intelligence or annoying facts. Simply make a few arrests and hold a public press conference. Charges could later be dropped. It didn't matter; by the time the news hit the airwaves and was printed up in the local newspapers, the damage had already been done.

It was the FBI's assertion that the action stopped by the arrests under that Arizona power line in late May, 1989, was to be a test run for a much grander plot involving Davis, Baker, Millet, and the group's leader, Dave Foreman. The FBI charged the four with the intent to damage electrical transmission lines that lead to the Rocky Flats nuclear weapons facility in Colorado.

"The big lie that the FBI pushed at their press conference the day after the arrests was that we were a bunch of terrorists conspiring to cut the power lines into the Palo Verde and Diablo

Canyon nuclear facilities in order to cause a nuclear meltdown and threaten public health and safety," explained Foreman.

In the late 1980s the FBI launched operation THERMCON in response to an act of sabotage of the Arizona Snowbowl ski lift near Flagstaff, Arizona that occurred in October 1987, allegedly by Davis, Millet and Baker. Acting under the quirky name, Evan Mecham Eco-Terrorist International Conspiracy (EMETIC)—the eco-saboteurs wrecked several of the company's ski lifts, claiming that structures were cutting in to areas of significant biological importance.

This was not the first act the group claimed responsibility for. A year prior EMETIC sent a letter declaring they were responsible for the damage at the Fairfield Snow Bowl near Flagstaff. The group's letter also included a jovial threat to "chain the Fairfield CEO to a tree at the 10,000-foot level and feed him shrubs and roots until he understands the suicidal folly of treating the planet primarily as a tool for making money."

The group used an acetylene torch to cut bolts from several of the lift's support towers, making them inoperable. Upon receiving the letter, the Arizona ski resort was forced to shut down the lift in order to repair the damages, which rang up to over $50,000.

But the big allegations heaved at these eco-saboteurs wasn't for dislodging a few bolts at a quaint ski resort in the heart of the Arizona mountains, or for inconveniencing a few ski bums from their daily excursions. No, the big charges were levied at the group for allegedly plotting to disrupt the functions of the Rocky Flats nuclear facility hundreds of miles away. Ironically, at the moment of their arrests, the FBI was simultaneously looking into public health concerns due to an illegal radioactive waste leak at the nuclear power site, which led Earth First! activist Mike Roselle to quip, " [the FBI] would have discharged its duty better by assisting in a conspiracy to cut power to Rocky Flats, instead of trying to stop one."

***

Gerry Spence climbed into his private jet in Jackson, Wyoming estate almost immediately after he heard about the FBI arrest of Dave Foreman in Arizona. Spence had made a name for himself among environmental activists in the late-1970s for his case against energy company Kerr-McGee, when he provided legal services to the family of former employee Karen Silkwood, who died suspiciously after she challenged the company of environmental abuses at one of their most productive nuclear facilities. Silkwood, who made plutonium pellets for nuclear reactors, had been assigned by her union to investigate health and safety concerns at a Kerr-McGee plant near Crescent, Oklahoma. In her monitoring of the facility, Silkwood found dozens of evident regulatory violations, including faulty respiratory equipment as well as many cases of workers being exposed to radioactive material.

Silkwood went public after the company seemingly ignored her and her union's concerns, even going as far as to testify to the Atomic Energy Commission (AEC) about the issues, claiming that regulations were sidestepped in an attempt to up the speed of production. She also claimed that workers had been mishandling nuclear fuel rods, but the company has covered up the incidences by falsifying inspection reports.

On the night of November 13, 1974, Silkwood left a union meeting in Crescent with documents in hand to drive to Oklahoma City where she was to meet and discuss Kerr-McGee's alleged violations with a union official and two *New York Times* reporters. She never made it. Silkwood's body was found the next day in the driver's seat of her car on the side of the road, stuck in a culvert. She was pronounced dead on the scene and no documents were found in her car.

An independent private investigation revealed that Silkwood was in full control of her vehicle when it was struck from behind and forced off to the side of the road. According to the private investigators, the steering wheel of her car was bent in a manner that showed conclusively that Silkwood was prepared for the blow of the accident as it occurred. She had not been asleep at the wheel as investigators initially thought. The coroner concluded she had not died as a result of the accident, but possibly from suffocation.

No arrests or charges were ever made. Silkwood's children and father filed a lawsuit against Kerr-McGee on behalf of her estate. Gerry Spence was their lead attorney. An autopsy of Silkwood's body showed extremely high levels of plutonium contamination. Lawyers for Kerr-McGee argued first that the levels found were normal, but after damning evidence to the contrary, they were forced to argue that Silkwood had likely poisoned herself.

Spence had been victorious. Kerr-McGee's defense was caught in a series of unavoidable contradictions. Silkwood's body was laden with poison as result of her work at the nuclear facility. In her death Spence vindicated her well-documented claims. The initial jury verdict was for the company to pay $505,000 in damages and $10,000,000 in punitive damages. Kerr-McGee appealed and drastically reduced the jury's verdict, but the initial ruling was later upheld by the Supreme Court. On the way to a retrial the company agreed to pay $1.38 million to the Silkwood estate.

Gerry Spence was not cowed by the antics of the Kerr-McGee Corporation, and when he agreed to take on Dave Foreman's case pro-bono, justice seemed to be on the horizon for the Earth First! activists as well.

"Picture a little guy out there hacking at a dead steel pole, an inanimate object, with a blowtorch. He's considered a criminal," said Spence, explaining how he planned to steer the narrative of Foreman's pending trial. "Now see the image of a beautiful, living, 400-year-old-tree, with an inanimate object hacking away at it. This non-living thing is corporate America, but the corporate executives are not considered criminals at all."

Like so many of the FBI charges brought against radical activists throughout the years, the case against Dave Foreman was less exciting than the investigation that led up to his arrest. The bureau had done its best to make Foreman and Earth First! out to be the most threatening activists in America.

Spence was not impressed and in fact argued as much, stating the scope of the FBI's operation THERMCON was "very similar to the procedures the FBI used during the 1960s against dissident groups." No doubt Spence was right. Similar to the movement disruption exemplified by COINTELPRO against Martin Luther King Jr., the Black Panthers and the American Indian Movement, the FBI's crackdown of Earth First! in the late 1980s had many alarming parallels to the agency of old.

"Essentially what we need to understand is that the Federal Bureau of Investigation, which was formed during the Palmer Raids in 1921, was set up from the very beginning to inhibit internal political dissent. They rarely go after criminals. They're a thought police," said Foreman of the FBI's motives for targeting environmentalists. "Let's face it, that's what the whole government is. Foreman's first law of government reads that the purpose of the state, and all its constituent elements, is the defense of an entrenched economic elite and philosophical orthodoxy. Thankfully, there's a corollary to that law—they aren't always very smart and competent in carrying out their plans."

The man who was paid to infiltrate Earth First! under the guise of THERMCON was anything but competent. Special agent Michael A. Fain, stationed in the FBI's Phoenix office, befriended Peg Millet and begun attending Earth First! meetings in the area. Fain, who went by alias, Mike Tait, posed as a Vietnam vet who dabbled in construction and gave up booze after his military service. On more than one occasion, while wearing a wire, Fain had tried to entice members of Earth First! in different acts of vandalism. They repeatedly refused.

During pre-trial evidence discovery the defense was allowed to listen to hours of Fain's wire-tapings, when they found that the not-so-careful agent inadvertently forgot to turn off his recorder. Fain, while having a conversation with two other agents at a Burger King after a brief meeting with Foreman, spoke about the status of his investigation, exclaiming, "I don't really look for them to be doing a lot of hurting people... [Dave Foreman] isn't really the guy we need to pop—I mean in terms of an actual perpetrator. This is the guy we need to pop to send a message. And that's all we're really doing... Uh-oh! We don't need that on tape! Hoo boy!"

Here the FBI was, acting as if these Earth First!ers were publicly vilifying them, while privately admitting that they posed no real threat. "[The agency is acting] as if [its] dealing with the most dangerous, violent terrorists that the country's ever known," explained Spence at the time. "And what we are really dealing with is ordinary, decent human beings who are trying to call the attention of America to the fact that the Earth is dying."

The FBI's rationale for targeting Foreman was purely political as he was one of the most prominent and well-spoken radical environmentalists of the time. Despite their claims that they were not directly targeting Earth First! or Foreman, and were instead investigating threats of sabotage of power lines that led to a nuclear power plant—their public indictment painted quite a different story.

"Mr. Foreman is the worst of the group," Assistant U.S. Attorney Roger Dokken announced to the court. "He sneaks around in the background ... I don't like to use the analogy of a Mafia boss, but they never do anything either. They just sent their munchkins out to do it."

But agent Michael Fain's on-tape gaffes were simply too much for the prosecution to manage, and the case against Foreman, having been deferred almost seven years, was finally reduced in 1996 to a single misdemeanor and a meager $250 in fines. The $2 million the FBI wasted tracking Earth First! over the latter part of the 1980s had only been nominally successful. Yet the alleged ring-leader was still free. Unfortunately, the FBI may have gotten exactly what they wanted all along. Dave Foreman later stepped down as spokesman to Earth First! and inherited quite a different role in the environmental movement—one of invisibility and near silence.

Peg Millet, Mark Davis and Marc Baker were all sentenced separately in 1991 for their involvement in their group EMETIC's acts of ecotage against the expansion of Arizona Snowbowl. Davis got 6 years and $19,821 in restitution. Millet got 3 years, with the same fine, while Baker only received 6 months and a $5,000 fine.

Little did these activists know that their capture and subsequent arraignments were only the beginning. THERMCON's crackdown of Earth First! would prove to be a dry-run for the Federal Bureau of Investigations.

–January 12, 2009

HOW TRE ARROW BECAME AMERICA'S MOST WANTED ENVIRONMENTAL "TERRORIST"

By Jeffrey St. Clair and Joshua Frank

That Tre Arrow, a tree-hugging vegan who espouses non-violence and lives by the airy and some nebulous philosophy of Gaia, would top the FBI's Most Wanted list, only reaffirms the notion that the Bureau's energy is being exerted in specious directions.

On August 12, 2008, after a tumultuous seven-year investigation, Arrow was sentenced in Federal court to six-and-a-half years for lighting three cement haulers ablaze at the notorious Ross Island Sand and Gravel in Portland, Oregon, as well as firebombing two trucks and one front loader owned by Ray Schoppert Logging Company near the timber town of Estacada, Oregon. The acts were in protest of the Eagle Creek timber sale in Mt. Hood National Forest in the late 1990s.

Located in a roadless area within Oregon's Clackamas River watershed, the streams that snake through the old growth groves of Eagle Creek provide drinking water for over 185,000 people in the greater Portland area. Critics of the plan to log Eagle Creek argued that the forest's steep slopes were in the "transient snow zone" and would likely lead to future landslides and mass flooding, which would ultimately spoil water quality during the region's frequent rain-on-snow events. Arrow was one of the most creative and articulate activists opposing the sale.

A grim-faced, 34-year-old Arrow listened warily as Judge James Redden read his sentence. At the behest of his lawyers, Bruce Ellison and Paul Loney, Arrow earlier signed off on a plea deal with the U.S. Department of Justice and accepted responsibility for his role in the arsons, even though for years he denied any involvement.

"[I'm] true to a higher power ... I don't feel I need to be rehabilitated," Arrow stated in a verbose speech to the court upon hearing the ruling. "Corporations have usurped much of the governmental power. Corporations seem to be able to get away with poisoning the very entity we rely on for our well-being with no punishment, or very little punishment," he declared.

"I don't know what happened to you but they were very serious crimes, and you know it," responded a disgruntled Judge Redden.

The closing of the case was seen as a major victory by the FBI, which had long promoted Arrow as America's most notorious and dangerous eco-terrorist.

"Now we know the truth, and we know he has to pay the price," Assistant U.S. Attorney Stephen Peifer brayed to reporters. "It sends a clear message that society doesn't tolerate it, that these cases are solved and these people are brought to justice."

***

Tre Arrow, born Michael James Scarpitti, was raised in Jensen Beach, Florida in a suburban community on the ritzy outskirts of sun-drenched Palm Beach, where grandiose mansions line the streets and luxury automobiles occupy the driveways. His mother was a real estate agent and his father owned a plumbing and air conditioning business. Arrow was seemingly your average middle-class kid who scored good grades in school and steered clear of trouble. As a young teen he was a star wrestler but later abandoned the sport to pursue his love for music, hoping to one day make it a fulltime career.

"My brother was always someone who had deep feelings and could express them very well," his older sister, Shawna, told *Rolling Stone* in 2006. "He was way mature for a teenage boy. If something moved him, he would cry about it without any shame at all."

Arrow's parents supported their Tre's aspirations but pushed him to enroll at Florida State University upon graduation. It wasn't long before he began dabbling in environmentalism, from initiating a recycling program at his dormitory to embracing veganism and speaking out against animal cruelty. Music, however, was still the young activist's passion, and his college band, Soya Bean Fields, played at coffeehouses and other venues in and around Tallahassee.

After completing an associate's degree at FSU, Arrow headed up to Cincinnati, Ohio where he fathered a child with a bandmate before heading off to Sedona, Arizona and then Boulder, Colorado. Arrow was in search of a place to call home, and that home would soon come in the form of the rain-soaked and tree-lined streets of Portland, Oregon.

"He just fell in love with the Northwest," said Arrow's father Jim Scarpitti. "Whenever [he] would write to us, he'd include all these drawings of the scenery, the white-capped mountains and the dark-green forests. He's a gifted artist, and his letters were like illustrated novels."

Arrow left behind a life he was trying hard to forget. He changed his name, disconnected from old friends and altered his lifestyle so as to be in more direct contact with the natural world. While still pursuing music, Arrow became more and more involved in environmental causes. He ditched his shoes, rarely showered and only ate raw, uncooked food. He embraced a new kind of religion, what some may call Deep Ecology—or that the living environment as a whole has the same rights as humans. But Arrow's beliefs were all his own, shaped by what he was witnessing first hand in the mountains of the Pacific Northwest—the ruin left in the wake of President Clinton's brutish Northwest Forest Plan, Option 9, which restarted the logging of ancient forests throughout the West.

It was hypocrisies and compromises such Clinton's that invigorated a new breed of radical, direct-action oriented environmentalism throughout the region. "If the federal forest agencies don't follow the plan, they'll end up in court. Or, if they ignore new scientific information demonstrating the need to revise the present plan, they'll end up in court," explained Andy Kerr of the Oregon Natural Resources Council at the time. But when legal tactics weren't successful, activists flung their bodies in front of bulldozers and set up canopies high in the giant Douglas Firs as a warning to loggers of their potential self-sacrifice to save the forest. It was an all out environmental war zone.

Forest activists and environmental lawyers viewed the Clinton plan as undermining the well-being of the Northern Spotted Owl and endangered salmon and steelhead trout. In retrospect, Option 9 was nearly as bad as proposals sought during the first and second Bush administrations. Some claimed, with justification, that it was actually worse. Portions of the plan were deemed illegal by federal courts, and scientists predicted that the policy would not halt the spotted owl's slide toward extinction. Bill Clinton, Al Gore and Secretary of the Interior Bruce Babbitt pushed their plan forward despite these concerns, steamrolling their former allies in big green groups. By 1994, new timber sales in old growth forests were being offered for sale to timber companies for the first time in six years—a feat that eluded Bush the Elder. These were Clinton-created clearcuts, and the administration boasted proudly of what they wrought.

The fight to save the wild forests of the Pacific Northwest was well underway by the time Tre Arrow arrived in Portland with his guitar strapped to his back. But it was in the midst of these worthy struggles that he became radicalized, witnessing first hand the unharnessed pillage of our national forests.

***

On the afternoon of July 7, 2000, Tre Arrow, perhaps unwittingly, became the idol of a reinvigorated environmental movement: one that was radically creative, action oriented, non-violent and boldly uncompromising. Passion for the wild drove the agile Arrow, barefoot in shorts and a t-shirt, to scale the wall of a U.S. Forest Service Regional Headquarters in downtown Portland, where he would remain perched on a small window ledge for 11 consecutive days.

Earlier that morning, in what the government saw as a huge victory against a batch of dangerous environmentalists who were fighting timber sales in the Mt. Hood National Forest—federal agents razed a camp and road barricades set up by Cascadia Forest Alliance to stop the logging of Eagle Creek. In the pre-dawn hours, Forest Service henchmen donned in camouflage and bearing assault rifles charged in on ATVs to bust up the blockades.

High above the forest floor, activists constructed an intricate swinging platform made up of rope and plywood that swayed back and forth between two large conifer trees. Thirteen people swung from oversized hammocks supported by the makeshift web. If the trees or ropes were cut, these forest defenders would have fallen to their deaths. Many activists surrendered immediately upon the feds' arrival. But not all. Emma Murphy Ellis, who called herself "Pitch", wrapped a noose around her neck and threatened to commit suicide if the armed agents moved any closer. Ellis's tactic held the officers off for more than seven hours.

In response to the feds' interruption, thousands of protestors began to amass thirty miles away in Portland in front of the Forest Service's regional headquarters building. Tre Arrow was more than sympathetic to the Eagle Creek cause, gathering supplies and rallying support around the city. He often visited the resistance site, helping to build the structures that hung between two large conifer trees. Many activists deemed the site to be the spiritual nucleus of their movement. Like so many, Arrow was galvanized by the experience and joined the rally outside Forest Service headquarters to carry on the struggle against the logging of Eagle Creek. But the stagnant protest seemed to be going nowhere.

"Tre was saying, 'Man, something else has to happen,'" said Arrow's friend and fellow forest activist Samantha Waters. "I nodded my head, then turned away for a moment, and when I turned back, Tre was already halfway up the wall."

Perched on his ledge, Arrow became an immediate media sensation. News broadcasts and papers across the country told of his act, and the Forest Service was forced to make the next move. The agency had to decide how best to pursue the government's tenuous plan to reintroduce logging in the Mt. Hood forest.

"They raided our camps—the pods we had set up—and that's one reason I went on the building when I did, to protest the way they handled our activists out there," Arrow explained.

Comrades on the ground set up shop and passed a bullhorn and banners to Arrow who hung the signs below his feet for the world to see. From above the crowded sidewalk, Arrow articulated the concerns of many who opposed the logging. With every word, it seemed, more support flooded to the cause. Arrow spent hours on a cell phone talking to reporters, telling them what was happening to the forests he had grown to love.

After agreeing to abide by a court order, a weary Arrow finally rappelled down from his lofty post, telling the mob of supporters and passer-bys, "This is not over by a long shot. Everyone get on buildings! Everyone get to the woods! I love you!"

Arrow's spontaneous act of resistance was not only passionate, but articulate. He got his point across and brought more attention to the plight of Eagle Creek than all previous actions combined. He didn't have the luxury of media access or the backing of a big environmental group. He did not own a law degree or hire a public relations team craft his message. Arrow had only his rage against a corporate machine he saw destroying, not only the fragile ecosystem of Eagle Creek, but the vitality of the entire planet.

"There [are] just not enough activists, not enough public involvement to stop this yet. Even though we might save an area here or there, they're cutting everywhere. The result is there's less than 4% of our native forests remaining in national forests," Arrow said in an interview with Miriam Green not long after he came down from his ledge sit. "And on state land it's even worse. There's about 1% of native old growth forest left in Oregon. Everything has been slaughtered. The ecosystems are severely devastated and they give us these wicked clearcuts with stumps and debris."

Almost overnight, Tre Arrow became the Mick Jagger of the radical environmental movement. And he reveled in it.

***

The campus of Portland State University was bustling with left-wing co-eds in the fall of 2000. Many cut their teeth as young activists a year earlier when they hopped on buses and jammed into cars to race up the I-5 corridor to protest the World Trade Organization in Seattle. Some choked on pepper spray for the first time while others were arrested and brutalized by violent cops dressed in black stormtrooper gear. The smell of rebellion was still fresh in the air.

At the same time, the Earth Liberation Front (ELF) was dispatching regular communiqués through its unofficial spokesman, Craig Rosebraugh, who lived in Portland. Since 1997, the secret members of the ELF took credit for virtually all of the eco-arsons throughout the country. Typically, one or two days after ELF activists tagged the group's initials near one of their alleged fire-bombings, Rosebraugh would receive an anonymous statement that he, in turn, would submit as a press release to the local and national media outlets. Needless to say, Rosebraugh drew a lot of attention.

"While innocent life will never be harmed in any action we undertake, where it is necessary we will no longer hesitate to pick up the gun to implement justice and provide the needed protection for our planet that decades of legal battles, pleading, protest and economic sabotage have failed so drastically to achieve," one incendiary press release read after an arson in Pennsylvania. "The diverse efforts of this revolutionary force cannot be contained, and will only continue to intensify as we are brought face to face with the oppressor in inevitable, violent confrontation."

The aftershocks of the ELF's frequent actions reverberated throughout the Northwest, and the amorphous band of rebel enviros soon won many sympathizers up and down the west coast. Rosebraugh was their collective voice. With his wire-rimmed glasses, shaved head and punk rock persona, the scrawny vegan with a tattoo wrapped around his arm gave the ELF underground legitimacy—and more importantly, sex appeal. He was quoted frequently in the press defending the group's numerous actions. Aside from Tre Arrow, the sharp-tongued Rosebraugh was perhaps the most revered militant environmentalist on the West coast. And like Arrow, he was getting addicted to the spotlight.

"It seems that the ELF was formed to provide what some individuals considered to be a needed addition to the US environmental movement," writes Rosebraugh in his book, *Burning Rage of a Dying Planet*. "Using elements of guerrilla warfare, limited to property destruction, the first individuals conducting ELF actions in the United States had a most definite mission—to start a movement that could not be stopped."

If Rosebraugh and the fire-starters at ELF represented the militant wing of the radical environmental movement in the Northwest, Arrow and the Cascadia Forest Alliance were viewed as the acceptable alternative by many radicals. The philosophy Arrow espoused publicly was that of peace and non-violence and finding harmony with nature. He disavowed property damage and arson. Arrow's antics largely deemed legitimate in the public eye, especially when they were compared against the ELF's long rap sheet of burned buildings.

It was also a presidential election year and Ralph Nader's campaign for president was filling arenas across the country. Eddie Vedder, Susan Sarandon, Michael Moore and a host of celebrities were supporting Nader's campaign. So too was Tre Arrow. The Pacific Green Party (PGP) got word and approached Arrow to entice him to run for US Congress from the state's Third District against incumbent Democratic Representative, Earl Blumenauer. Arrow agreed, and from his stage the wild-eyed Green lambasted the Clinton administration for passing Option 9 and was quoted in *The Oregonian* as calling Al Gore's Portland stump speech on the environment, "A total lie."

Arrow was a star activist and fast became the public face of the PGP—an image not all members were willing to embrace. "When Tre Arrow ran for congress, the PGP was eagerly searching for candidates willing to run for public office. There was not, at that time, a thorough vetting process for examining the background and campaign strategy of individual candidates, nor was the party endowed with any significant financial resources," said Lloyd Marbet, a local Green Party activist, who himself has run for office several times. "Tre raised important forest issues that resonated with party members but he lacked political experience and I do not think he ran a well organized political campaign."

"So he climbed up on a ledge and crapped in a bucket," exclaimed another critic, "my 2-year-old can do that, but does that mean she's qualified to run for Congress?"

Yes, responded Portland-based lawyer and devoted Nader supporter, Greg Kafoury. "What Tre Arrow did was to risk his life (by climbing the Forest Service building) over a rather extended period of time for an issue he believed in. That's a pretty serious message, and in an age where politicians are processed like cheese, someone who is real carries a lot of weight," Kafoury told *Willamette Week* in an interview during Arrow's election bid. "If he was at any risk of winning, then you'd evaluate him differently. I'm saying this: When the party is in a position where its candidates are not just raising issues but need to be taken seriously as potential elected officials, then you go from dreamers to more practical and technically knowledgeable people."

He may not have been politically knowledgeable candidate but the only progressive that seemed as popular as Nader around Portland that year was Tre Arrow. Arrow's congressional campaign was run a lot like his Eagle Creek protests. He became a frequent agitator at local Democratic campaign events. When the band Everclear rocked a rally in support of Al Gore at PSU, there was Arrow swinging high above it all, gripping on to scaffolding with one hand and brandishing a bullhorn with the other, criticizing the Democrat's damaging environmental policies.

In the end, Arrow's run for Congress garnered more votes throughout Portland than did Ralph Nader's. He continued to make frequent visits to speak to local campuses and became an icon at PSU among the school's activist cliques, where he spoke at meetings put on by Students for Unity, among others. One of the PSU coeds Arrow befriended at the time, Jacob Sherman, would later prove to be an unfortunate acquaintance.

***

Sherman, a Portland native, was not unlike many of his cohorts. The shadows of the great forests he grew up beneath were dwindling, and the young college freshman knew exactly who the culprit was: corporations and their political allies. As the FBI would later argue, it was under the spell of one Tre Arrow that Jacob Sherman was seduced into radical environmentalism.

In the fall of 2000, Jacob Sherman became intensely involved in Ralph Nader's presidential campaign and was active in several progressive organizations on campus. Over the course of Sherman's first term at Portland State, he was drawn to issues ranging from a living-wage to the independence struggle of the Zapatistas in Chiapas. Sherman and Arrow became close. By winter quarter Sherman not only adopted a few of Arrow's granola routines, such as refusing to bathe and going barefoot, he also began mimicking his forms of protest.

In the Portland suburb of Clackamas, Sherman helped to lead a protest in February of 2001 against an old growth timber sale that was to take place in the Mt. Hood National Forest. Like the action Tre Arrow had carried out almost a year earlier, Sherman climbed to the top of the logging company's building and rallied the crowd that amassed below. "Sherman initially refused to come down from the roof," the FBI later wrote in a court affidavit, "but later agreed to cooperate with authorities in lieu of being arrested."

As the FBI and media outlets would later tell it, Sherman was under the persuasive sway of Tre Arrow. He was seen as an obedient pawn who followed Arrow into battle, which was ignited two months later at Ross Island Sand & Gravel in Southeast Portland. On the night of April 15, 2001, three of the company's rigs were destroyed by fires sparked from gas-filled milk jug bombs. Investigators later learned that Sherman sent Craig Rosebraugh an anonymous note a week later claiming responsibility, and blamed the company for "stealing soil from the earth." Rosebraugh released a press statement, claiming members of the ELF had been responsible.

***

In the fall of 2001, Tre Arrow and the Cascadia Forest Alliance turned their focus from Mt. Hood to the mossy rain forests of the Oregon coast, where the Acey Line timber sale, consisting of over 120 acres of some of the oldest trees in Oregon, was slated to be cut in what known as Gods Valley, nestled in the heart of the Tillamook State Forest.

"It is part of what little remains, on the coast, of an actually intact forest. Even though it was logged more than a century ago, it has naturally reseeded itself," Arrow explained at the time. "It is lush, it is biologically diverse and full of life, it's perfect habitat for wildlife. This is a rain forest. The forest floor is like a sponge ... The U.S. Forest Service and ODF (Oregon Department of Forestry) figure that most citizens don't care much if it's just trees being cut from public lands. Unfortunately, they're right, most people are too busy to pay attention to the complexities of forest management."

Over 2.5 million board feet of timber was purchased by Christian Futures Inc. of Springfield, Oregon for the meager sum of $400,000. Several conservation groups earlier in the year contested the plan, arguing that logging trees in Gods Valley would further endanger marbled murrelets (a seabird that nests only in old-growth forests) and northern spotted owls, both of which are federally listed as threatened species. Activists, including Arrow, descended on the area in hope of disrupting the logging operations.

Forest management on state lands in Oregon leaves little room for the public to weigh in and voice objections. The public is not allowed to comment on sales of state land to timber companies and there is no way to appeal them once they are in place. The Endangered Species Act, however, does apply to state land in Oregon, and most fights against such land deals challenged in the courts stem from these federal protections. But when those battles in the legal world fall short, forest activists take it upon themselves to stand up and defend what they rightly see as an environmental injustice.

On the morning of October 4, Arrow and his fellow members of Cascadia Forest Alliance and Hard Rain Alliance, came head to head with forest officials in Gods Valley to protest the Acey Line sale. In typical Arrow fashion, Tre taunted loggers and the ODF, leading them on a wild chase through the forest, climbing 80-feet up a tree to escape being caught. The reaction became a defining moment to save Gods Valley. Arrow remained high in the hemlock tree for two days where he was exposed to physical, emotional and physiological torment. "We're not sleepin', so you're not sleepin," yelled the men below. When fellow activists attempted to pass up food and water they were arrested immediately. The plan was to cut Arrow out of the tree or keep him awake so long that he would end up collapsing, plummeting to his death.

"A logger began to cut the lower branches of the tree I was in, working his way up the tree as he cut. I became seriously concerned about my ability to stay in the tree safely. When the logger was right below me with his chainsaw and I jumped to the next tree over. Once I was in that tree, the logger proceeded to cut the first tree into three sections, taking it completely to the ground," Arrow told *Alternatives* magazine shortly after the incident.

"They then made an announcement over their bullhorn that they were going to cut all the trees around me. I jumped into a third tree, the largest in that group of three, to try to protect it. At that point, the loggers proceeded to cut every tree within a thirty-foot radius around me, including trees only a few feet away from me. It was dangerous," he said. "That night, I tried to sleep but the activities of the men on the ground made it impossible. They'd call out 'Knock knock! Wake up! Wake up!' on their bullhorn and do the siren thing, and smash things against the tree … What resulted was exhaustion and sleep deprivation due to their deliberate tactics of keeping us activists awake day and night. Finally, at 2:00 a.m. on the morning of October 6th, I fell out of the tree I was in from roughly 100 feet height."

Arrow barely survived the fall. He suffered a fractured shoulder, severed pelvis, torn knee ligaments and broken ribs. His brain and internal organs were bleeding. His lung was pierced and collapsed. The forest officials did their best to kill Arrow, most likely in an attempt to teach his fellow activists a lesson, forcing them to retreat from Gods Valley. "We don't know where he started his fall," says Clatsop County Sheriff John Raichl, "but they heard the crashing. Even with the floodlights, it was dark.

One of the deputies is an emergency medical technician and started working on him. He is very, very lucky to be alive."

While they threatened a sleep-deprived, malnourished tree-hugger with the threat of violence, Arrow and his friends reciprocated only with defiance, not aggression. At one point during the tree-sit, a logger climbed up to coax him down when Arrow noticed that another official on the ground was pointing a rifle at him. He knew if he were to come down he was not going to be embraced with open arms.

"I am totally confident we did the right thing," Sheriff Raichl told *The Oregonian*. Oregon Governor John Kitzhaber wasn't so sure, and ordered an investigation into the matter while the logging continued. Arrow was charged with trespassing on public land and interfering with a forestry operation. After his weak body smashed on the ground, Arrow was rushed to the emergency room where he was put critical care.

As Arrow was nursing his injuries in a hospital bed, FBI agents were investigating an arson that took place six months prior. On the night of May 31, 2001, Jacob Sherman borrowed his mom's truck, told her he was going to run some errands and picked up Arrow along with two other fellow PSU students, Angie Cesario and Jeremy Rosenbloom. They headed to the timber town of Estacada, where the Eagle Creek logging contractor, Ray Schoppert, kept the company's logging trucks.

"Jake (Sherman) told [his girlfriend] that, on that same night, Jake, Jeremy and Angie went with Tre to a place where logging trucks were parked," government investigators would later assert. "Jake kept saying he didn't want to do it. Tre said they were here to do this and that's what they were going to do."

Sherman was boastful and told several girlfriends in brutal detail his version of the events that took place that night. As he told it, Cesario was the lookout and stayed in the truck, while Rosenbloom, Arrow and Sherman took eight gasoline-filled jugs and positioned them under the logging trucks. As Sherman lit one jug it flared up dramatically and scorched his eyebrows, hair and clothing. They then immediately left the scene, leaving four of the incendiary jugs unlit. The other four milk jugs ended up burning two trucks and one frontloader, causing a total of $100,000 in damage.

Sherman had not been an especially careful saboteur. The truck smelled of gasoline and he dumped his clothes in the trash bin when he returned that night at 2:00 am, asking his brother to tell his parents that he had returned home at 10:30 pm.

Sherman's father, Tim Sherman, who did not live with the family, contacted the FBI telling them he believed his son was involved in the arson. To this day it is unclear as to what prompted Tim to believe his son was involved. The day after his father phoned FBI, agents interviewed Sherman's parents and friends. But it is still uncertain if the FBI was also looking into Arrow's involvement at this time. Arrow wasn't hard to find during most of the investigation, from October to November he was essentially captive in Emanuel Hospital in Portland, healing his battle wounds from his fall in Gods Valley.

During FBI questioning, Sherman buckled and pegged Arrow as the ringleader, who along with Sherman allegedly burned the Ross Island Gravel trucks. In July 2002, Arrow, Sherman, Rosenbloom and Cesario where indicted for their alleged participation in the firebombing in Estacada. But Arrow somehow escaped the FBI's Joint Terrorism Task Force dragnet, despite the fact that his lawyer Stu Sugarman was helping Arrow with civil lawsuits in challenging the Gods Valley incident and was arranging to have his client appear in court at the same time.

A trial and conviction could have meant 30 years in prison. The defendants were strong-armed into striking plea deals, all eventually pointing the finger at Tre Arrow to reduce their sentences. This was a departure from earlier testimonies, when both Cesario and Rosenbloom did not name Arrow as the instigator, but Jake Sherman.

Rumors floated through activist circles that Arrow was in fact an agent provocateur who infiltrated the group and passed back information to the feds. This, some claimed, was why he was not been captured early on. But Arrow fled across the country. The FBI believed Arrow might have been involved in many ELF actions from Colorado to Pennsylvania. But his friends at Cascadia Forest Alliance didn't buy it. All of the activists who were called before the Grand Jury to indict Arrow pled the Fifth Amendment, refusing to turn on their friend and fellow activist.

In the end, the Schoppert fire in Estacada proved to be a huge boost for the plight of Eagle Creek. Timber sales in the forest began to unravel immediately after the flames torched the logging trucks, with several timber outfits pulling out of their deals. The arsons seemed to have forced the companies to reconsider logging in an area that was so contentious, exactly the outcome many active in the struggle were hoping for.

Radical environmentalism had been successful, at least for the moment, a fact not many people inside or outside of the movement were willing to admit. While the media may portray radical activists that turn to violence to defend the Earth as deranged psychopaths, there is an underlying ethic that drives their actions. Radical environmentalists believe the culture and economic system are inherently exploitative and corrupt. They believe we are making far too many intrusions on the natural world and must stop at once. Focusing their efforts to stop logging on public lands is only one tactic in the greater struggle to bring human existence back into balance with the natural order.

***

Now Tre was no longer dangling from a limb to save a tree; he was on the lam to avoid being imprisoned. On October 18, 2002, Jake Sherman was indicted on four counts, including the fires at Ross Island Sand & Gravel. Since Sherman claimed Arrow was involved, the charges against the AWOL environmentalist immediately doubled. Arrow's parents hadn't heard from him in months, few friends admitted to having correspondence. It was clear Arrow, now a fugitive, was trying to avoid arrest. His story appeared on *America's Most Wanted* and the FBI was confident their man would come out of hiding at any moment.

It wasn't until March 13, 2004 that the FBI learned exactly where Tre Arrow was. He hadn't turned himself in, but he was in handcuffs. Arrow had been caught stealing bolt-cutters from a hardware store in Victoria, British Columbia. He had been on the run for 19 months. "The only thing I was going to use the bolt-cutters for was to 'liberate,' as we call it, dumpsters [and share the waste]."

Canadian officials ran Arrow's prints and fast became aware that he was a wanted man in the States. Arrow immediately began to fight extradition, as he felt that he would not receive a fair trial in the paranoid and punitive post-9/11 political climate. "'The media has already convicted me not just of the crimes, but of eco-terrorism," Arrow told *Willamette Week* from his jail cell. "They don't bother to use the word 'alleged' or 'accused,' just flat-out 'terrorist' with my name attached."

He outright denied involvement in any firebombings or affiliation with the ELF. "I emphatically express that I am not involved in the ELF and never have been. And at the same time, I don't condemn the activists that are involved in the ELF for the actions they engage in," he said. "[People who know me] know I don't burn anything. The ELF, it has its place. I recognize it does have an impact. It's very telling that the FBI regards the ELF as a bigger threat than the white supremacist groups."

Meanwhile several of Arrow's alleged associates were already serving time. From his small cell Arrow essentially embarked on a protest-fast, as a strict raw vegan diet was continuously denied. He lost nearly 40 pounds, and many were concerned about his deteriorating health. Arrow approached a Canadian immigration panel seeking to be awarded refugee status because he and his lawyers claimed he'd already been labeled guilty by the media and would not receive a fair trial. The motion was denied.

Arrow spent much of his time fleeing the FBI by roaming around Canada. "When he showed up in Halifax, Arrow said he had an aunt living just outside the city. He came from the West Coast and didn't talk much about his past. I got to know him as Josh Rivers, the ever-so-vegan couch surfer who defended Mother Earth," writes Chris Arsenault in *This Magazine*. "He spent nights tearing around the city on a borrowed bicycle to scavenge paper from recycling bins so we wouldn't have to print leaflets on 'dead-tree bleached sheets' … [Some] respected and admired him, while others found him off-the-wall if not downright offensive … He was kind and diligent, yet overzealous and a little hot-headed; passionate and contradictory. While incarcerated, he refuses cooked food, in part because of the fossil fuels used in cooking. Yet he chomps bananas shipped from Latin America at a far greater environmental (and social) cost. Lots of fury, a little short on thought."

Eventually Arrow stopped fighting extradition and accepted a plea agreement, stating he had been involved in both the Ross Island and Schoppert arsons. On August 12, 2008 Arrow was sentenced to 78 months in federal prison, but was given credit for the time he had already served in Canada. Arrow would walk free in four years. He could have faced 40 years in prison and been forced to pay a fine of $500,000.

"Some may look at this non-cooperation plea agreement as a victory. Some may see it as a defeat. It's really neither! It's simply another step in this journey as i (sic) walk my path of conscience," decried Tre Arrow in a message to his supporters after he agreed to the plea deal. "You see, it's never been about me. From before the days of the ledge-sit, right thru 'til today, this has been and will always be about the commitment to leave our Earth Mother in a healthier, more beautiful state then when i (sic) arrived. This is about taking back our power from the government and corporate entities that would have us believe that monetary wealth and the acquisition of material objects is more important than the health of the planet."

– August, 28, 2009

ON THE FRONT LINES OF THE CLIMATE CHANGE MOVEMENT: MIKE ROSELLE DRAWS A LINE

By Jeffrey St. Clair and Joshua Frank

The beard is graying. The hair is clipped military-short. He is a large man, oddly shaped, like a cross between a grizzly and a javelina. It's Roselle, of course, Mike Roselle—the outside agitator. He and a fellow activist have just spread an anti-coal banner in front of a growling bulldozer in West Virginia on a cold February morning in 2009. He's in this icy and unforgiving land to oppose a brutal mining operation and will soon be arrested for trespassing. Massey Energy, the target of Roselle's protest, is the fourth largest coal extractor in the United States, mining nearly 40 million tons of coal in Kentucky, West Virginia and Tennessee each year.

The arrest was nothing new for Roselle, who cut his teeth in direct action environmental campaigns decades earlier as a co-founder of Earth First!, a top campaigner for Greenpeace US and later as the wit behind the tenacious Ruckus Society. Unlike most mainstream environmentalists, you are not likely to see Roselle sporting a suit and lobbying Washington insiders on the intricacies of mining laws—you are more apt to see this self-proclaimed lowbagger (one who lives light on the land, works to protect it and has few possessions to show for their hard work) engaged in direct, but nonviolent, confrontations with the forces of industrialization, using tactics honed during the Civil Rights Movement of the 1950s and 1960s. And his dissent in West Virginia is more than justified.

The mountaintops of the Appalachia region, from Tennessee up to the heart of West Virginia, are being ravaged by the coal industry—an industry that cares little about the welfare of communities or the land that it is chewing up and spitting out with its grotesque mining operations.

The debris from the mining pits, often 500 feet deep, produce toxic waste that is then dumped in nearby valleys, polluting rivers and poisoning local communities downstream. Currently, no state or federal agencies are tracking the cumulative effect of the aptly named "mountaintop removal," where entire peaks are being blown apart with explosives, only to expose tiny seams of the precious black rock.

On December 22, 2008, a coal slurry impoundment at the Tennessee Valley Authority's Kingston coal fired power plant in Harriman, Tennessee, spilled more than 500 million gallons of toxic coal ash into the Tennessee River. The epic spill was over 40 times larger than the Exxon Valdez in Alaska. Approximately 525 million gallons of black coal ash flowed into tributaries of the murky Tennessee River—the water supply for Chattanooga and millions of people living downstream in the states of Alabama and neighboring Kentucky. The true costs—environmental and social—of the spill are still not known.

As a result of the ongoing destruction of this forgotten region of Appalachia, Roselle and others affiliated with his latest group, Climate Ground Zero, have set up shop and vow not to end their actions until this mining practice has been outlawed. But the West Virginia media, long in the pockets of Big Coal, has not depicted Roselle as a nonviolent activist who has been pushed to act because his conscience has forced him to. On the contrary, Roselle has been portrayed as a potential eco-terrorist and a threat, not only to jobs in the region, but to human life as well.

"A quick search of Roselle's name on the internet produces pages of accusations that he will go to any length for his cause, vandalism that could put lives in danger," reported WSAZ-TV on February 11, 2009.

Fox affiliate WCHS-TV8 went even further in a story they aired on the same date stating, "Roselle has been called an 'eco-terrorist' by some because of his tactics. He's someone we think you should know about. Tomorrow night don't miss the 'Roselle Report' when we'll take a closer look at how this man's radical methods of protest may put lives at stake in West Virginia."

Being labeled a terrorist isn't a new accusation for Roselle, who has been at the forefront of dozens of nonviolent direct action environmental campaigns throughout the past several decades. "I have been arrested over forty times in twenty states," Roselle remembers with a smirk. "My longest time in jail is four months in South Dakota for an action on Mt. Rushmore against acid rain."

Even anti-environmentalist Ron Arnold, who coined the term eco-terrorist in *Reason* magazine in the early 1980s, came out with a statement in opposition to Roselle's terrorist label.

"I don't agree with him, but he's no terrorist. I've covered Roselle since 1995 and even devoted dozens of pages to his protest activities in my 1997 book *EcoTerror: The Violent Agenda to Save Nature*," said Arnold. "I covered his actions to distinguish between radicals and terrorists. I say he's a radical environmentalist, not an eco-terrorist. It's not a crime to be a radical and Roselle has never been charged with any violent crime."

Despite Arnold's clear distinction between terrorism and environmentalism, western states like Idaho and Oregon seem to disagree.

***

Saving Idaho's wilderness had come to this: Two militant greens standing in the middle of an isolated, snow-crusted road in a place where machines should never be, bracing their bodies against a train of logging trucks, snowmobiles and Forest Service jeeps groaning at the gate, demanding entry, willingly subjecting themselves to arrest by Idaho troopers armed with automatic weapons, Billy clubs and a draconian and subconstitutional new law. All in a last-gasp attempt to halt a vastly destructive timber sale in the heart of the nation's largest roadless area called Cove/Mallard, a timber sale two federal judges already found to be a brazen assault on our national environmental laws.

Charged with felony conspiracy to commit a misdemeanor, Roselle and Tom Fullum, of the Native Forest Network, faced a possible five-year prison terms and $50,000 fines under Idaho's so-called Earth First! Statute—a law geared to smother popular dissent against the transgressions of multinational timber companies by slamming the jailhouse door on anyone bold enough to bodily protest logging on federal lands in the Potato State. The bill was signed into law in 1993 by then-Gov. Cecil Andrus, a noted liberal who called the Cove/Mallard protesters "just a bunch of kooks."

The 90,000-acre Cove/Mallard roadless area is a biological cradle in the mountains, a rolling landscape of ponderosa pine forests, meandering streams and wet meadows that serve as a critical biological and migration corridor between the Salmon River and the high country of the Gospel Hump and Selway Mountains. One of the most wild places in the lower 48, its brisk streams are home to steelhead, Chinook salmon, bull trout, rainbow trout and cutthroat, while the broad meadows harbor some of the best elk country in the Northern Rockies. Bighorn sheep and mountain goats inhabit the tall mountains and the entire area is a key part of the Central Idaho grizzly bear and gray wolf recovery areas. In fact, over the past ten years, the Fish and Wildlife Service has documented numerous confirmed wolf sightings in the Cove/Mallard roadless area.

Federal and state governments have long targeted the civil rights of environmentalists. In the mid-1980s, swaths of new laws were passed that targeted the acts of direct, action-oriented, environmental protests. The laws followed a tree spike incident in Sonoma County, California, during the height of the battles to save the ancient redwood forests. As a worker thrust his blade into the trunk of a mighty tree, the blade hit a spike, snapped and flung back only to strike the logger. The media and logging industry called it eco-terrorism. But it wasn't an environmentalist that hammered that spike into the tree; it was a furious local right-wing landowner who had no part in the protests to end logging of the redwoods in the state. He was just pissed it was happening in his own backyard. Nonetheless, the tree spiking opened up attacks by the media, treating the incident as legitimate terrorism. The timber behemoths lobbied hard and the result was a series of laws that were meant to deter activists from targeting the logging industry in any way in any form.

The problem with most of these laws is that they do not decipher between acts of civil disobedience and vandalism. There is no line drawn, for example, between property damage like arson and chaining oneself to a logging truck. States across the West followed California's and Oregon's lead, making it a crime to hinder or delay any timber sale on public or private land. Activists that shut down logging operations directly, even by nonviolent means, were soon being deemed eco-terrorists, and not only by the media, but by the state laws themselves.

"Some of these laws, like the Earth First! Statute, made it a felony to conspire to or advocate any of those actions," recalled Roselle. "During debates on the House floor, outraged legislators said the law was intended to apply to professional radical environmentalists who recruited innocent kids from college campuses, and sent them off to block legal-logging operations, and take food out of the mouths of working families. Imagine!"

The Noble timber sale was one of nine big timber sales slated for the Cove/Mallard. These sales called for 200 different clear-cuts, the logging of 81 million board feet of timber and the construction of 145 miles of new logging roads. The Cove/Mallard timber sale planned to leave behind only an empty infrastructure: its web of roads a lethal impediment to the migration of wolves and elk, its eroding swaths of bare land quietly smothering salmon and trout.

The evidence of an imminent ecological collapse of Idaho's river systems in the area is overwhelming. In one of America's wildest state, more than 70 percent of the streams are out of compliance with the standards of the Clean Water Act, dozens of stocks of salmon gasp along with the bull trout at the brink of extinction. This means that every additional clearcut or mine gouged into these watersheds creates a necrotic wound in the fragile ecosystem. This was the emergency situation to which federal Judge David Ezra responded with an injunction to halt the logging.

Of course, the predictable backlash swiftly erupted in rural Idaho when news of the injunction was leaked to local timber contractors, ranchers and mining companies by the Forest Service. Local papers played up the inevitable chest beating by a mongrel assortment of tree cutters, ranch hands and placer miners from towns with names like Challis, Dixie and Kamiah. Then came the apocalyptic assessments of the ruling by mega-corporations such as Boise/Cascade, Potlatch and Hecla Mining: Mills and mines will be closed, they warned; thousands will be thrown out of work; bars will run dry and already impoverished communities will be driven deeper into destitution. Environmentalists and not greed were to blame.

The injunction also became a pretext for yet another round of vituperative cant from Idaho's reactionary Congressional delegation against outside agitators like the hippie Roselle. On the floor of the Senate, Dirk Kempthorne (who would later become Idaho's governor and then interior secretary under Bush the Younger) bellowed that he would seek Congressional action to shred the injunction and "the ill-conceived laws it was based on." Meanwhile, Rep. Helen "Call-Me-Congressman" Chenoweth denounced the injunction as the work of "animal worshipping nature cults." And the stentorious Larry Craig, the ex-senator with the wide stance, amplified the volume of his "forest health" crusade—a cruel hoax on the public in which the last roadless forests in the West will be stripped of the meager protection provided them by current environmental laws and opened to indiscriminate chainsaw surgery in the name of medicating the ecosystem.

The response to Idaho's Earth First! law was predictable said Roselle, "We went to a bunch of college campuses … we intended to recruit a bunch of new students to block, impede, halt, obstruct, and otherwise obliterate logging in the Cove/Mallard Timber Sale. We continued to block the road until the US Forest Service was halted, impeded, blocked and obliterated in Federal court. It turned out that the logging in Cove/Mallard never was legal after all."

Perhaps surprisingly, Idaho's anti-environmentalist statues aren't the worst you'll find out here in the Northwest. In fact, the neighboring state of Oregon has pushed the envelope so far that home invasions, felony charges and police brutality have become the norm, not the exception, to how law enforcement reacts to environmental campaigners. And like Idaho's egregious Earth First! law, Roselle is also at the center of Oregon's attempt to paint environmental civil disobedience as eco-terrorism.

***

It was during the State legislative session of 1999 when the Oregon Cattlemen's Association and the Oregon timber industry joined forces to lobby their allies at the capital in Salem to pass special criminal legislation, worthy of a felony charge, for any individual or group that interfered with business operations. Entitled "Interference with Agricultural Operations," (Ag-Ops law) the new statues prohibited any activist, sans union or labor disputers, that knowingly or intentionally "obstructs, impairs or hinders or attempts to obstruct, impair or hinder agricultural operations."

Call it Oregon's version of Idaho's Earth First! law, or at least its latest incarnation, and like Idaho's statute, Mike Roselle found himself in the middle of the liberal state's crackdown on pesky enviros.

In March of 2005, activists traveled to Josephine County, Oregon, near the quiet town of Ashland, to protest what they believed to be illegal logging operations. Like good direct action environmentalists of old, they blocked public roads that led to the cut in the Siskiyou National Forest where the Biscuit timber sale was taking place. The logging operations were being contracted by the United States Forest Service (USFS) to private timber outfits that were looking to cash in on a rather dismal occupation.

Like the untouched forests of Idaho, the Siskiyou National Forest is one of the most biologically diverse landscapes in the continental United States. It houses five nationally designated wild and scenic rivers, as well as one of the healthiest stocks of native salmon in the country. The plan introduced by the USFS included extensive logging in 12 roadless areas, which covered well over 12,000 acres of taxpayer-managed land.

In all, the USFS placed 1900 acres of public land on the auction block and, of those, 1160 were mapped out for demolition. The venture, titled the "Biscuit Fire Recovery Project," was the largest forest service sale in US history. In all, almost 30 square miles of federal land was handed over to chainsaw-happy timber barons.

Not surprisingly, the Forest Service wanted onlookers to believe these types of logging operations are for "restoration" purposes only, not profit, as this patch of old trees in the Siskiyous fell victim to massive natural wild fires in the summer of 2002. During a meeting among timber, conservation and USFS officials on July 26, 2006, over lawsuits the groups had filed regarding the Biscuit sales, eco-activists were simultaneously erecting a 75-foot tall tree platform and a large road blockade in hopes of halting access to "Indi," the first salvage sale site set for cutting by the beginning of August.

"Logging is not restoration," said activist Kay Pittwald as she hung from her suspended platform high above the soggy forest floor. "The future of this remote area is healthy salmon, clean water and a thriving tourist economy. It is not a place for an out-of-country timber grab to ship wood products to Asia."

US District Judge Michael Hogan, who handled the lawsuits, was of little comfort to the conservationists that attempted to stop the logging in the courts. Indeed, Hogan, one of the most conservative federal judges in the Ninth Circuit, has a long history of siding with extractive industries (and later being overruled on appeal). In 2001, he called for the delisting of threatened Coho salmon, and in 2002 he allowed logging in Montana's Bitterroot National Forest to proceed after talks between Big Greens and industry officials.

Forest fires, like the one in the Siskiyou National Forest, became stigmatized only when forests began to be viewed as a commercial resource rather than an obstacle to settlement. Fire suppression became an obsession only after the big timber giants laid claim to the vast forests of the Pacific Northwest. Companies like Weyerhaeuser and Georgia-Pacific were loath to see their holdings go up in flames, so they arm twisted Congress into pouring millions of dollars into fire-fighting programs. The Forest Service was only too happy to oblige because fire suppression was a sure way to pad their budget.

In effect, the Forest Service's fire suppression programs (and similar operations by state and local governments) have acted as little more than federally-funded, fire insurance policies for the big timber companies, an ongoing corporate bailout that has totaled tens of billions of dollars and shows no sign of slowing down, even under President Obama. There's an old saying that the Forest Service fights fires by throwing money at them. And the more money it spends, the more money it gets from Congress. Sadly, the Biscuit Fire Recovery Project was no different.

"Their world-view dictates that 'healthy forests' equal tree farms," said George Sexton, who worked as the Conservation Director for the Klamath-Siskiyou Wildlands Center at the time. "Industry wanted a train wreck at Biscuit."

In the eyes of the activists who blocked the logging road that March afternoon in 2005, they had been successful. Logging was halted for the moment. But when logging operations stop, law enforcement officers are dispatched to get the chainsaws running again and, in order to do so, activists are arrested and charged, often with trespassing (on private lands) or disorderly conduct. But in this case, with a new law in their arsenal, the Biscuit protesters, Roselle included, were charged with disrupting logging operations, a potential felony. For those arrested, the court imposed sentences of two to four days in custody, additional fines and probation for 18 months.

"[One] problem with [the Ag-Ops law] is that it does not forbid 'hindering' an agricultural operation to the point of cessation, property damage, or any other tangible point," wrote Lauren C. Regan and Misha J. Dunlap of the Civil Liberties Defense Center in their appeal brief, which claimed the law used to sentence the defendants was unconstitutional. "Instead, it leaves the person conducting the 'agricultural operation' free to decide when a group of people shall be dispersed and/or arrested. The point at which there is harm (or 'hindrance') under [the law] is not readily identifiable and, in fact, reaches to protected conduct of peaceable assembly at sites of agricultural operations. This clearly violates Article I, section 26 of the Oregon Constitution. The constitutional right to publicly assemble in a public forum cannot be proscribed by a statute that is intended to protect commercial interests. Commercial interests do not trump fundamental constitutional rights."

The lawyers also argued in their brief that the law is aimed at the content of one's speech and targets that speech based on the content. In the context of the statute used, it does not prohibit all speech aimed at disrupting agricultural operations, but only certain types of speech—that which does not relate to labor protests.

On October 28, 2009, the Oregon Supreme Court ruled in favor of the Biscuit protesters, striking down the Ag-Ops Law as unconstitutional. The court ruled that the law unfairly singled out environmental demonstrators as a separate class, in violation of the equal protection clause. Labor protests, for example, were specifically excluded from the law.

"The overwhelming majority of people prosecuted under the law were environmentalists," said Dan Kruse, an attorney for the protesters.

***

Back in West Virginia, Mike Roselle sat back and conducted one of his many radio interviews by telephone. Empty beer cans were piled up in the kitchen. Roselle's rental home has become the headquarters for Climate Ground Zero. In this particular interview, Roselle spelled out his defense of the tree sitters who are attempting to halt Massey Energy's mining operations by setting up camp in their blast zone. It was an unusually busy summer for Roselle, as hundreds of boisterous activists descended on West Virginia to voice their objections to mountaintop removal. The fight has heated up, so much so that even Roselle is surprised at the grassroots outpouring. There have been dozens of arrests and several major protest actions. Yet, Roselle is still sympathetic to the workers' concerns and shrugs off the negative media coverage as par for the course.

"Those who are not involved in the mining industry are almost unanimously opposed to it. And even a lot of the folks who work for Massey Energy are not really happy with what they're doing, but they're kind of—because this is one of the poorest states in the country, they don't have many choices. There are no other jobs," Mike Roselle told Amy Goodman on Democracy Now! in April 2009. "I don't think there's really that much support throughout West Virginia for destroying the mountains. There is support, I think, for supporting the coal industry ... the best way to maintain coal jobs in West Virginia is to end mountaintop removal immediately, because it employs a lot less people than underground mining. Underground mining is a lot less destructive to the environment, and it could be even less so if more regulations were enforced and new ones put in place."

So, his fight to save the mountains of Appalachia continues. Laws may attempt to deter Mike Roselle as accusations of terrorism attempt to tarnish his reputation. Yet, he soldiers onward, and will do so until he sees an end to mountaintop removal. In the meantime, however, you can expect Massey Energy, in conjunction with Democratic Sen. Jay Rockefeller of West Virginia, who receives hundreds of thousands of dollars from the coal industry in his state, to do their best to outlaw the actions taken by Roselle's Climate Ground Zero campaigners. Even if it means trampling over their civil rights in the process.

– February 17, 2010

THE FBI'S "OPERATION BACKFIRE" AND THE CASE OF BRIANA WATERS

By Jeffrey St. Clair and Joshua Frank

Smoke billowed as a wing of the University of Washington's Center of Urban Horticulture burned in the early morning hours of Monday, May 21, 2001. It was not the result of a science experiment gone awry—it was arson.

Situated under a tree, safe from the heat of the blazing inferno, were boxes of little snakes stacked neatly on top of one another, prompting former UW researcher Valerie Easton to wonder "who would torch 20 years of research and plant and book collections, yet take the time to save a couple of pet snakes?" They must have been amateurs she thought, not entirely certain why anyone would want to burn the research center to the ground.

The group of five men and women, associated with the covert Earth Liberation Front (ELF), broke into the building through a window, connected a digital timer to a 9-volt battery, which in turn was hooked up to an igniter that was positioned to spark tubs filled with gasoline. When the timer went off the igniter clicked and the gasoline blew. The result was a small, yet fierce explosion that spread fast through the University's modern science facility.

The flames, first spotted by campus security, were so intense that it took fire-fighters two hours to quell, but the damage was done. UW claimed over $3 million in losses. Botany labs burned and decades of scientific research was lost. Investigators had no leads and only suspicions of who was behind the mysterious arson.

Five days after the fire investigators got their first tip in the form of a press release dispatched by Craig Rosebraugh in Portland, which claimed the ELF was behind the attack. The target was

UW professor Toby Bradshaw, who received funding from the timber industry to develop fast-growing cross-pollinated poplar trees, which are used to produce paper and lumber products. The genes Bradshaw identified through trial and error cross-pollination experiments were used by Oregon State University professor Steve Strauss who took the genes, often resistant to specific diseases, and inserted them into poplar seeds creating genetically engineered (GE) organisms. Bradshaw in turn grew these poplar trees in greenhouses at UW.

Many environmentalists believe GE trees are, as the ELF's communiqué stated, "an ecological nightmare." The development of GE applications in nature, in the absence of environmental safeguards, is a recipe for disaster. Wild trees can interbreed with GE trees causing problems scientists can only speculate about. Genes from GE poplar trees, for example, are free, just like pollen or seeds that blow with the wind and can invade forests, spreading fast and disrupting the genetic diversity that allows forest ecology to evolve naturally over time.

The ELF activists targeted Professor Bradshaw's lab for this reason, but they missed their mark. The fire did not damage the majority of Bradshaw's actual scientific research. He made backups of all of his work, which was previously targeted by anti-GE activists during the WTO protests in 1999. Bradshaw was not happy about being on placed on the ELF's shitlist.

"It's very hard to have a discussion with [these types of environmentalists]. The most vocal critics don't know very much about the science," Bradshaw publicly bemoaned. "They don't have the ability to distinguish good science from bad science or even non-science. They just don't have the background … In order to support (the) ELF, you have to espouse terrorism as a tactic which after Sept. 11, I think is pretty untenable."

And just like that the radical environmentalists who besieged Bradshaw's work at UW were deemed a terrorist threat even though they were meticulous in the execution of their act, making sure nobody would be injured. Their target was property, not human life. They did their homework, ensuring that janitors were not on duty that night, and despite what the mainstream media reported about Bradshaw's research, they knew exactly what type of science the professor was practicing and where his research funds originated.

"[These people are] anti-intellectual bigots incapable of making a reasoned argument in a public forum, but capable only of throwing a firebomb in the dead of night," Bradshaw wrote in a sternly worded opinion piece for the *Seattle Post-Intelligencer* shortly after the incident.

The angry professor remained undeterred, but it was clear the ELF act had struck a nerve.

***

The UW research facility was just one in a string of attacks by the nebulous group, and as a result in 2004 the FBI merged seven of its on-going investigations into "Operation Backfire" in an attempt to round up the eco-bandits who allegedly struck a Vail ski resort, a horse slaughterhouse, and even an SUV dealership.

"Investigating and preventing animal rights and environmental extremism is one of the FBI's highest domestic terrorism priorities," said then-FBI Director Robert Mueller. "We are committed to working with our partners to disrupt and dismantle these movements, to protect our fellow citizens, and to bring to justice those who commit crime and terrorism in the name of animal rights or environmental issues."

Until the FBI coordinated efforts with local authorities and other agencies, they didn't have much to work with in regard to the UW fire. No real evidence was left behind, and any that did exist went up in smoke. They needed someone on the inside to come forward, who would name names and point fingers. The FBI found the informant they needed in late spring 2003, heroin addict Jacob Ferguson.

Ferguson was a tattooed strung out drifter who traveled across the country, apparently leaving nothing but ashes behind. He admitted to over a dozen arsons, mostly in Oregon where he spent the majority of his time. He claimed to know almost every member of the ELF, and became the FBI's go-to guy in amassing hours upon hours of tape recordings of conversations he had with his friends. As a drug abuser, Ferguson likely came forward ready to tell all, or make up stories, in order to cash in the reward of $50,000 the FBI announced in May of 2004 that they would offer anyone with information about the UW blaze.

Ferguson's drug use may have made him vulnerable to the FBI's persuasive ways, and money is usually a great impetus for junkies with heroin habits. Over the course of almost two years Ferguson was showing up in places he had not been seen before. He'd been sighted at environmental law conferences and Earth First! outings, events he avoided in the past, likely wired the entire time, recording conversations that had nothing to do with the FBI investigation.

When news broke in late December 2005 that Ferguson was a "government witness", anger spread like an ELF fire across the Pacific Northwest environmental community. Acquaintances turned to enemies, and some even left responses about their former ally on Portland's Independent Media webpage in contempt for his actions.

"The entire [investigation] ... seems to rest on the words, actions and credibility of this one man, a man we now learn has lived a double life. In a community where there is consensus distrust, even disgust for the federal government and especially its law enforcement operatives, Jake pretended he was one of us. He was and is one of them," commented a poster named Mongoose. "How long has Jake been a federal narc? The reason this issue is critical turns on the fact that some of the alleged arsons may actually have been planned or implemented with federal law enforcement help. That could well constitute entrapment."

It wasn't long after Ferguson turned informant that the FBI began rapping on doors of environmental activists across the country, picking up where Ferguson left off. He was leading them straight to his friends, people who welcomed him into their homes and around their dinner tables. It seemed as if Ferguson would do whatever it took to keep himself out of prison, even if that meant losing those people who were closest to him.

The chase started by Ferguson eventually led to the front stoop of a wholesome violin teacher living in Berkeley, California in 2004. Briana Waters, 32 at the time, was not someone you'd peg for a terrorist. She simply didn't look the type. A strung out Ferguson, on the other hand, with a pentagram tattoo sprawled across his balding head, fit the stereotypical profile a bit better. He looked like an arsonist. Waters looked like a young mother, which she was.

Raised in suburban Philadelphia, Waters came from an upper-middle class household and left her family behind to attend college at Evergreen State College in Olympia, Washington in the late 1990s. Evergreen is a bastion of progressive activism and has a strong reputation for turning out radical students, with the list including Rachel Corrie who lost her life while standing up to an Israeli Defense Force bulldozer in an attempt a spare a Palestinian home from demolition in 2003. Waters and Corrie were Evergreen students at the same time, and like Corrie, Waters was a committed, well-known activist on campus.

Waters headed up the animal rights group at Evergreen and was committed to naturalist education, leading hikes through the nearby forests on weekends teaching people about the native flora. By her senior year Waters was becoming a seasoned environmental activist, cutting her teeth as a tree-sitter in an effort to stop the logging of Watch Mountain, an old-growth preserve in the Cascade Mountain range in Washington.

Tree-sitting was a frequent tactic of environmentalists in Oregon and even British Columbia, but Washington state was not accustomed to this type of direct action:

"These tree-sitters, calling themselves the Cascadia Defense Network, don't like the government's plan to give 25 square miles of heavily forested mountain land on the west slope of the Cascades to the timber company in exchange for 75 square miles of prime hiking land near Snoqualmie Pass," reported Robert McClure for the *Seattle Post-Intelligencer* in August 1999. "Loggers for generations, many local residents have stood by as the local mill closed and timber companies began shipping timber overseas for processing. Like the protesters, they are not happy with big timber companies."

Waters and her green comrades were not only confronting the logging industry and the government, they were also tossing dirt in the face of big environmental groups in Seattle who signed off on the deal let Plum Creek Timber Co. log Watch Mountain, near the small town of Randle, Washington. It may have been Waters' first real brush up with the radicals of the Northwest environmental movement, one that would later be used to discredit her true intentions.

"We just want to sit up there in those trees and be a spectacle for you," fellow activist Tim Ream told local Washington residents about the protest his group organized. "We're going to sit up there until there are chainsaws buzzing all around us and they take us to jail. And we're not going to make it easy for them."

The direct action worked, after five long months the Cascadia Defense Network was victorious and Waters caught the victory on film for his senior project at Evergreen. Her heartfelt footage documented the struggle with the timber barons as well as friendly relationship between the activists and the local townsfolk. Over 28,000 acres of prime wilderness was ultimately saved and the public land was never handed over to Plum Creek Timber.

***

The FBI was out to track down the perpetrators of the UW fire and they were more than ready to use the testimony provided by cooperating witnesses to do so. Two of the government's key informants in the UW case were 31 year-old Lacey Phillabaum, a former editor of *Earth First! Journal*, and Jennifer Kolar, 33, a millionaire yacht enthusiast with a master's degree in astrophysics. In order to shorten their own sentences, Kolar and Phillabaum agreed to testify against Waters, claiming she was the lookout for the arson and borrowed a car to drive to the campus that night. They even insisted Waters lived on the property where the explosive device was assembled by her boyfriend at the time,, Justin Solondz.

On February 11, 2008 at Western U.S. District in Tacoma, Washington, the government's case against Briana Waters began with U.S. District Judge Franklin D. Burgess presiding. The location of the trial was moved from Seattle, as prosecutors believed she'd have a less sympathetic jury outside the Emerald City. The jury was selected during the first day and at 9:00am the on February 12 the courtroom theatre began, with a packed room full of Waters' friends, family, and supporters.

The prosecution was led by Assistant United States Attorney Andrew Friedman and First Assistant United States Attorney Mark Bartlett. The duo's opening remarks to the jury painted Waters as a dangerous environmental extremist who was willing to do whatever it took to terrorize their target, Professor Toby Bradshaw.

"What the defendant and her accomplices did that night was wrong in every way," Friedman told the 12-person jury as he described Waters as the lookout that night. "… If there was one building in Seattle that helped the environment, it was probably the Center for Urban Horticulture. They plotted [their attack] for weeks and built complicated firebombs at a house the defendant rented," Friedman continued. "She had her cousin rent a car to use in the action and they drove it to Seattle, ate dinner, drove to the Urban Horticulture building, near a residential area, parked on a hill in the residential neighborhood a block away from the building. Waters stayed in the bushes with a radio while the others broke into an office [and planted the firebomb]."

The defense team, made up of attorneys Neil Fox and Robert Bloom, claimed the federal prosecutors were barking up the wrong tree and the hunt for the real perpetrators led them to an innocent woman. They argued that the evidence was simply not there to support the prosecutor's claims.

"Not only has Briana Waters pleaded not guilty, she is not guilty ... She is completely innocent, not involved in this or any other arson. The government's proof is what is on trial," Bloom asserted to the jury. "The government must prove beyond a reasonable doubt ... Ms. Waters is innocent not because of some technicality, but because she was not involved with this group of people in any arson, in any discussion of arson ... that's not what happened."

While prosecutors seemed to draw on guilty by association tactics, Waters' defense cautioned jurors to look at the facts of the case, not just the illegal actions of her former acquaintances. Both Kolar and Phillabaum began cooperating with the FBI shortly after their initial roundup along with five other environmentalists for a separate Oregon arson in 2005. In exchange for helping the government build its case against fellow activists by wearing a concealed wire, prosecutors promised to cut them a deal. Minimum sentences for arson alone carry a statutory minimum of 30 years with the threat of a maximum life term. It's little wonder why Kolar and Phillabaum felt pressured to name names, even if those people were close friends and legitimate fellow activists.

Problem was, Kolar, when first interviewed by the FBI in December 2005, only fingered four other participants in the UW arson. Kolar even told the FBI what each of their aliases were. Briana Waters was not on her list. A surprising lapse in memory considering Waters supposedly drove to the site of the arson that night. It was only later, after being pressured by government prosecutors, that Kolar named Waters as the lookout. According to the FBI's notes provided to Waters' defense team, Kolar was interviewed five or six times before identifying Waters as the lookout.

As Jennifer Kolar sought to strike a plea bargain with the feds she abruptly "remembered" who the lookout was that night. In mid-January 2006 Kolar was shown a photo of Waters, which she recognized by name, but did not say Waters was involved in the incident. It was almost a full month later, in March 2006, that Kolar informed the FBI of Waters alleged participation.

Aside from the testimonies of Kolar and Phillabaum, the FBI had little to work with. Their original informant, Jacob Ferguson had a drug problem, which would certainly dispel any legitimacy he would have on the stand, plus he was not even directly involved in the UW incident, he only led the FBI down Kolar and Phillabaum's trail. Anything he confessed would be hearsay. The alleged ringleader of the UW arson, argued the prosecution, was Bill Rodgers, known to others as Avalon, a man who committed suicide by wrapping a plastic bag over his head in his jail cell shortly after being arrested in Arizona in December 2005. There was simply no hard evidence that tied Waters to the crime scene that night. No fingerprints were left behind, no minuscule strain of DNA. Nothing. All the prosecutors had were suspicion and the testimony of two activists who struck plea deals in order to save themselves from decades in prison.

Lacey Phillabaum's fiancé, Stan Meyerhoff, a friend of Jacob Ferguson, was a cooperating witness in other ELF cases. While Meyerhoff didn't participate in the UW arson, he attended secret Book Club meetings leading up to the event and said Waters was not involved in the UW arson. The Book Club, hosted at different locations, served as the organizing nucleus for the group's covert actions. Meyerhoff even ratted on the love of his life, Lacey

Phillabaum. He did not seem to be holding any information back from the FBI.

"Within twenty-four hours [of being arrested], with no deal of any sort on the table, Stan was supposedly squealing like a pig," said Lauren Regan, a lawyer with the Civil Liberties Defense Center in Eugene, Oregon. "Given that Jake had a heroin-riddled mind; Stan was able to fill in a lot of blanks for the prosecution."

But apparently when the blanks weren't filled in to the Justice Department's liking, they simply invented scenarios based on innuendo and stories told by cooperating witnesses who were copping plea deals. On March 17, 2006, Stan Meyerhoff, handed over to the FBI by his pal Jacob Ferguson, was questioned by the feds and shown pictures of people who were under investigation for numerous ELF actions. One of those photos was of Briana Waters. Meyerhoff told investigators that the woman in the photo looked familiar but stated that she was not involved in any action. He was sure of it. The case, according to Water's defense, should have ended right there. Meyerhoff admitted to being intimately involved in numerous ELF acts and knew all the players, but stated outright that Waters was not one of them.

This little bump in the road didn't stop the prosecution, however. Waters did know Bill Rodgers, which was the cornerstone of the FBI's case against her. Rodgers, like Waters, was also an above ground environmental activist who was often strapped for cash and had credit problems. As a result Waters purchased a cell phone for him and paid his phone bills to help him out. Prosecutors argued that Rodgers and ELF were cautious and meticulous in all of their crimes. They left no trail, absolutely nothing that could lead authorities to their whereabouts.

So why would Briana Waters purchase a cell phone for Bill Rodgers if she was worried about being caught? Rodgers, according the FBI's profile, would not have asked Waters to buy him a phone if she was in anyway connected to any illegal activities. They weren't that careless. That was the case Waters' defense attempted to make: purchasing a phone and paying its monthly bill is not a crime, and in no way put Waters at the scene of the crime that night. But what did, the prosecution countered, was the vehicle she had her cousins rent for her that Waters allegedly used to drive from Olympia, Washington to UW's campus in Seattle.

***

On February 15, 2007 Lacey Phillabaum took the stand. Expressing sympathy for all involved, Phillabaum was still clear why she was testifying against Briana Waters. "I had regrets and did not want to spend 30 years in jail," she told the prosecutor.

An entire day on the stand and Phillabaum did her job in implicating Waters in the UW arson.

She claimed Rodgers vouched for her since she never attended any of the underground Book Club meetings. Phillabaum said that Waters and her saw the "clean room" where the bomb device was constructed by Rodgers and Waters' boyfriend, Justin Solondz. Waters, according to Phillabaum, was put in charge of procuring a car for the drive to the UW campus. On her second day of testimony, Phillabaum told of regret for what she did and her tumultuous transition back into ordinary life with Stan Meyerhoff.

"[Stan Meyerhoff and I] got to know each other and began reintegrating back [into] mainstream [culture], it was hard to do," Phillabaum said. "First part of getting uninvolved [with the ELF] was admitting to each other that we didn't want to be involved. Which was hard to do having met in this context … After 9/11 I decided it was intolerable to be involved with anything like this. We shared a mutual reinforcement of values."

Phillabaum, whose parents are both lawyers, was certainly primed for the barrage of questions the defense peppered her with. Phillabaum, insisted the defense, slept with Waters' boyfriend Justin Solondz. Phillabaum told Waters' defense attorney

Robert Bloom that she did not remember Waters ever confronting her, where Waters yelled, "how dare you have an affair with my boyfriend!"

"I think the implication is that we had a sexual interaction. That is not correct," Phillabaum told Bloom. "I never gave him a blowjob either if that's what you're implying." To which Bloom replied, "It is about whether you bear ill-will toward Briana … Briana called you all kinds of names. 'Disrespectful, unprincipled, not fit to be involved with the movement.'"

"I bear no ill-will toward Briana Waters," she protested.

Later Bloom asked, "If you stay with your deal, the best sentence for you is three years, the worst is five years right?"

"Yes," Phillabaum responded.

"…One of the inputs of the sentence is what the prosecutors tell the judge about how well you do on the stand, right? It's fair to say you have an incentive to please the prosecutors," defense attorney Bloom asked.

"I am not particularly motivated by my plea deal," Phillabaum explained to Bloom. "I am committed to fulfill it, but emotional and moral commitment which drives me to be honest is to the researchers who I victimized. I would rather do three years than five, but I will do no more than five no matter what I say."

Overall Bloom's questions to Phillabaum were not overly interrogating. She held her composure and stuck to her story. Briana Waters, Phillabaum recalled, was involved in obtaining the vehicle for the night and met with all involved for dinner at the Green Lake Bar: Justin Solondz, Bill Rodgers, Jen Kolar, Briana Waters and herself. Had she not implicated Waters, claimed defense attorney Bloom, Phillabaum would face up to 35 years in prison.

The real linchpin in Waters' trial was not Lacey Phillabaum, but Waters' cousin Robert Corrina. On February 19, Corrina was called to testify against his cousin. He was repeatedly interviewed by the FBI, with varying stories leading up to the trial. At first

Corrina said he did not know Waters, even though he lived with him and his wife when she first moved to Olympia. In preceding interviews he said he did, but didn't know anything about a rental car which was in fact rented by his wife on Waters' behalf and even deposited $200 cash for it the week before.

Defense attorneys insisted that since Corrina told contradictory stories to the FBI on numerous occasions that "now the feds hold your life in their hands." To which Corrina responded, "Not true." The FBI even went to his wife's place of employment and threatened them both with the possibility of a perjury charge, a felony offense. Like their case against Briana Waters, the feds also had Corrina cornered.

As Corrina squirmed in his seat while he was grilled with questions, the Waters defense seemed to be unraveling. The jury did not seem to be buying the fact that Corrina was bullied by the FBI to indict his cousin in order to save both him and his wife from prison. What the jury was presented with by the prosecution was a soft man who was telling the truth after having initially lied in an attempt to protect his cousin. Corrina's early statements to the feds only portrayed Waters as having done something wrong.

On the Sunday night of the arson, recalled Corrina for the first time under oath, her boyfriend Justin Solondz drove Waters in the rental car to the Emergency Room because Waters was having abdominal pains. Olympia's hospital wouldn't admit her, so she drove to Seattle, allege Corrina. It was the first time Waters was alleged to have been with Solondz on the same night as the arson. It was damning testimony, and it sent the defense's case for a tailspin. Now they didn't only have to argue that Phillabaum was lying to save herself, they had to say her cousin was too.

Waters' ER story also didn't hold up well under the prosecution's scrutiny. Neither hospital Waters reportedly sought treatment at had any records of her visit.

Jennifer Kolar was up next, whose testimony, despite the fact that she had at first not included Waters as involved in her FBI interrogation, did not help Waters' cause. When questioned about her memory trouble, Kolar replied, "I contradicted myself and my memory." The defense backed off right at the very moment they should have pounced. They painted Kolar as a cold-hearted rich girl who, unlike Phillabaum, had little remorse for the actions she committed as a clandestine member of the Earth Liberation Front. But however cold Kolar was on the stand, the defense did not attack her truthfulness in such a way that would convince the jury that she was lying to reduce her own sentence.

Waters' case was falling apart at the seams. Her cousin Robert Corrina put her in the car he helped obtain and Phillabaum and Kolar put her at the scene of the arson as a lookout. Despite a lack of hard evidence, Waters did not have a solid alibi. As for boyfriend Justin Solondz, the one person who could have either corroborated or confirmed Waters' whereabouts that night—he was long gone, having fled after the initial arrests and was a fugitive on the FBI's Most Wanted list.

On February 25, FBI Special Agent Tony Torres took the stand as a witness for the prosecution. Torres was the note-taker for Jennifer Kolar's interview on January 12, 2006 where she was shown a photo of Briana Waters and recognized her, but did not say she was in any way involved in the UW arson. After a long, evasive testimony, Torres was forced to admit that Kolar never named Briana Waters as a participant until well after the FBI already fixed on her as a suspect.

According to Torres' interview with Jennifer Kolar, she recalled events that were in direct contradiction to Phillabaum's testimony. Not only did Kolar not originally recall Waters being involved, she also thought that Budget rental car used for the night's event was obtained by Bill Rodgers, not Waters. Also, Phillabaum testified that the car was scrapped while speeding out of the neighborhood where they parked near UW, but Kolar did not recall this happening, nor could Special Agent Torres provide any evidence from Budget that the car returned by Robert Corrina sustained any damage. Torres also testified that Phillabaum told the FBI that both Briana Waters and Justin Solondz acted as lookouts during the UW arson, in contrast with the government's allegation that Waters alone acted as a lookout.

The big gap in Torres' testimony was that the FBI did not record Jennifer Kolar's questioning, even though it is FBI protocol to do so. He also admitted he stopped taking notes in the middle of the interview in an attempt to avoid the "confusion" that resulted in major discrepancies between him and Special Agent Ted Halla's notes from their interview with Jennifer Kolar's on December 16, 2005. Defense attorneys accused Torres of falsifying documents in order to set up their case against Waters.

It wasn't a smoking gun, but Torres was perhaps the weakest link in the prosecution's case against Briana Waters. He confirmed that the FBI's two main witnesses' stories did not match up with one another and had not from the inception of the FBI's investigation. Kolar changed her account of events numerous occasions. She didn't recall a scrape on the car, nor did she even remember that they used a rental car, as she told the FBI originally that they drove a van to UW, a much more realistic vehicle given the number of people allegedly involved in the arson and the equipment they had to bring along.

Both Phillabaum and Kolar also said that Waters and crew met at the Green Lake Bar on the night of the crime. Kolar said they met "around 9 at night, 8 at night," while Phillabaum testified they met in the "early evening." Defense lawyers challenged both Kolar and Phillabaum's recollection and presented a bank card receipt which put Waters 60 miles away in Olympia at 7:12 p.m, and given that their was a Seattle Mariners game and construction that evening, it was unlikely, with even normal traffic on Interstate 5, that Waters would have been able to drive to UW in time to meet the others at the bar.

While Briana Waters took the stand in her own defense, a wave of trepidation filled the air, even sending Judge Burgess into an afternoon siesta. Supporters in the courtroom were convinced there were simply too many conflicting testimonies and evidence to convict Waters of any crime. It was now Waters' turn to speak in her own defense. She denied any involvement whatsoever in the UW arson, or any arson for that matter. She did not attend any Book Club meetings. She knew Bill Rodgers, but only for his above ground activities. Waters did not believe that arson was a legitimate form of environmental activism, something she realized during her time on Watch Mountain as she worked with others to organize local communities against proposed logging.

As the defense and prosecution laid out their final arguments for and against Briana Waters, a fire erupted in a posh Seattle development project called Street of Dreams and the ELF claimed responsibility. Perhaps it was more than poor timing. Or perhaps it set by contractors in an attempt to cash in on some insurance money before the housing boom reached their cul-de-sac. Regardless, it certainly did not help Waters.

The prosecution went first, admitting that Jennifer Kolar's memory was suspect, but that she was certain Waters was a lookout for the arson. They cautioned the jury to see past Waters' soft veneer and to see her as a domestic terrorist willing to use the threat of violence to spread her anti-establishment message. It was their duty, prosecutors insisted, to put Waters behind bars where she belonged, even though all they really ever accused her of was holding a walkie-talkie as a lookout. But domestic terrorism is serious, they contended, and she must be punished for her actions, no matter how minor they may seem.

The defense believed they provided the jury with numerous examples that ought to lead to reasonable doubt. Enough that would set Briana Waters free. They pointed out Kolar's mangled testimony and Special Agent Torres' bad note taking habits. They said the fact that they had a receipt from Waters in Olympia made it virtually impossible to meet at the Green Lake Bar with the rest of the arsonists. They pointed out that cooperating witness Stan Meyerhoff, second only under Bill Rodgers, said Waters was never involved in any actions. They said that the cell phone payments and her cousin's rental car was not evidence that she committed the crime. There were just too many unanswered questions and too much innuendo to find Briana Waters guilty, the defense argued. Lastly there was no hard evidence that put Waters at UW that night.

On June 2, 2008, Waters' defense attorneys filed a motion which they claimed revealed that Jennifer Kolar patently lied and deceived the FBI and jury, and that an investigation was required to determine what action needed to be taken in light of such a disclosure. The defense motion was based upon documents the government disclosed after the trial. The new information, the defense attested, should have resulted in a mistrial.

Unfortunately, Judge Burgess didn't agree and jurors were unable to convict on all counts, but they did find Waters guilty on two counts of arson. While awaiting her sentencing, Waters' lawyers asked that she be released until her sentencing so she could spend more time with her partner and 3-year-old daughter. The U.S. attorney's office opposed the request, and claimed they had new evidence that Waters was involved in more than one arson, insisting that Lacey Phillabuam's fiancé Stan Meyerhoff, who said before that Waters was never involved, claimed that Waters participated in an attack at the Litchfield Wild Horse and Burro Ranch in Susanville, California.

On Thursday, June 19, 2008, Briana Waters was sentenced to 6 years in prison. Letters of support and a tearful plea by her own mother could not keep her out of prison. Lacey Phillabaum and Jennifer Kolar dramatically reduced their sentences, with Phillabaum received 36 months and Kolar 60 months.

"Prosecutors used scare-mongering to get the jury to convict an innocent person," Waters' lawyer, Robert Bloom, told Salon shortly after the trial ended. "This is really a study in American prosecution. It was an absurdly slanted American prosecution."

***

Waters' conviction was later overturned on appeal in 2008, but in June 2012, when faced with a retrial, Waters signed a plea and was sentenced to four years in prison. With the plea, she agreed to testify against Justin Solondz and claimed she perjured herself during her 2008 trial. She also admitted UW wasn't her only firebombing. She said she helped torch the the Litchfield Wild Burro and Horse Corrals in 2001. In return for her plea, the feds agreed not to charge her with the arson in California. Did the feds force Waters into the plea deal in an attempt to get Solondz? We'll never know for certain. Waters was released from prison in 2013.

Justin Solondz was sentenced to seven years in prison in 2012, this after spending two years in a Chinese prison on local charges. Solondz was released from prison in the US in early 2017.

– June 23, 2017

DESIGNER PROTESTS AND VANITY ARRESTS IN DC

By Jeffrey St. Clair

The scene was striking for its dissonance. Fifty activists massed in front of the White House, some of them sitting, others tied to the iron fence, most of them smiling, all decorous looking, not a Black Blocker or Earth First!er in the viewshed. The leaders of this micro-occupation of the sidewalk held a black banner featuring Obama's campaign logo, the one with the blue "O" and the curving red stripes that looks like a pipeline snaking across Kansas. The message read, prosaically: "Lead on Climate: Reject the KXL Pipeline." Cameras whirred franticly, most aimed at the radiant face of Daryl Hannah, as DC police moved in to politely ask the crowd to disperse. The crowd politely declined. The Rubicon had been crossed. For the first time in 120 years, a Sierra Club official, executive director Mike Brune, was going to get arrested for an act of civil (and the emphasis here is decisively on civil) disobedience.

Brune had sought special dispensation for the arrest from the Sierra Club board, a one-day exemption to the Club's firm policy against non-violent civil disobedience, The Board assented. One might ask, what took them so long? One might also ask, why now? Is the Keystone Pipeline a more horrific ecological crime than oil drilling in grizzly habitat on the border of Glacier National Park or the gunning down of 350 wolves a year in the outback of Idaho? Hardly. The Keystone Pipeline is one of many noxious conduits of tar sand oil from Canada, vile, certainly, but standard practice for Big Oil.

The Sierra Club has an image problem. Brune's designer arrest can be partially interpreted as a craven attempt to efface the stain of the Club's recent dalliance with Chesapeake Energy, one of the largest natural gas companies on the continent and a pioneer in the environmentally malign enterprise of hydraulic fracturing or "fracking." Between 2007 and 2010, Chesapeake Energy secretly funneled nearly $30 million to the Sierra Club to advocate the virtues of natural gas as a so-called "bridge" fuel.

Bridge to where is yet to be determined. By the time this subornment was disclosed, the funders of the environmental movement had turned decisively against fracking for gas and the even more malicious methods used to extract shale oil. The Sierra Club had to rehabilitate itself to stay in the good graces of the Pew Charitable Trusts and New York Mayor Michael Bloomberg, who had lavished $50 million on the Club's sputtering Beyond Coal Campaign.

As the cops strolled in to begin their vanity arrests, they soon confronted the inscrutable commander of these delicately chained bodies, Bill McKibben, leader of the massively funded 350.Org. McKibben had repeatedly referred to this as the environmental movement's "lunch counter moment," making an odious comparison to the Civil Right's movement's courageous occupation of the "white's only" spaces across the landscape of the Jim Crow era, acts of genuine defiance that were often viciously suppressed by truncheons, fists and snarling dogs.

But McKibben made no attempt to stand his ground. He allowed the PlastiCuffs that tied his thin wrists to the fence to be decorously snipped. He didn't resist arrest; instead he craved it. This was a well-orchestrated photo-op moment. He was escorted to the police van, driven to the precinct station, booked, handed a $100 fine and released. An hour later, McKibben was Tweeting about how cool it was to be arrested with civil rights legend Julian Bond. But are you really engaged in civil disobedience if you can Tweet your own arrest?

Beyond the fabric of self-congratulation, what's really going on here? The mandarins of Big Green blocked nothing, not even entry to the White House grounds. It was a purely symbolic protest, but signifying what? Directed at whom? Even Derrida would have a hard time decoding the meaning of a demonstration that so effusively supported the person it supposedly targeted.

Of course, Obama, who was in North Carolina during the designer arrests, had no such problem. He correctly divined the impotence on display. In a matter of weeks, he delivered a State of the Union Address pledging to expedite oil and gas drilling on public lands and off-shore sites, nominated pro-nuke and pro-fracking zealots to head the EPA and Department of Energy.

Predictably, the Sierra Club, which now functions as little more than an applause machine for the administration, praised both the State of the Union address and the dubious appointments to EPA and Energy. Here we have what Jean-Paul Sartre called "the mirage of an opposition."

Then the coup de grâce: the State Department issued its final report endorsing the pipeline as an ecologically-benign sluice toward economic prosperity. This was swiftly followed by an order from the White House to the EPA demanding that the agency withdraw the stern new standards on greenhouse gas emissions from powerplants.

So Obama screwed Gang Green while their mugshot selfies were still fresh. But, like Pavlovian Lapdogs, the Enviro Pros will lick their wounds, cash a few checks and within two weeks be back to issuing press releases touting him as the Greenest President of All Time. Rest assured, Obama feels terrible about these setbacks and will move decisively to fix them in his third term.

– April 17, 2013

WHY ONE COMMUNITY'S CRIES FOR HELP AGAINST CANCER AND OTHER DISEASES ARE GOING UNANSWERED

By Joshua Frank

This may be considered flyover country for most eco-minded Americans, but smack dab in the middle of eastern Oklahoma there's an environmental rebellion afoot.

Residents of the rural community of Bokoshe, population 450, are none too happy with the huge heap of blackened coal ash that is piled in a pit a mile from their quaint little Main Street. They claim the combustion waste is poisoning water, polluting their air, and causing asthma and cancer among those who live nearby. In fact, of the 20 households in closest proximity to the dump, 14 people have been diagnosed with cancer and many others have died since the site was opened eight years ago.

An outfit that goes by the shameless name of Making Money Having Fun LLC (MMHF) operates the toxic coal ash pit. MMHF hauls the noxious debris by truck to Bokoshe from the nearby AES Shady Point Generation Plant. In a single day as many as 80 truckloads of coal ash are driven down Main Street and dumped at the site.

Each year coal-fired power plants in the U.S. produce almost 140 million tons of scrubber sludge and coal waste, as well as additional combustion waste from the burning of the fossil fuel. This coal ash, which contains numerous toxins such as arsenic and lead, is contaminating groundwater, drinking supplies and wetlands in hundreds of communities and in dozens of states. Currently there are no federal regulations of coal waste disposal, but some Oklahomans aren't having it.

"Making Money Having Fun might be having a good time dumping their coal ash in Bokoshe, but I assure you that the citizens are not having any fun at all," says Tim Tanksley, who lives in Bokoshe and has been vocal in his opposition to the site. "The fly ash is in our air and in our water; it is flowing into our creeks, streams and eventually into the Arkansas River."

When MMHF applied for a commercial permit to dump ash near Bokoshe, it claimed there were no towns with a population under 20,000 within a three-mile radius. Except, of course, there were, and hundreds of folks lived in homes a lot closer than three miles away.

From the beginning, residents claim, the company has been flat out lying. It lied about what it was dumping and now it is lying about its potential harm to human and environmental health. MMHF and AES are simply not acknowledging that their waste site, which is also allowed to have oil and gas water, could potentially be killing the citizens of Bokoshe.

"They just told everybody it was dirt, that you could put it on your peanut butter and jelly sandwich," Tim Tanskley says. In December, students at Bokoshe Elementary in Oklahoma teamed up to ask AES to stop dumping fly ash from its Shady Point Generation Plant near their homes. Their teacher, Diane Reece, believes the coal ash has caused many of her students to develop debilitating asthma.

"When I found out that nine kids out of seventeen in my sixth grade [class] had asthma," says Diane Reece, "I knew there was a problem."

Last year the townspeople invited Obama's regulatory czar Cass Sunstein to visit their town to check out the site. They signed petitions, wrote letters, lobbied their local officials and cried out for help in every way they knew. Their request to Sunstein and the Obama White House was simple and to the point: The government should regulate coal ash and deem it the hazardous substance that it is.

The Obama administration has not responded. But Tim Tanskley has not been deterred. Last April, Tanksley, along with John Wathen of Tuscaloosa, Alabama and Elisa Young of Meigs County, Ohio set off for Washington to meet with Sunstein's office. Sunstein, unsurprisingly, was a no-show, and the trio was only allocated a few minutes to make their case.

"It was a dog-and-pony show for us to feel better when we left," Wathen said.

However, it was likely a classic DC dog-and-pony show for a good reason.

Cass Sunstein, a former law professor and close friend of the president, has a sordid history when it comes to environmental health problems. As Sunstein wrote in his 2002 book *Risk and Reason*, "It remains unproven that the contamination of Love Canal ever posed significant risks to anyone."

Sunstein holds this belief despite the fact that the EPA claims that even 25 years after the Hooker Chemical Company stopped using Love Canal for an industrial dump, "82 different compounds, 11 of them suspected carcinogens, have been percolating upward through the soil, their drum containers rotting and leaching their contents into the backyards and basements of 100 homes and a public school built on the banks of the canal."

Sunstein has gone so far as to state that the American public overreacted to Bush's unpopular decision to suspend the arsenic rule issued during the Clinton years.

"If a Republican nominee had these views, the environmental community would be screaming for his scalp," Frank O'Donnell, president of Clean Air Watch, a Washington-based advocacy group, said in an interview prior to Sunstein's nomination hearing.

The response MMHF gives to critics of its operations in Bokoshe has been callous at best, but the real culprit has been the owner and operator of the plant itself. A global energy giant, with over 120 projects worldwide, AES has been working hard to keep coal ash waste from being regulated by the federal government.

AES is a member of the American Coal Ash Association (ACAA), an umbrella lobbying organization that represents all coal ash interests that includes other major coal burners such as Duke Energy, Southern Company and American Electric Power. The group argues that the so-called "beneficial-use industry" would be eliminated if a "hazardous" designation was given for coal ash waste.

ACAA has also set up the pro-coal front group Citizens for Recycling First, which argues that using toxic coal ash as fill in other products like concrete and home insulation is safe, despite mounting evidence to the contrary.

AES defended its practices to local media outlets in Bokoshe last December. Company spokesman Lundy Kiger told reporters that he was 100 percent convinced that fly ash is not hazardous to human health.

"We drink the same water. We breathe the same air," Kiger said. "We have an outstanding environmental record over the past 20 years."

The Oklahoma Department of Environmental Quality has acknowledged that the coal ash may be impacting people in Bokoshe, but has refused to act. The state's Department of Mines has not been of much help either and has denied that MMHF's ash pit could possibly be leaking contaminated wastewater.

Bokoshe citizens have also asked for help from Oklahoma Senator James Inhofe, a global warming denier, and Representative Dan Boren, to no avail. Senator Inhofe was gracious enough to reply, "The fly ash is temporarily mounded while it is mixed with water to form slurry. Ultimately, the mine will be transformed into a pasture. Therefore, the fly ash mound is temporary and will disappear once the reclamation is complete."

Meanwhile, both Inhofe and Boren do not want to see AES' dumping ground shut down anytime soon.

"If you are going to an economically depressed area and killing people with this coal combustion waste just to feed the big cities with cheap electricity … this is not right, this is not social justice," says a concerned and determined Tim Tanskley. "There is nothing right about that process."

– January 28, 2011

HANFORD'S TOXIC AVENGERS

By Joshua Frank

Once home to the nation's largest plutonium-making facility, Hanford, Washington, is now one of the most toxic nuclear-waste sites in the world. The U.S. Department of Energy (DOE) is currently spending $2 billion a year to clean up the 586-square-mile reservation. However, not all is well on Washington's dusty southeastern edge: Whistle-blowers are stepping forward, claiming that taxpayer money is being spent recklessly on a project riddled with potentially deadly design defects.

Donna Busche, who has been employed by contractor URS (originally known as United Research Services) as acting Manager of Environmental and Nuclear Safety at Hanford's Waste Treatment Plant (WTP) since 2009, is among the latest of these senior managers to speak out about what she sees as the silencing of those who raise concerns about possibly lethal safety issues. Last November, Busche filed a complaint of discrimination under the federal whistle-blower protection statutes with the U.S. Department of Labor, alleging retaliation against her for reporting problems at the WTP, which one day will turn Hanford's 56 million gallons of highly hazardous radioactive waste into storable glass rods through a process known as vitrification.

Climbing the corporate ladder in the male-dominated engineering world was no easy feat. But Busche, as numerous co-workers say, is tough, politically savvy, and scientifically skilled. After attending graduate school at Texas A&M and before arriving at Hanford, Busche was the Chief Nuclear Engineer and Manager of Nuclear Safety at the DOE's Waste Isolation Pilot Plant in Carlsbad, New Mexico.

Busche's job at Hanford is to ensure that the site's contractors produce adequate documentation to support the contractor's compliance with federal environmental and nuclear-safety laws, meaning that virtually no aspect of construction can take place at the WTP until Busche says it is safe to do so. "I'm where the nuclear-safety buck stops," says Busche.

If Busche says "Stop," the work must stop. But saying "Stop" to the wrong guys, Busche claims, has gotten her in a heap of trouble with Hanford higher-ups.

Among her grievances, Busche claims that she has been sexually harassed by URS manager Bill Gay. In Busche's official complaint, she explains that Gay made inappropriate and sexist comments to her in an unscheduled meeting, "including comments that women react emotionally while men use logical thinking." Gay also allegedly told Busche that, as an attractive woman, she should use her "feminine wiles" to better communicate with her male cohorts. Gay apparently also said that if Busche were single, "he would pursue a romantic relationship with her." Busche notified Human Resources shortly after Gay made these remarks, at which point he reportedly apologized. Gay would not comment on the allegation.

Perhaps even more damaging are Busche's claims that, beginning in 2010, the lead contractor at Hanford, Bechtel National Inc., shirked safety compliance, signing off on shoddy work in order to meet deadlines that would earn the contractor large financial incentives. For example, radioactive-waste stirrers called pulse jet mixers have had numerous design problems, such as erosion and potential leaking. Despite these concerns, Bechtel pushed through testing saying they were sound.

Their timing was impeccable: It was late June 2010, and by having their plans finalized by the end of the month, the company would receive a $5 million bonus for reaching cost and schedule goals. Busche says that during this time she was viewed as a roadblock to meeting these goals. As a result, Busche's concerns were suppressed and Bechtel managers allegedly sought ways to retaliate against her.

But management at Bechtel and the DOE didn't know whom they were dealing with. In October 2010, Busche took her concerns to the Defense Nuclear Facilities Safety Board (DNFSB), an independent governmental organization that oversees health and safety issues at the DOE's nuclear facilities. After her comments were made during a public hearing with DNFSB on October 7, Busche says she was "openly admonished by former DOE Assistant Secretary Inés Triay for her testimony."

In her Department of Labor complaint, Busche alleges that after her testimony, Triay told her "If [your] intent was to piss people off [with your testimony, you] did a very good job." (Triay, now a Visiting Scholar at Florida International University, did not respond for comment after multiple phone calls and e-mail requests.)

When Busche showed up for a second day of hearings, she claims she was approached by Frank Russo, who runs the WTP project for Bechtel; Bill Gay; and Leo Sain, a senior URS vice president. They all urged her to recant her earlier testimony when she met with the DNFSB. She replied that she would not.

Even worse, when Busche returned to work after the hearings, she alleges WTP management kept her isolated and out of meetings that she was both authorized to and required to attend. She also says that since Bechtel "controls the work and supervision of persons assigned to [her]," that the company has "actively sabotaged her work since [Bechtel] employees go around her, defy her efforts to supervise them … all without consequence."

She is currently awaiting a response from the Department of Labor about her complaint. Busche's story—when coupled with that of the DOE's Dr. Don Alexander, as outlined in *Seattle Weekly* ("The Nuclear Option," October 19, 2011)—provides ample evidence that management at both Bechtel and the DOE are at best ignoring, and at worst actively retaliating against, experts with inconvenient opinions. And because it's nuclear waste that's being dealt with, their alleged negligence could ultimately prove deadly.

The government's manufacturing of plutonium to fuel the atom bomb was a scientific feat unlike any that came before it. At the nucleus of this gargantuan undertaking was Hanford. The roaring Columbia River provided the much-needed water to help keep its reactors consistently cool, and Hanford's remoteness allowed the facility to operate with scant international attention.

Today Hanford no longer produces plutonium for nuclear weapons. Instead, the scientific and engineering minds employed there are tasked with an equally, if not more, daunting endeavor: cleaning up one of the largest radioactive nuclear-waste sites in North America.

The DOE manages the Hanford project for the federal government, but contractors such as Bechtel and URS act as the design and contract specialists for the site's most important undertaking, the construction of the WTP. Once the glass rods roll out of the WTP, which will be a first-of-its-kind operation, they are to be stored in a safe place where a radioactive leak is far less likely than it is today—Hanford's waste currently remains in old, underground tanks that are decades past their lifespan.

While Bechtel holds the primary contract with the DOE to build the WTP, URS acts as their subcontractor, and the companies split all fees 50/50. URS also holds another contract for managing Hanford's Tank Farms, where the 56 million gallons of radioactive waste are held. Over the duration of the WTP contract, from 2001 to today, Bechtel has raised their proposed budget from $4.3 billion to $12.263 billion, with more increases likely to come: In late August the DOE's Construction Project Review team estimated an extra $800 to $900 million would likely be needed to finish the job. Watchdog groups, like the Seattle-based Hanford Challenge, say the final cost could top $20 billion.

Either Bechtel drastically underestimated the cost to build the WTP, or they blatantly misled DOE when they said they could complete the project for $4.3 billion. This is not the first time Bechtel has increased a government contract and failed to deliver: In March 2006, the Special Inspector General for Iraq Reconstruction (SIGIR), an oversight group set up by Congress to keep an eye on government contracts in Iraq, found that Bechtel was mismanaging a hospital project that was way over budget.

In mid-October 2004, Bechtel scored the contract to build an Iraqi children's cancer hospital for $50 million, promising to complete the construction by late December 2005. However, SIGIR's report found that Bechtel likely wouldn't finish work on the hospital until at least July 2007, with a final price tag of $169.5 million. After SIGIR's report on Bechtel's gross mismanagement, the government canceled the company's contract for the hospital. Another contractor later completed the hospital construction in 2010.

This incident wasn't unique: A 2007 SIGIR report found that fewer than half of Bechtel's projects had met their original objectives. Additionally, the majority of Bechtel's Iraq projects were canceled, reduced in scope, or never completed at all.

Now a number of engineers and scientists, like Don Alexander, are wondering why Bechtel isn't coming under the same kind of congressional scrutiny for its even larger contract to build the WTP.

***

A high-ranking DOE scientist at Hanford, Alexander first spoke out in this publication to express his concerns with managerial and operational aspects of his work at the WTP, as well as the plant specifications that had been carelessly accepted as safe and sound. In one instance, Alexander pointed out the DOE's and Bechtel's refusal to re-evaluate their so-called pulse jet mixer design, which is supposed to keep the radioactive waste at the WTP constantly moving, after his own studies showed that the containers that held the mixers would erode, potentially causing a lethal radioactive leak. Alexander says that following the article, the DOE is now paying close attention to the issue, and has assigned one expert from the Massachusetts Institute of Technology, nine full-time staffers, and 11 Bechtel employees to resolve these design problems.

But new evidence has emerged in a lawsuit, filed last May in Washington state court by Dr. Walter Tamosaitis of URS, that implicates high-level DOE employees in the silencing of Tamosaitis, who was removed from his management position at the WTP after he raised concerns about the plant's faulty design. In a deposition taken in this lawsuit in July, Bechtel's Frank Russo verified the names of DOE officials with whom he had discussed Tamosaitis: Dale Knutson, federal project director for the DOE at Hanford; DOE Deputy Secretary Daniel Poneman; and Inés Triay, who served as Assistant Secretary for Environmental Management under Secretary of Energy Stephen Chu until July 2011. Triay and Poneman were Obama appointees.

In the deposition, Tamosaitis' lawyer, Jack Sheridan, asked Russo whether or not he had, via e-mail, told his boss, Bechtel President David Walker, that Triay, Poneman, and Knutson all "understood the reason for Walt's departure" and that "DOE can't be seen as involved." Russo confirmed this, admitting to telling Walker that he had briefed Triay and Poneman on the issue.

In early November 2011, Tamosaitis filed a second lawsuit against Bechtel and the DOE in federal court. Among other things, Tamosaitis' suit alleges that Bechtel management and DOE brass were concerned that the issues Tamosaitis was raising could put an additional $50 million of WTP funding in jeopardy.

Additionally, in early December, Tamosaitis testified in front of the U.S. Senate's Homeland Security and Governmental Affairs Subcommittee. At the hearing, he explained how he was removed from his job and forced to work in an offsite windowless basement office as a warning of sorts to others who were contemplating speaking out.

The DOE says they do not comment on issues related to pending litigation, such as that levied by Tamosaitis. But now, for the first time, two veteran Hanford scientists are adding their experiences to this unfolding saga by blowing the whistle on what they see as blatant corruption and mismanagement at Hanford's WTP. With these endeavors, the new whistle-blowers claim, DOE management is not only complicit, but taking direct actions to hide glaring technical problems from the public—problems that could lead to a catastrophic nuclear accident.

***

At 78, longtime Hanford nuclear chemical process engineer David Bruce says his enthusiasm to do his job right is as great as ever. Many of his co-workers past and present see Bruce, who has worked for various Hanford contractors for more than 46 years, as a mentor of sorts—a man whose words are worth heeding.

"The pursuit to stay on schedule has crippled the entire operation," Bruce says of the WTP. "This sucker is not going to run as currently designed, plain and simple, and a heck of a lot of people around here know it but are too afraid to speak up."

Last December, Bruce decided he'd had enough. He was aware of glaring technical flaws, such as problems in the mixing design that could lead to lethal leaks at the WTP and prevent it from ever running properly. These problems had not yet been addressed, and in a meeting with top management, including Russo, Bruce stood up and made his points.

"After that meeting, [Frank] Russo came up to me and asked to meet with me later to discuss the issues that I raised," Bruce says. He was a bit surprised; it was the first time anyone that high up in Bechtel management had seemed concerned with the issues he was raising. While he thought the meeting went well and felt that Russo heard him out, he still has very serious doubts about whether necessary changes will ever be made.

Russo and Bechtel would not comment directly on the claim that management continues to override technical staff, but the company insists that "[Bechtel's] responsibility to the American taxpayer is to ensure that balance in designing and building a plant that will safely and effectively operate to protect people and the environment from the hazards of and risks from the radioactive waste."

Yet on January 13, the DOE's Office of Health, Safety and Security (HSS), which is tasked with overseeing work carried out at the DOE's nuclear sites, released what some—including a DOE employee who did not want his name to appear in this piece for fear of reprisal—have called the most scathing review of Hanford ever to come out of the independent oversight committee. The document was direct in its criticism of the culture that permeates Hanford's work environment, finding that "only 30% of all survey respondents feel that they can openly challenge decisions made by management." The report goes on to state, "There is a strong perception that you will be labeled or red-flagged, and some individuals indicated that they were transferred to another area by their supervision after having raised concerns."

Russo responded to the HSS report by telling his employees in a letter, "I want to re-emphasize how important it is for everyone to have a questioning attitude, to stop and ask questions if something doesn't seem right, and if there is a concern, to raise it so it can be addressed."

Getting Russo to acknowledge even this much had proven an arduous slog. In late September 2009, frustration with their supervisors' failure to address ineffective designs had grown so high that Bruce and URS Senior Advisory Engineer Murray Thorson, both devout Christians, retreated to their work cafeteria to pray together. Their request to their Lord was simple: They asked Him, if their perceptions were correct, to expose what they saw as waste and corruption within the DOE and contractor management.

During the previous six months, the two had worked diligently to come up with a design to eliminate precipitation in the ion-exchange system at the WTP. Buildup of precipitation in the feed to the ion-exchange columns, integral parts of the process of turning nuclear waste into glass, would cause the columns to plug or fail to function, jeopardizing the operability of the entire WTP facility.

Starting in 2007, Bruce and Thorson had reached out to management with their concerns. But after being repeatedly ignored, they met with the DOE to outline the serious technical flaws in Bechtel's proposed design. Only then did Bechtel agree to do something about it.

An ad hoc group was then formed, with Bruce and Thorson on one team and another set of engineers from Bechtel and URS on another. The two pursued a fix for the buildup of precipitation, which became known as the Equipment Option, while the other group developed an alternative Operating Solution. The Equipment Option was projected to take five fewer years to process Hanford's nuclear waste into glass. At an operating cost of roughly $1 billion per year, that's a $5 billion savings for taxpayers. The Operating Solution, on the other hand, might temporarily fix the issue, but would provide less reliability and less flexibility and increase the amount of time needed to process the nuclear waste. More important to Bechtel, however: The Operating Solution would have cost less in construction dollars to implement.

Bechtel took both options to the DOE, stating their recommendation of the Operating Solution option. DOE, however, ended up opting for Thorson and Bruce's design.

Tamosaitis, then serving as URS management advisor for the precipitation study teams, says, "Murray [Thorson] and Dave [Bruce] had the undisputed answer to the problem. Everyone knew it, but despite this fact, Bechtel management did not want to accrue the costs of the fix. So they picked the cheaper, less adequate solution.

"Bechtel knew darn well DOE would [not pick the Operating Solution], and would go with the Equipment Option," Tamosaitis continues. "But they pursued this approach anyway, so that DOE would ultimately cover the cost"—because, according to their contract, if the DOE picks a more expensive solution to a problem, they, rather than Bechtel, have to cover the costs by adding funds to Bechtel's [baseline] budget.

"Bechtel is the best at playing the game of getting the most taxpayer money to address technical issues that are their responsibility," says Tamosaitis. "They wait for DOE to give them more money. This maximizes their profits at taxpayer expense. If they don't get the money, they just move on. It's the only business where not doing it well leads to more profits—all of which is taxpayer money."

Bechtel spokesperson Suzanne Heaston defends her company via e-mail, stating, "The Operations option fully met all technical requirements and had a lower installed cost."

"Bechtel was not very excited about our approach," Bruce says with a chuckle before turning serious. "Murray Thorson is a brilliant engineer, one of the best I've ever worked with, and the fact that Bechtel didn't even really want to hear what we had to say on the issue was very disheartening, to say the least."

Thorson's other accomplishments at the WTP are well-documented. From 2002 to 2008 he led a highly successful effort that resulted in changing the type of resin used in the WTP's ion-exchange columns. This resin acts as a sponge to separate radioactive cesium from the waste, helping to decontaminate Hanford's radioactive material before it is processed into glass. Bechtel was not supportive of Thorson's efforts, however, because more than $11 million worth of research and testing was required to develop and qualify the resin, despite its potential long-term savings of billions of dollars. Another resin already existed, and despite all its problems and associated high cost, Bechtel contended it was acceptable, and told Thorson to stop the development effort.

All indications were that the original resin was not going to work—it gummed up, potentially plugging and causing the system to fail. Even so, URS and Bechtel management disagreed with staff recommendations and claimed the resin was fine as it was. The DOE thought otherwise, and the agency's federal director at the time, John Eschenberg, authorized the group Thorson was working in to move ahead with the new resin development, agreeing to cover the research costs, which were added to Bechtel's WTP budget. After several years of research and testing, Thorson's efforts paid off, and his resin was demonstrated to be a tremendous success.

The new resin was substantially less expensive than the original resin. When all is said and done, Thorson's resin will save taxpayers at least $3 billion.

***

Shortly after the DOE chose Thorson and Bruce's Equipment Option, Thorson wanted out. He did not feel his work was being adequately appreciated at the WTP, though he'd saved the project billions of dollars. When an opening arose at Hanford's Tank Farm, which handles the underground storage containers that hold the toxic site's remaining nuclear waste, Thorson went after it, even though it carried a lesser title.

"I want to be clear: Bechtel did not force me to leave my job at WTP," says Thorson. "But the environment they created there, where good work isn't recognized, was one that I could no longer [work in]. I wanted WTP to operate properly, and believed my new job would continue in these efforts."

Thorson's new job was to work on an oversight group called CLIN 3.2, responsible for looking at long-term operability issues at the WTP. Though technically still a URS employee, Thorson would be working for a company called Washington River

Protection Solutions (WRPS), which led CLIN 3.2's evaluations. WRPS is a joint company accountable under their contract to URS.

CLIN 3.2 stands for Contract Line Item Number 3.2, which was included in Hanford's Tank Farm contract between the DOE and URS, the company put in charge of Tank Farm operations. The Tank Farm contract is separate from the WTP contract. Bechtel is not involved in the Tank Farm contract, but URS acts as its lead contractor, responsible for safely retrieving, treating, storing, and disposing of Hanford's Tank Farm waste, which currently sits in 177 underground concrete tanks that are grouped into 18 "farms." The Tank Farm contract is worth $7.1 billion.

Waste from the Tank Farms will one day move to the WTP through piping and different treatment facilities. The final phase of this process will turn this processed waste into glass. So the Tank Farm and the WTP are to work in conjunction to ensure optimum success. In the Tank Farm contract, CLIN 3.2 called for the establishment of biannual independent evaluations to ensure the WTP would run properly.

"This isn't your typical project design," says Thorson, referring to areas in the WTP called black cells that hold piping and equipment. Once sealed, these cells will be off-limits to maintenance. If something like erosion causes a radioactive leak in these vessels, nothing can be done.

One of the primary tasks assigned to the CLIN 3.2 evaluation group was to ensure everything inside these black cells would function as designed. Two sources, who worked as managers and engineers at Hanford and are familiar with the contract, say that CLIN 3.2 was a "top objective" of the Tank Farm contract, which would help ensure that Bechtel was kept honest since they would have a stake in both the Tank Farm and the WTP contracts.

The first CLIN 3.2 report was issued in September 2010 and found numerous risks, including problems with reliability, operability, maintainability and throughput, hydrogen-vent control, precipitation of solids that could plug equipment, control-system documentation, and contamination control.

After the report was issued, Bechtel said they would not answer design questions or support any reviews, asserts Thorson. "Since DOE did not require them to do so—which Bechtel argued was not required by their contract—it really knocked the wind out of us." Though the reviews would benefit the WTP's potential success, Bechtel claimed they had no money to do reviews unless the DOE handed over more funds. Essentially, CLIN 3.2 was an elite technical review board without any real teeth.

The DOE would not comment on Thorson's claim that they did not require Bechtel to address the issues raised in CLIN 3.2's first report. But, says Thorson, "It was clear that Bechtel was not pleased with the long-term operability issues we had raised [regarding the WTP]. DOE was simply not supportive of [CLIN] 3.2's original scope."

WRPS soon reduced CLIN 3.2 from a 12-person operation to half that. Even with the significant downsize, Thorson and others continued to work to put together an annual report—the "Annual Waste Treatment and Immobilization Plant (WTP) Operational Support Report (For Fiscal Year 2011)," released last September. Once again, the evaluation found serious vulnerabilities with the WTP that would likely require design changes and testing to remedy. The results of the report were briefed to the DOE.

At that point, however, the report's classification was revised, then reissued as "business sensitive" and for "official use only," rather than being released publicly as intended. "The stated reason from the DOE at the meeting was to keep it out of the hands of potential critical reviewers such as the [DNFSB]," says Thorson.

"Why wouldn't they want it in the hands of [DNFSB]?," says Tamosaitis. "Because it would bring a big spotlight to the whole WTP operation."

Asked about the delay in releasing the September report, DOE spokesperson Carrie Meyer did not directly address the allegation, saying "The report will be checked for factual accuracy, and released in the spring."

"[Bechtel and DOE] do not want to look at long-term operability of WTP," Thorson adds. "They'd rather build the thing and let the problems be fixed later. But you can't do that in the black cells. This is not a normal construction job, it's a first-of-a-kind with a lot of unforeseen issues if it doesn't work right."

Seattle Weekly has obtained a copy of the September report. It is the same as the version now classified as "official use only," a DOE source notes. The report's authors identify numerous vulnerabilities, including the potential for hydrogen buildup due to faulty venting that could lead to a shutdown of the WTP—or worse, an explosion.

Despite such potential calamities, at the end of 2011 the DOE verbally requested in a meeting that all CLIN 3.2 evaluations of the WTP in the form of annual reports be stopped for the indefinite future. Thorson says that he and others were also instructed by management to halt work on CLIN 3.2. Additionally, a draft alteration to WRPS's contract with the DOE has been circulated outlining this change in CLIN 3.2's work scope.

No immediate justification was given by the DOE, but Meyer states that the DOE is now going to implement a "one-system integrated approach" that does not eliminate the CLIN 3.2 analysis, but rather combines work and safety reviews of the Tank Farm with those taking place at the WTP.

"Despite what they say, they aren't going to allow us to do any more long-term operability analysis at all," Thorson responds. "Since Bechtel doesn't believe a factual accuracy check is in their contract, there is no mechanism to ever release the report or get the issues addressed—apart from DOE direction."

***

One reason the DOE may be supporting Bechtel's decision to largely ignore CLIN 3.2's work could have to do with a March 2011 paper titled the 2020 Vision. *Seattle Weekly* has obtained an internal copy of the 2020 Vision plan, which was primarily put together by WRPS, DOE, and Bechtel personnel who, as the documents state, were "tasked with identifying the optimum approach to startup, commissioning, and turnover of WTP facilities for operations."

The plan, marked "Business Sensitive and Proprietary," reads in part "An important feature of our proposed approach is acceleration of the transition" of activities "from the WTP line item to operating expense." The goal, the 2020 Vision notes, is to ensure that the WTP cost is capped at $12.263 billion. With this, the 2020 Vision lays out a plan for Bechtel to stay within their proposed budget.

What this means is that the WTP will be shifting some of their research work to the Tank Farms, says a URS employee who wishes to stay anonymous for fear of retribution. Unlike Bechtel's WTP contract, the URS Tank Farm contract is not nearly as strapped for cash. By moving some work to the Tank Farm contract, Bechtel and the DOE can publicly contend that they have kept their WTP costs lower than they actually are.

Giving the appearance that the WTP budget is not growing provides cover for the project, protecting against interrogation from outside watchdog groups and organizations like the Government Accountability Office and DNFSB, says Tamosaitis.

"[Bechtel] management here turns over every three years, and guys like me stay around to see the damage they've caused," claims an engineer who has worked for Bechtel for well over a decade and wishes to remain anonymous for fear of being fired for speaking out.

"The Bechtel mantra is 'Build Something, Be Paid, Be Gone,'" adds Tamosaitis.

Turnover at Bechtel typically occurs within management. For example, Bechtel has changed out project presidents on four separate occasions since they took over the WTP contract in 2000, most recently installing Russo as director just over two years ago. The anonymous Bechtel engineer says this is a clear sign that they don't have the project under control, and the DOE's Alexander admits his agency does not have enough technical staff to oversee the WTP project.

With the CLIN 3.2 oversight group's objective essentially being dismantled, Murray Thorson is once again frustrated. As is David Bruce. "If Bechtel won't listen to the issues I am raising, I'm going to make a big, big stink," he promises, saying that if he isn't given a fair hearing, he'll identify many more design flaws. "[Management's] shenanigans have gone on for far too long."

Research support for this story was provided by the Investigative Fund of the Nation Institute and was first published by Seattle Weekly.

– February 21, 2012

DEFENDER OF THE BIG WILD

By Jeffrey St. Clair

A few years ago, I was sitting at a campfire in the foothills of the Bridger Mountains of western Montana, with a few close friends, sipping whiskey while watching a dazzling sunset dissolve behind the ragged peak of Haystack Mountain on the distant horizon. It was my 50th birthday and there was no better place to mourn the passing of the years.

Most of us circled around that crackling fire of lodgepole pine were grizzled veterans of environmental battles and we looked the part. The decades had taken their toll: Bad backs, hip replacements, busted ankles, arthritic wrists, failing eyeballs. One of us stood out, though. He was lean, sinewy and sported the implacable, no bullshit gaze of an auditor at the IRS. His name was Mike Garrity and he was by far the most dangerous figure on the mountain that night, except, perhaps, for the young grizzly that had been sighted rummaging through a berry patch just up the slope earlier in the week.

Garrity was a professional killer. He killed timber sales and mining projects, grazing allotments and oil wells, dams and ski lodges. Garrity was the executive director what had long been my favorite environmental group, the Alliance for the Wild Rockies: an outfit as fierce, lean, unflinching and fleet-footed as Garrity himself.

As coyotes gossiped under the starlight, Garrity began to talk about his vision for the sprawling region known as the Northern Rockies, a landscape that stretches from northern Utah, up through Wyoming and western Montana, to Idaho and across Hells Canyon into eastern Oregon and Washington. This was a region that contained the last vestiges of the real American wilderness in the lower 48: wild rivers and rugged mountain ranges, ancient forests and high deserts, alpine lakes and vast marshes. This was the last stronghold of the American bison, the gray wolf, and grizzly. It was also a region under siege on all fronts.

Garrity thinks big. He doesn't merely want to protect high-profile scenic parcels of the region. His goal is to secure permanent protection for all of the untrammelled spaces, some 18 million acres combined, and link them together with biological corridors. This isn't some grandiose fund-raising ploy geared toward squeezing grants from East Coast foundations or Bay Area tech billionaires with a fetish for bison. It's the only real option for saving the wild landscapes of the Northern Rockies as functioning ecosystems, instead of what our mutual friend Steve Kelly dismissively calls "postcard ranges." Toward that end, the Alliance has crafted the Northern Rockies Ecosystems Protection Act (NREPA), one of the most visionary pieces of environmental legislation since the passage of the Wilderness Act itself.

In the meantime, many of those forests, ranges and rivers are under immediate threat from clearcutting, road building, oil leasing, cattle grazing and mining. Most of Garrity's time and energy are devoted to fending off these destructive schemes, which he does with a relentless efficiency. One former Forest Supervisor in Montana told me that "the Alliance for Wild Rockies was our biggest pain in the ass. They were always looking over our shoulder. Scrutinizing every detail, looking for any vulnerability. Garrity is one tenacious SOB. After a few years of being shell-shocked by appeals and lawsuits, even our biggest timber beast grew to respect the guy. They didn't like him, but viewed him as an honorable opponent."

I first ran into Garrity in the late 1990s when he was working as a staffer for one of the rarest birds in Congress, Rep. Merrill Cook. Cook was a Republican from Utah. No surprise there. Here's the catch: Cook was also an ardent conservationist. He hired Garrity shortly after Mike finished his course work at the University of Utah for a doctorate in environmental economics.

"I figured I could protect more land as an activist, than as a professor," Garrity told me.

While working for Cook, Garrity helped expose one of the great acts of political flim-flam of Clintontime: the President's Roadless Area Rule. The Clinton Roadless Rule was a sloppily stitched together executive order issued in 1999 that was designed to placate the environmental lobby which had grown restless with Clinton's despicable record on the environment. The problem was the roadless rule itself was rather toothless and it left out many hundreds of thousands of acres of imperiled wilderness lands, especially in the Rocky Mountain West.

Merrill Cook was the perfect politician to lead the offensive and Garrity provided him with the ammunition. In congressional hearings, Cook mercilessly raked the Clinton administration officials over the coals, savaging the roadless rule for being a weak and politically expedient measure that left vitally important lands unprotected. In the end, Cook, with Garrity's guidance, succeeded in winning protection for 250,000 acres of roadless lands in the sprawling Dixie National Forest of southern Utah. With this victory under their belt, Cook and Garrity went after the Forest Service, which was feverishly attempting to log off tens of thousands of acres of ecologically unique old growth forest in Utah, even though the timber sales violated the Endangered Species Act and other laws. Eventually, the Forest Service backed down and quashed the logging projects. It was a stinging defeat for the agency, but a dramatic win for environmentalist in a state where such victories are exceedingly rare.

Garrity has a unique gift for getting unlikely folks to take couragous stances in the defense of the environment. For example, in 1996, Garrity helped convince the Southern Utah Loggers Association to sign onto a letter to the Chief of the Forest Service calling for the protection of all roadless lands from logging. Their logic was two-fold: first, they had a legitimate concern about protecting the environment; second, they argued that timber sales in roadless areas were most likely to be bought and logged by large out-of-state corporations.

Garrity pulled a similar coup in the Northern Rockies when he almost single-handedly convinced the Teamsters and Operating Engineers Unions of eastern Washington, to back a plan drafted by the Alliance that called for reintroducing grizzly bears to central Idaho and western Montana, as well as protecting all roadless lands and ripping out more than 3,500 of existing logging roads that pose a threat to fish and bears.

In 2002, Mike Garrity became the new executive director of the Alliance for the Wild Rockies. He was no interloper. In a region obsessed by familial origins, Garrity can boast of being a fifth generation Montanan. That gave him a certain cachet with locals that many other environmentalists who immigrated to the region from the coasts can never attain. Moreover, Garrity has never been bound by political ties to the Democratic Party. From the first day on the job, Garrity proved willing to confront Democrats, like Jon Tester (and Barack Obama, for that matter), whose environmental policies on forests, wilderness, oil drilling and endangered species are often indistinguishable from the Republican ultras. Since Garrity took over the helm of the Alliance for the Wild Rockies, he has slimmed the organization down. Made it leaner, meaner and more effective. He moved the headquarters of the Alliance from the rarified atmosphere of the university town of Missoula to Helena, the state capital, where politics is rough-and-tumble. This simple move not only saved the Alliance overhead, but put the extraction industries on notice: the oil, timber and mining lobbies were going to be watched and challenged on their own turf.

For many years, I've told people that pound for pound, the Alliance for the Wild Rockies is the most tenacious and visionary environmental group in the country. They don't blow through money on development directors, public relations staffers or membership coordinators. They fund appeals and lawsuits targeted at stopping the destruction of endangered wildlands and wildlife, from wolves to lynx to bull trout. Under Garrity's tenure, the Alliance is even tougher. As we've seen, Garrity is good a building coalitions, but he is also a talented street-fighter who knows the pressure points of his opponents and how to strike them. It shows in the Alliance's incredible record of legal victories in a region where the courts are distinctly hostile to most environmental litigation.

Garrity and his savvy cohort of lawyers, activists and citizen ecologists are so good at winning lawsuits and administrative appeals that the Government Accountability Office once investigated them to determine how they did it. The GAO confirmed what many of us knew intuitively: that the Alliance was the Forest Service's most relentless foe. A GAO audit revealed that the Alliance for the Wild Rockies, under Garrity's leadership, filed and won more lawsuits against the agency than any other organization. In fact, the study disclosed that 28 percent of all environmental suits won against the Forest Service were filed by the Alliance for the Wild Rockies.

Garrity doesn't just fire off lawsuits hoping they'll hit something, use the press headlines to raise money and then surrender the injunctions when the political heat gets too intense. They file suits aimed at stopping incursions into wildlands or timber sales that pose immediate threats to rare wildlife. The object is to win. And win they do. Over the past decade or so, the Alliance for the Wild Rockies has won 85 percent of its lawsuits and appeals. That's an eye-popping record of success, but it also serves as a rather chilling indictment of the Forest Service and the Bureau of Land Management as lawless agencies doing the devious bidding of the extraction industries.

The proof is on the ground. In the past few years, the Alliance has saved tens of thousands of acres from ruin by filing lawsuits as a last resort. Among their string of victories: in Montana, they won a federal court case stopping a 10-year long logging scheme that would have cut 3,000 acres of forest in Bozeman's municipal watershed; they scored a huge victory in the rugged Big Belt Mountains halting an atrocious 2,289-acre logging project; they won a precedent-setting federal case in the East Boulder Range stopping 650 acres of logging in critical habitat for lynx; they won a key injunction outlawing wolverine trapping in the state and successfully pushed the Fish and Wildlife Service to propose listing the wolverine for protection under the Endangered Species Act; and they scored a dramatic victory by cutting off federal payments for low-level helicopter flights aimed at hazing (read: terrorizing) Yellowstone's iconic bison herd.

In Idaho, perhaps the most environmentally-hostile state in the West, Alliance won a spectacular victory where they saved 7,000 acres from logging in lynx habitat on the Targhee National Forest near Yellowstone Park. Moreover, court injunction prevents the Forest Service from any future timber sales in 400,000 acres of lynx habitat in the region. And down in Utah, near the extraordinary Grand Staircase-Escalante National Moment, the Alliance swooped in and stopped the Forest Service from proceeding with a vast logging project across 4,000 acres on the north slope of Boulder Mountain, which functions as critical winter habitat for elk and migratory birds.

That's an unrivaled record of success for any environmental group. It certainly overshadows the paltry achievements of the Sierra Club, an organization with 1.4 million members, 550 paid staffers and an annual budget massive enough to return the $26 million it was outed for surreptitiously taking from Chesapeake Energy, one of the country's most notorious frackers for natural gas. Recall the Alliance operates on a modest budget with only a single fulltime staffer: Mike Garrity. But winning isn't about budgets, glossy magazines, or political connections. It's about guts, smarts and determination. And those qualities are the calling of Mike Garrity and his team at the Alliance for the Wild Rockies.

As the embers of our fire began to fade on that June night, a sliver of moon ascended over the dark outline of Sacajawea Peak. Then we heard a faint howl, deep and mournful, that echoed eerily down the canyon. Not the shrill yapping of a coyote. This was an ancient lupine voice that would have been familiar to Sacajawea herself: a primeval call to defend the wild.

–Feburary 24, 2014

THE RACHEL CARSON OF THE ROCKIES

By Jeffrey St. Clair

If you wanted to locate the frontlines for the battle to protect the future of wild nature in the lower-48 states, you could do worse than tuning your Google map to the Swan Range in northwestern Montana. This rugged and remote swath of the Northern Rockies rambles from the border of Glacier National Park southward for nearly 100 miles. Bounded on the west by the Mission Mountains and Flathead Lake and the vast Bob Marshall Wilderness to the west, the valleys, alpine slopes and forests of the Swan Range retain much of the natural character of the Rockies at the time when Lewis and Clark first encountered the Salish people in 1805.

The landscape looks roughly—very roughly, from some vantages—the same. And most of the wildlife the Corps of Discovery saw, described and often shot as they crossed the Continental Divide, is still present, though in greatly reduced numbers. The Swans still harbor populations of wolves, lynx, mountain goats, wolverines, bobcats, moose, elk and grizzlies. In short, the Swan Range is one of the last redoubts of wild America, one of those rare places that still has most, if not all, of its key ecological parts, from the top of the food chain on down to newts and salamanders, forest lichens and glacial wildflowers.

But it is also hotly contested terrain, craved by logging companies, mining operations, resort developers and politicians, like Democratic Senator Jon Tester, who want to carve it up as payback to the corporadoes who finance their campaigns. And hovering over it all is the meta-threat of climate change, already making its menacing presence felt through melting glaciers, disappearing tree species, such as whitebark pines, prolonged droughts and intensified wild fires. It is a region under the gun.

Fortunately, the Swans have a very capable and fearless defender. Arlene Montgomery moved to northwestern Montana in 1987. She and her husband wanted to live closer to the "big wild." She worked a variety of jobs from bartending to office bookkeeping, eventually settling in the tiny mountain town of Swan Lake, population 250 or so in the busy summer months, not including wayward ballet dancers.

Montgomery was shocked to discover that she had moved into a landscape that was under siege by logging companies, rushing to clearcut the sprawling Flathead National Forest.

"I had lived for many years in western Washington and had witness the butchery of industrial forestry by the likes of Weyerhaeuser," she told me. "But when we moved to Montana I was shocked to find the same kind of brutal logging taking place on public lands. I was outraged. How could they do this when there are grizzlies here. So I threw myself into the mix."

The timber beasts on the Flathead Forest would soon live to regret awakening the sleeping giant known as Arlene Montgomery. Over the next dozen years, Arlene made stopping clearcuts on the Flathead a top priority. By the year 2000, largely due to the dogged persistence of Montgomery and her rag-tag band of cohorts, including Keith Hammer and Steve Kelly, the Flathead Forest had been compelled to stop all logging of old-growth groves, one of the most decisive environmental victories in the history of Montana forest politics.

But Montgomery's most important work, the place where she would make her mark as one of the most creative environmentalists in the country, came not in fighting timber sales but in protecting fish. One fish in particular, a little known salmonid with a rather unalluring name: the Bull Trout. In a region revered for its fly-fishing, the bull trout remains something an outsider. Part of this has to do with the fish's confusing nomenclature. For decades it was called a Dolly Varden, as if it were a bad Broadway musical. Worse, the region's fishing elites, the so-called Orvis cabal, despised the bull trout. Why? Because the bull trout is a mean son-of-a-bitch. It doesn't rise to the bait of elegantly casted dry flies, preferring instead to lurk in cool deep pools and await tastier fare. You see: the bull trout is piscivorous. In other words, it eats other fish. Often the very brook, cutthroat and rainbow trout prized by the hip-wading jet set.

So the Montana anglers paid little attention to the status of the bull trout, either out of indifference or outright loathing. Fortunately, a couple of wildlife biologists in the region had been paying attention and what they learned was very troubling indeed. While doing surveys on the Flathead River, the fish biologists recorded a sobering decline in redd counts for bull trout—redds are essentially trout egg nests on gravel stream bottoms. The data suggested that bull trout were in a state of precipitous decline, their numbers falling by as much as 65 percent in some streams. Neither the Forest Service nor Fish and Wildlife Service showed the slightest interest in this disturbing trend. Recall this was in the early 1990s, during George HW Bush's presidency, when Manual Lujan ran the Interior Department. Lujan had famously declared that the last thing he wanted to see was "another fucking fish landing on the Endangered Species list."

Frustrated by the Bush administration's bureaucratic antipathy toward wildlife, in 1992 the biologists leaked their data to Montana environmentalist Mike Bader, then director of the Alliance for the Wild Rockies, who used the data to file a petition to list the bull trout as a threatened species. This was a bold move because the bull trout's habitat stretched from Montana to Puget Sound, Puget Sound to southern Oregon, and Oregon to the Jarbridge River in Nevada. In other words, almost all of Northern Rockies and the Pacific Northwest. The bull trout suddenly rose from obscurity to become a bigger threat to the looting of the West than the northern spotted owl.

Into this contentious mix walked Arlene Montgomery. In 1993, she became director of the Friends of the Wild Swan, a small but militant environmental group based in Bigfork, Montana, and soon made the protection of the bull trout her top priority.

What's so special about the bull trout? For starters, the bull trout is big, by far the largest and most aggressive trout to be encountered in the streams of the Northern Rockies. One biologist called it the grizzly of the rivers. It's also wide-ranging, with some bull trout migrating more than 100 miles up and down streams and rivers to spawn. But most crucially bull trout require pristine water to breed. They are highly intolerant of sediment that slides into rivers and streams from logging operations and road—building project. Bull Trout and clearcuts can't coexist.

"Arlene is a dogged researcher and fearless advocate for wildlife and wildands," long-time Montana environmentalist Steve Kelly told me. "When she sinks her teeth into an issue she doesn't let go."

When the Fish and Wildlife Service sat listlessly on Bader's bull trout petition, Montgomery sprang into action. She hauled her own copying machine to the Fish & Wildlife Service's regional offices in Portland and began printing out reams of documents on the status of the imperiled trout. What Montgomery uncovered became the basis for one of the longest-running legal battles in American history.

Over the course of the next 22 years, Montgomery, working closely with Missoula-based attorney Jack Tuholske, waged a relentless war against the intransigence of federal and state wildlife agencies. These lawsuits had one common result: Montgomery's team won them all. First, there were the three victorious lawsuits forcing the feds to list the trout as a threatened species, with the ultimate victories coming in 1998 and 1999. Then there was another decade long legal fight to secure critical habitat designations for the trout, a battle which pitted Montgomery against Julie McDonald, one of the most corrupt and venal members of George W. Bush's hatchet team at the Interior Department. Montgomery prevailed in 2010 when the agency was forced to designate vast areas of the Northwest as critical habitat for the trout, including 19,729 miles streams and rivers across five states, 754 miles of marine shoreline in Puget Sound and 488,000 acres of ponds and lakes. Equally important, this total included many miles and acres of currently unoccupied bull trout habitat to be protected as migratory corridors and ecological connectors between distinct populations.

But the battle for the future of the bull trout wasn't over. The Obama administration soon revealed itself to be just as obstructive as the Bush administration. "The Endangered Species Act is a three-legged stool," Montgomery said. "It requires the listing of a species, the identification of critical habitat for the species and a recovery plan for saving the species from extinction. If even one leg is missing or hollow, the whole thing falls apart."

What was missing from the Obama administration is a recovery plan that makes any kind of positive strides toward saving the Bull Trout from extinction. According to Montgomery, the draft recovery plan, released in September 2014, has a number of fatal flaws, most glaringly the it allows for the existing Bull Trout population to fall by another 25 percent and still be considered "recovered." That's right. The plan of the man the Sierra Club dubbed the "greatest environmental president in history" will consider the bull trout to be thriving if its population plunges 25 percent below the level that caused the fish listed as being threatened with extinction.

Expect Montgomery to be back in court and expect her to win—win big.

***

Swan Lake is a small town where everybody knows everybody else's business. For many years, the Post Office was located in the General Store, where Montgomery would regularly run into her neighbors. Most weren't too pleased by her environmental activism and the more lawsuits she won, the more intense local feelings became. "I wasn't the most popular person in town," Montgomery said. "But occasionally some of the people in town would pat me on the back and say 'good work.' A few even joined Friends of the Wild Swan."

A very few. Friends of the Wild Swan has fewer members than the summer population of Swan Lake—about 200 or so and many of them don't pay their dues all that regularly. The group's annual budget is about $46,000 a year—or about a third of the salary for the CEO of a big time environmental outfit like the National Wildlife Federation. Yet this tiny group based in a small seasonal town hidden in the Northern Rockies has won more decisive legal victories for wildlife and wildlands than the National Wildlife Federation (annual budget $88 million), National Audubon Society (annual budget $90 million)and Defenders of Wildlife (annual budget $30 million) combined.

And the bull trout saga is only the crown jewel on Montgomery's resume. Over the last 20 or so years, Montgomery has helped block road-building on 36,700 acres of grizzly bear habitat, moved to block a logging in another 500,000 acres of grizzly occupied forest, sued to force a recovery plan for lynx, filed legal challenges against the feds' failure to list both the fisher and wolverine as threatened species, won a major Clean Water Act case forcing the clean up hundreds of miles of "impaired waters" across Montana, forced Montana to implement its first forest management plans for state forests and to adopt rules for management of old-growth forests and advocated tirelessly for the passage of the Northern Rockies Ecosystem Protection Act (NREPA), a visionary piece of legislation that would protect most remaining wildland in the region as designated wilderness and connect big blocks of wilderness and national parks through ecological corridors.

"Arlene is the go-to activist for protection of forest carnivores, including pine marten, fisher, wolverine, lynx, and grizzly bear," says Keith Hammer of the Swan View Coalition in Kalispell. "She has worked tirelessly to help insure that, as roads are closed to protect grizzly bear habitat, culverts are removed to protect water quality and fish from their inevitable blow-outs. And she remains at the forefront to stop logging that removes trees standing, dead and fallen that forest carnivores call home. As an anecdote, when local Roadless Area hearings were held in Kalispell in the early phases of what became Clinton's Roadless Rule, Arlene and her testimony received the loudest and most rowdy boos of anyone testifying in front of the 'wise-use' dominated crowd wherein Sheriff's deputies were posted to keep the peace. She's one tough cookie and an honor to work with!"

By any standard, this is a dazzling record of accomplishment, a stunning string of victories won against long odds versus hostile bureaucracies in an embattled region where the stakes are as high as they get. In decades to come, Arlene Montgomery may come to be known as the Rachel Carson of the Rockies. But not just yet. She has much more work to do.

– March 6, 2015

SNIPERS AND INFILTRATORS AT STANDING ROCK: QUASHING PROTESTS AT TAXPAYER EXPENSE

By Joshua Frank

The inner-workings and cost of the government's militant and violent crackdown on peaceful Standing Rock protesters have been trickling in these past few months, yet it hasn't received the headlines it all deserves. In March, MUCKROCK was provided with an unredacted look at Indiana's Department of Homeland Security's EMAC (Emergency Management Assistance Compact) operation at Standing Rock, and later files and photos obtained by journalist Mike Best from Ohio's State Highway Patrol confirm that at least one sniper was deployed on a nearby hill, overlooking the protests.

First, here's a look at Indiana's EMAC, which was asked to join North Dakota's efforts to silence Standing Rock protests at taxpayer expense. For 18 days, from October to November of last year, 37 officers from Indianapolis PD were sent to North Dakota's Morton County. Estimates of the cost of sending these cops, including their equipment, transport and commodities, exceeded $725,000. Wisconsin's Dane County Sheriff's Office also sent 13 deputies, with a total cost of $91,166 per day for an eight day stint.

Here's a list and cost breakdown provided by MUCKROCK of the weapons and materials Indiana sent along with their forces to Standing Rock.

- 42 "sidearms" (judging from the individual officer's paperwork, these are various Glock models): $16,464
- 37 (one for each officer!) Bushmaster AR-15's: $14,504
- 16 outfits of riot gear: $9,408

- 23 shotguns: $9,016
- 21 pairs of Gen III night vision goggles: $8,232
- 37 seemingly department issued cell phones: $6,160
- 21 pairs of binoculars: $1,029
- 10 spotting scopes (possibly used as part of a sniper team): $490
- 2 tear gas launchers of different sizes: $784
- 1 TAC 700 pepper ball launcher: $392
- 1 thermal imaging camera: $784

The official police photos below come from Mike Best's request from the Ohio State Highway Patrol. While it is widely known that pepper spray and dogs were used to intimidate and terrorize Standing Rock activists, these new photos give us an inside look at government efforts to quash the uprising against the Dakota Access Pipeline. The photos show that at least one sniper had his sights set on #NoDAPL activists below, they also indicate that the protest itself was likely infiltrated by law enforcement personnel. No doubt all of this is just the tip of the iceberg.

ALL PHOTOS BY MIKE BEST.

EPILOGUE: THE END OF ILLUSION

By Jeffrey St. Clair and Joshua Frank

In the spring of 2017, the carbon dioxide readings at the Mauna Loa observatory in Hawai'i cracked 410 parts per million, an all-time record and a frightening one. On Earth Day, climate marches took place in cities across the world. Trump's policies didn't drive the spiking CO_2 levels, but they did propel tens of thousands onto the streets for a few hours of fun. Where were those people during eight years of Barack Obama, an oil and gas man of some distinction? Where were they during eight years of Bill Clinton, one of the greatest environmental con men of our time?

Has Donald Trump finally shattered our illusions, so that we can see clearly the forces—economic, political and technological—that are plunging the planet toward a man-made heat death? Is he, in fact, a kind of clarifying agent for the real state of things?

One can hope so.

Except one mustn't hope.

As Kafka, the High Priest of Realism, admonished his readers, "There is hope. But not for us."

Hope is an illusion, an opiate, an Oxycontin for the masses.

Instead of hope, we need a heavy dose of realism. A realism as chilling as reality itself.

Twenty-five hundred years ago, the Buddha instructed us that the world is suffering, and indeed it is. He also advised us that the cure for suffering is empathy, especially for those living beings—among which we would include redwood trees, sea coral and saguaro cacti—which have no defense against the forces that are inflicting that globalized torment.

That's where we come in. Defenders of the Earth need to abandon all hope before entering the fray. Hope is a paralytic agent. Hope is the enemy.

The antidote is action.

Action, however, is not marching in a parade a couple of times a year, featuring puppets, vagina hats and signs printed up by the Sierra Club©.

Action is not taking selfies with a celebrity in the back of a police wagon after a designer arrest.

Action is not typing your name on a MoveOn e-petition or voting for a Jill Stein-like candidate in safe states like Oregon or California.

Action is standing arm-in-arm before water cannons and government snipers on the frozen plains of North Dakota. Action is hanging from a fragile perch 150-feet up in Douglas-fir tree in an ancient forest grove slated for clearcutting, through howling winter storms. Action is chaining yourself to a fracking rig in rural Pennsylvania or camping out in the blast zone at a Mountain Top Removal site in the hills of West Virginia. Action is intervening when police in storm trooper gear are savagely beating a defenseless woman on the streets of Portland. Action is jumping into the Pacific Ocean with a knife in your teeth to cut the vast trawler nets ensnaring white-sided dolphins and humpback whales. Action is stopping bad shit from going down, or trying to.

The time for protests is over.

Protests will not prick the conscience of the unmasked beast called Donald Trump. Trump has no conscience to arouse, no shame to trigger, no remorse to cultivate. Trump is a full-frontal menace, that dangerous object in the mirror that is closer than it appears. It is the old threat, coming at us faster than before and from all directions at once. An unchained beast that will not be moderated by regulations, social conventions or appeals to common decency.

We are witnessing the wet-dream of Steve Bannon—the Trump Whisperer—made manifest: the dismantling of the regulatory state. This new reality compels us—for those who are willing to look—to confront the shedding of another illusion, an illusion that mainstream environmentalists have been marinating in since the 1970s, when our most progressive president, Richard M. Nixon, cynically created the modern environmental regulatory state in order to split the anti-war movement, pacify the Left and smother a much more radical defense of the natural world.

The green regulatory state—as personified by the EPA, the Fish and Wildlife Service, the Forest Service and the BLM (Bureau of Livestock and Mining), as well as thousands of laws, administrative rules and regulations, the meaning of which can only be divined by lawyers, lobbyists and professional environmentalists—has not slowed the decimation of native forests, the extirpation of wildlife or the poisoning of our air and water. It has simply codified and systematized the destruction, allocating the looting to a coterie of well-connected corporations large enough and shrewd enough to navigate the legal labyrinth for their own bloody profits.

At the same time, the creation of the regulatory state effectively neutered the once potent environmental movement as a real threat to the System. As their budgets swell, often fattened by the largess of grants from foundations linked to the fossil fuel industry, the big DC-oriented conservation groups become more and more complicit with the political fool's gold of neoliberalism. Try finding a lobbyist from NRDC with calluses on their hands and a trace of mud on their boots.

As Trump begins the demolition of the regulatory state, we start to see how hollow many of Gang Green's alleged environmental victories of the past—from coal mining and air quality regulations to endangered species protections and new national monuments—really are. They are being wiped out with a slash of the pen.

As the archdruid David Brower used to say: "When we win, it's only a stay of execution, when they win it's forever. Thus we must be eternally vigilant." These days the corporate environmental movement is vigilant about only one thing: claiming fake victories in their sustained barrage of fund-raising appeals.

But the days of the laptop environmentalism are numbered. Trump is creating a battlefield where professional conservationists will fear to tread, a direct, face-to-face confrontation with the machinery of ecocide.

And we know who will rise to the call. The ones who always have in the past: the indigenous, the altruists and the anarchists. Those are the ones who will fight as if their lives depend on the outcome, because, of course, they do.

If we are to believe the sociobiologists, such as E.O. Wilson, the altruistic gene may only be present in three percent of the human population—*may their gene pool increase!* But, hell, that's still three times as many people as the one-percenters who are running the show! If you want hope, there's a microdot to swallow.

Small, scruffy and unruly as it is, we've seen the power of our movement in the past. When our backs are—often literally—against the wall, when the battle lines are clear from the immobilizing fog of liberal rhetoric and free from the timid advice of professional compromisers. We've seen it emerge from the Lacandon jungle to say enough is enough and overtake the streets of Seattle to shut down the World Trade Organization. We've seen grandmothers and housewives expose the toxic crimes of Love Canal and corn farmers shut down nuclear power plants. We've taken the international timber industry to its knees on its home turf, blocked strip mines, pipelines and river killing dams. We've thrown monkey-wrenches big and small into the gears of the System. It has been done and it will be done again and again. No grant applications or protest permits needed.

As Ed Abbey used to say: there's no battle more important, no fight more fun waging, no comrades more trusty-worthy than those in the trenches with us when we rise up together in defense of life on earth. To crib a line from Leonard Cohen: "we may be ugly, but we've got the music."

So draw a line and take a stand—almost any place will do, since the whole shebang is under threat—and let loose an old battle cry so that others will know where to come join you: Earth First!

INDEX